THE
HIRAM
CODE

THE
HIRAM
CODE

RON PHILLIPS, DMin

CHARISMA
HOUSE

Most CHARISMA HOUSE BOOK GROUP products are available at special quantity discounts for bulk purchase for sales promotions, premiums, fund-raising, and educational needs. For details, write Charisma House Book Group, 600 Rinehart Road, Lake Mary, Florida 32746, or telephone (407) 333-0600.

THE HIRAM CODE by Ron Phillips
Published by Charisma House
Charisma Media/Charisma House Book Group
600 Rinehart Road
Lake Mary, Florida 32746
www.charismahouse.com

Scripture quotations marked PHILLIPS are from The New Testament in Modern English, Revised Edition. Copyright © 1958, 1960, 1972 by J. B. Phillips. Macmillan Publishing Co. Used by permission.

Scripture quotations marked THE MESSAGE are from The Message: The Bible in Contemporary English, copyright © 1993, 1994, 1995, 1996, 2000, 2001, 2002. Used by permission of NavPress Publishing Group.

Cover design by Vincent Pirozzi
Design Director: Justin Evans

Visit the author's website at www.ronphillips.org.

Library of Congress Cataloging-in-Publication Data:
Phillips, Ron M.
  The Hiram code / by Ron Phillips. -- First edition.
      pages cm
  Includes bibliographical references.
  ISBN 978-1-62998-212-0 (trade paper) -- ISBN 978-1-62998-213-7 (e-book)
  1. End of the world. 2. Hiram, King of Tyre, active 969 B.C.-936 B.C.--Miscellanea. 3. Hiram Abiff (Biblical figure) I. Title.
  BT877.P45 2015
  236'.9--dc23
                               2015021975

While the author has made every effort to provide accurate Internet addresses at the time of publication, neither the publisher nor the author assumes any responsibility for errors or for changes that occur after publication.

16 17 18 19 20 — 98765432
Printed in the United States of America

*I dedicate this book to the descendants of the great
Phoenician people, now known as Syrians, and
to their great history and heritage in Israel. May
God spare the people from the terror they now
experience. They were on these shores among the
First Nations peoples long before Europe's colonies.*

*I further dedicate this book to the great Cherokee nation,
whose ancient history is part of America's prehistory,
though largely untold—and to all First Nations peoples
and their heritage. I dedicate this to the memory of
the Cherokee prophetess Sister Ada Wynn, whose
prayer shawl I brought home from Oklahoma to her
family's ancestral grounds in Chattanooga, Tennessee.*

*Further, I dedicate this book to the minorities that
have no one to tell their story. God sees and knows.*

*God bless Israel and all of Abraham's
descendants through Jesus Christ our Lord.*

CONTENTS

SECTION FIVE

THE DAVID FACTOR FOR END-TIMES VICTORY

INTRODUCTION

YES, THERE IS HOPE FOR
THE LAST DAYS!

I RECENTLY TALKED TO a very prominent leader in the energy business. There has been found in America another huge oil and gas reservoir that is as large as or larger than the Dakota discovery. The Dakota discovery and the fracking there has moved America toward energy independence. These new finds will make our nation an economic powerhouse.

America is awash with energy resources, so much so that if the government allowed us to bring them up, our wealth as a nation would dwarf the rest of the world and turn our nation back to its place of economic authority.

This would take our enemies' hands from around our throat and bring down energy costs. America would experience the greatest boom in its history. I believe God is ready to bless America and the world if we will begin to stand by faith on the principles that we know work. I believe in the Rapture and Second Coming, yet it is time we put our hands down and understand we are not leaving this world as losers. Jesus said, "Occupy till I come" (Luke 19:13, KJV). How then can we live confidently in these last days? We can embrace biblical hope!

Several years ago there was an article in *Parade* magazine that made an impact on me. It was the story of self-made millionaire Eugene Lang, who greatly changed the lives of a sixth-grade class in East Harlem, New York. Mr. Lang had been asked to speak to a class of fifty-nine sixth graders. What could he say to inspire these students, most of whom would drop out of school? He wondered how he could get this group of predominantly black and Puerto Rican children even to look at him. Scrapping his notes, he decided to speak to them from his heart. "Stay in school," he admonished, "and I'll help pay the college tuition for every one of you." At that moment the lives of these students changed. *For the first time they had hope.* Said one student: "I had something to look forward to, something waiting for me. It was a golden feeling." Nearly 90 percent of that class went on to graduate from high school.[1]

Hope is such an interesting word. By definition it means, "to desire with expectation of fulfillment; to expect with desire." All real hope must have a foundation to stand on. I might tell you that I hope to play center field for the Atlanta Braves next season, but you and I both know that is not hope based on a firm foundation—that's called wishful thinking.

Proverbs 13:12 says, "Hope deferred makes the heart sick, but a longing fulfilled is a tree of life." Paul wrote to the church at Thessalonica about the end times. Many in his day were afraid they had missed the Rapture. Their deferred hope was making their hearts sick and fearful. Although his main focus was on the theme of judgment, Paul continued to encourage the church constantly about their future hope:

+ He gave them hope and joy about the return of Jesus (1 Thess. 2:19).

+ He exhorted them to live holy lives in anticipation of His coming (1 Thess. 3:13).

+ He declared that we do not have to be shaken or disturbed but that we can live in hope (Titus 2:11–13).

WE ARE CALLED TO LIVE IN HOPE AND NOT FEAR

As a pastor for more than four decades, I have witnessed many changing events in the world. As I pen these words, ancient hatreds continue to boil to the surface in the Middle East. The war in Iraq has left many confused and dazed as to our purpose for being there. The war in Afghanistan continues to drag on, while Iran thumbs its nose at the international community. It continues to build a nuclear weapon for the purpose of annihilating Israel. Many believers have failed to recognize the conflict is being waged on a higher level. It is a conflict of immense spiritual proportions.

The world is on fire. People are living in fear and without much hope. Sad to say, this sense of hopelessness has infected the church. Instead of believing that darkness will overwhelm us, we in the church must recognize that the *truth of the Word of God* will always triumph over the infernal forces of the enemy!

My purpose in writing this book is to give hope back to the body of Christ and outline strategies that not only will enlighten you, but also

give you a clear direction for the future. In the following chapters you
will discover

- A clear "sound" has been released to this generation—a
  sound of hope and not fear;

- God is not finished with the nation of Israel;

- The connection that exists today between the ancient civilization of Phoenicia and Israel;

- Who King Hiram was and why he was important;

- The lessons we can learn from Isaac, and how he was able
  to walk in the hundredfold blessing;

- How to face your giants;

- And so much more!

My prayer is that the truth in this book will replace fear with faith
and we will have a hope firmly grounded in the truth of God's Word
that will cause us to remember we are on the winning side!

SECTION ONE

BLOW THE TRUMPET IN ZION

CHAPTER 1

UNLOCKING THE SIGNS
OF THE LAST DAYS

VOLUMES HAVE BEEN written over the last five decades about the signs of the end times. Furthermore, strange astronomical events such as blood moons and solar eclipses happening in rapid sequence have caught the attention of many.

Luke wrote both the Gospel that bears his name and the Book of Acts. In both he references these cosmological signs. Also, Luke gives three distinct passages that relate to the end times. Two of these passages have been dealt with by many writers.

Luke 17:20–37 reveals that the last days will be like the days of Noah before the Flood. We have very little information about the pre-Flood civilization except that it was wicked and demonically infested worldwide. (See my book *Unexplained Mysteries of Heaven and Earth*, chapter 2: "Days of Noah.")

Likewise Luke mentions the days of Lot (Luke 17:28–32). These were days very similar to our own. Ezekiel 16:49–50 describes them this way:

> Look, this was the iniquity of your sister Sodom: She and her daughter had pride, fullness of food, and abundance of idleness; neither did she strengthen the hand of the poor and needy. And they were haughty and committed abomination before Me; therefore I took them away as I saw fit.
>
> —NKJV

Notice the sins included pride, abundance, idleness, neglect of the poor, and sexual perversion. Furthermore in Luke 21:20–36 the writer lists the very familiar signs of Israel's destruction in AD 70 and the scattering of the nation. Other signs include cosmic phenomena; distress; and fearful, unsolvable dilemmas.

Luke includes the fact that these signs herald the rescue and final redemption of God's people: "Now when these things begin to happen, look up and lift up your heads, because your redemption draws near" (Luke 21:28, NKJV).

The church is called to be watchful and is promised an escape from the coming tribulation: "Watch therefore, and pray always that you may be counted worthy to escape all these things that will come to pass, and to stand before the Son of Man" (Luke 21:36, NKJV).

I have given this brief summary of the signs most often dealt with by prophecy teachers. Luke, as well as others, offers some other interesting signs of which we must be aware.

UNFOLDING UNUSUAL SIGNS

Most students of prophecy are aware that the Middle East is boiling with terror, Israel is surrounded by Islamic enemies, Iran and North Korea are in league trying to build nuclear weapons, and strange weather and climate disasters are increasing. Besides these we are familiar with, there are some others hidden away in Scripture, or completely neglected.

RAPID INCREASE IN KNOWLEDGE AND TRAVEL

Our society has seen remarkable advances in knowledge and communication in the last thirty years. Having served for thirty-five years at a growing church, I can remember a time with no computers, cell phones, Facebook, Twitter, or any of the other advances in technology we enjoy today. (I have a veritable library on my iPad!)

Furthermore, one can get on a plane and be on the other side of the world in a matter of hours. Daniel saw this coming and listed it as a sign of the end:

> But you, Daniel, shut up the words, and seal the book until the time of the end; many shall run to and fro, and knowledge shall increase.
>
> —DANIEL 12:4, NKJV

Speaking of our cities and roadways, listen to the prophet Nahum:

> The chariots rage in the streets, they jostle one another in the broad roads; they seem like torches, they run like lightning.
>
> —NAHUM 2:4, NKJV

ECONOMIC AND JOB WOES

In chapter five ("The Latter Rain and Israel") I will discuss this in greater detail, but I want to mention in this list as well the sign no one talks about. It is found in James 5:1–4:

> Come now, you rich, weep and howl for your miseries that are coming upon you! Your riches are corrupted, and your garments are moth-eaten. Your gold and silver are corroded, and their corrosion will be a witness against you and will eat your flesh like fire. You have heaped up treasure in the last days. Indeed the wages of the laborers who mowed your fields, which you kept back by fraud, cry out; and the cries of the reapers have reached the ears of the Lord of Sabaoth.
>
> —NKJV

Clearly God is concerned about the proper treatment of workers. Furthermore, notice the mention of gold and silver and the selling and hoarding of it today as a hedge for the future. Scripture says there is no final security in wealth.

PUBLIC RIDICULE FOR THE TRUTHS OF GOD

> Knowing this first: that scoffers will come in the last days, walking according to their own lusts.
>
> —2 PETER 3:3, NKJV

Here we find the phrase "last days." Peter gives us a new sign for the end of the age, a sign that fits our Western culture. Notice that these people are described as "scoffers." The Greek word here is *empaiktoi*. This word comes from two words that mean "in making fun." It could be an ancient word from which our word *imposter* is derived. It carries the idea of a teacher making fun of the Second Coming.

Mocking people who embrace the truth is a weapon being used by liberals today. Left-wing entertainers and comedians mock all truth and those who hold to the truth. Also, these scoffers model immoral lifestyles. This sign includes "walking after their own lusts." The word *walking* is *poreomai*, which means "to journey upward or to the top." These scoffers have a burning desire—a lust to get to the top in the world system.

Here are leaders who will laugh at and treat with sarcasm the things of the Spirit and of doctrine. They allow their human lusts for sex, for power, and for material things to drive their lives!

Can you see that our Western culture mocks holy things? God-hating, mocking, immoral voices are heard across the vast spectrum of politics, business, and entertainment.

DEMONIC INVASION AND PERIL

> But know this, that in the last days perilous times will come: For men will be lovers of themselves, lovers of money, boasters, proud, blasphemers, disobedient to parents, unthankful, unholy, unloving, unforgiving, slanderers, without self-control, brutal, despisers of good, traitors, headstrong, haughty, lovers of pleasure rather than lovers of God.
>
> —2 TIMOTHY 3:1–4, NKJV

According to Webster's Revised Dictionary, the word *perilous* means "full of, attended by, involving extreme danger and hazards." A second meaning describes people who are willing to be daring and reckless in their approach to life.

The Greek word *chalepos* gives the idea of bringing such terror and danger that it sucks the life and strength out of someone! The root word, *chalao*, means "to lower into a void" or into a hopeless position.

It comes from the ancient word *chasma* from which our English word *chasm* is taken, meaning "impassable interval." It is the word used to describe the position of the rich man in hell:

> And besides all this, between us and you there is a great gulf fixed, so that those who want to pass from here to you cannot, nor can those from there pass to us.
>
> —LUKE 16:26, NKJV

It is interesting that this same word is found in Matthew 8:28 to describe the spirit of the two demonized men of Gadara:

> When He had come to the other side, to the country of the Gergesenes, there met Him two demon-possessed men, coming out of the tombs, exceedingly fierce, so that no one could pass that way.
>
> —NKJV

The words *fierce* and *violent* are the same words as *perilous*. Seeing this, we begin to understand what these perilous times mean and where they come from.

Perilous describes a life that is

+ lived in extreme danger;

+ hazardous;

+ lived with lowered expectation;

+ separated by a void from God;

+ tormented; and

+ controlled by the demonic.

Both the rich man in Luke 16 and the demonized man in Mark 5 were divided from what they could be by forces of darkness and evil. "But know this, that in the last days perilous times will come" (2 Tim. 3:1, NKJV). These "perilous" times cause extreme social and community breakdown manifested by the fallen demonic spirits.

FIVE END-TIMES DEMONIC PERILS

1. Spirit of greed and pride

> Lovers of themselves, lovers of money, boasters, proud, blasphemers.
> —2 TIMOTHY 3:2, NKJV

Materialism rules the culture.

2. Spirit of rebellion

> Disobedient to parents, unthankful, unholy.
> —2 TIMOTHY 3:2, NKJV

Here we see a wild and godless generation of young people taking over the culture.

3. Spirit of perversion

> Unloving, unforgiving, slanderers, without self-control, brutal, despisers of good.
> —2 TIMOTHY 3:3, NKJV

Notice all these words that have to do with loving pleasure more than God.

4. Spirit of religion

> Having a form of godliness but denying its power. And from such
> people turn away! For of this sort are those who creep into house-
> holds and make captives of gullible women loaded down with sins,
> led away by various lusts.
>   —2 TIMOTHY 3:5–6, NKJV

Here the church is perverted into something that can perform but
inside is empty of the Holy Spirit. Gullible people are taken in by phony
religious types that can put on a good show.

5. Spirit of demonic wisdom

> Always learning and never able to come to the knowledge of the
> truth. Now as Jannes and Jambres resisted Moses, so do these also
> resist the truth: men of corrupt minds, disapproved concerning the
> faith; but they will progress no further, for their folly will be mani-
> fest to all, as theirs also was.
>   —2 TIMOTHY 3:7–9, NKJV

Here the intellectual elder always questions the truth of God under
a pseudointellectual guise. The Bible says they are "disapproved," which
means in Greek, "undocumented and not authentic."

"Perilous times" means that demons are operating with strategies now
to take down the work of God. The word *times* is *kairos*, which means
"season of opportunity." Unfortunately the demons are looking for seasons
of opportunity to advance their peril on this earth. (See Ron Phillips's book
Angels and Demons from Charisma House.)

THE LAST DAYS AWAKENING OF THE CHURCH

Luke's final passage on the last days is found in Acts 2. In this account
the Holy Spirit fell in the Upper Room upon 120 souls. The power
of God was visible and audible in cloven tongues of fire and a rushing,
mighty wind. Three thousand people were converted in a matter of
thirty minutes or so.

> Then those who gladly received his word were baptized; and that
> day about three thousand souls were added to them. And they
> continued steadfastly in the apostles' doctrine and fellowship, in
> the breaking of bread, and in prayers.
>   —ACTS 2:41–42, NKJV

When we examine Peter's message, we discover that it is drawn from Joel's prophecies of the last days (Joel 2). The context is found in Acts 2:17–21. Here is a promise of a last-days outpouring that will look like the Day of Pentecost. What can the church expect to see in the last days? What will the last-days church look like?

Notice the six markers that will identify the true church in the last days:

1. End-time outpouring of the Holy Spirit

> And it shall come to pass in the last days, says God, that I will pour out of My Spirit on all flesh; your sons and your daughters shall prophesy, your young men shall see visions, your old men shall dream dreams.
>
> —ACTS 2:17, NKJV

You will know it's the last days because of a mighty move of the Holy Spirit on "all flesh." It will be upon every race, age, gender, and nation.

God will pour out His Spirit on "all flesh"; upon the rich, poor, sinful, and sick.

God will move on people suddenly and powerfully.

2. End-time prophetic release on young people

"Your sons and daughters shall prophesy, your young men shall see visions."

This supernatural movement heralding Christ's coming will see children and young people moving in the gifts of the Spirit and speaking prophetically. Also, "visions" from God will come upon the young, and God will do mighty things according to those visions.

3. End-time recovery of the dreams of older people

"Your old men shall dream dreams."

There will be a restoration of health and strength to complete the dreams of youth and a rapid release of power to make God-given dreams a reality.

4. Ordinary working men and women will move in the gifts.

> And on My menservants and on My maidservants I will pour out My Spirit in those days; and they shall prophesy.
>
> —ACTS 2:18, NKJV

Here is an outpouring on all of us to release prophecy. The prophetic word releases new destinies for those who hear it and receive it. The days of "elite" ministries are over. The people will rise in prophetic power.

5. Signs and wonders in nature will be common.

> I will show wonders in heaven above and signs in the earth beneath: Blood and fire and vapor of smoke. The sun shall be turned into darkness, and the moon into blood, before the coming of the great and awesome day of the LORD.
>
> —ACTS 2:19–20, NKJV

As I said at the beginning, nature will herald this coming.

6. Millions will pray to receive Christ.

> And it shall come to pass that whoever calls on the name of the LORD shall be saved.
>
> —ACTS 2:21, NKJV

Here is the great promise of an end-time harvest. The latter rain of God's outpouring will release a last-days gathering in of the lost. The church must take Jesus's Word seriously.

> So he called ten of his servants, delivered to them ten minas, and said to them, "Do business till I come."
>
> —LUKE 19:13, NKJV

We must occupy until He comes. While all the signs are lining up around us, we will have powerful resources with which to fulfill our destinies. Watch for the signs and listen for the sound in the next chapter.

CHAPTER 2

MOVING AT THE SOUND

To have God speak to the heart is a majestic experience, an experience these people may miss if they monopolize the conversation and never pause to hear God's responses.[1]

—CHARLES STANLEY

LIEUTENANT PORTER B. Williamson recalls his life at the desert training center in California as preparations were made for the US military to enter World War II:

> Every evening, Gen. George Patton arranged a type of communication which united all soldiers. This "communication" united us with the soldiers of history! Gen. Patton had buglers blow Taps! Every unit down to a company of two hundred men had their own bugler. With over twenty thousand men sleeping on the ground over a thirty-mile strip of the desert valley, we had one hundred buglers.
>
> A bugle for communication during the day in a tank outfit was as practical as a feather in a hailstorm. No bugle call could be heard above the roar of tanks and trucks, but in the stillness of the evening, a bugle call would carry for miles. With sound traveling at the rate of eleven hundred feet per second, it was impossible for all the buglers to play Taps at the same time. It would take over five seconds for the first note of our Headquarters bugler to reach a bugler a mile away. Thus, with a hundred buglers blowing Taps at different places and times and with the echoes bouncing off the mountains, it was a sound to cause the mind of every man to pause for a moment in prayer. Those bugle calls made us feel as if we were a part of an organization which had the power of the armies of all the centuries.[2]

Biblical metaphors allow us to understand more clearly the mysteries of God. For example, when Paul spoke of the relationship between a husband and wife, his purpose was to reveal a deeper "mystery." The relationship a husband has with his wife is supposed to model a spiritual truth concerning Christ and His church.

This is only one of the metaphors Scripture uses to describe the church. There are nearly one hundred such images in the New Testament, images that reveal the church for what it is theologically. Four of the more significant metaphors reveal that the church's relationship with God is one of utmost closeness. In the metaphors of the church as a bride, a building, a body, and an army, we learn that our life as a community of disciples proceeds from within the life of the God who is Father, Son, and Holy Spirit. The first three metaphors unfold the mystery of Christ's intimate relationship with His beloved church. The fourth metaphor reveals the church as a mighty force on the earth.

1. *The bride of Christ.* This speaks of our intimacy with Him.
     2 Corinthians 11:2
     Ephesians 5:31–32
     Revelation 21:19; 19:7–8

2. *The body of Christ.* This speaks of function.
     Romans 12:4–5
     1 Corinthians 10:17; 12:27
     Ephesians 4:12; 5:30

3. *The building of Christ.* This speaks of structure.
     1 Corinthians 3:11; 16–17
     Ephesians 2:19–22
     1 Peter 2:5

4. *The army of Christ.* This speaks of our strategy against the enemy.
     Ephesians 6:10–18
     2 Timothy 2:3–4

The first three metaphors speak of our relationship and intimacy with the Father, but the fourth pictures our activity in pulling down strongholds of the enemy.

As followers of Christ, we are in a war against God's enemy. The enemy is not flesh and blood but spiritual forces arrayed against God's people. But that war must be fought by a corporate army.

The armor described in Ephesians 6 is meant to be worn by the church; it's not just given for individuals. We are soldiers in God's army, and Jesus Christ is our captain and commander in chief. Spiritual warfare is a corporate exercise. The weight of it belongs on the shoulders of the church, not the individual soldiers.

For too long individual believers have tried to take on the forces of hell and have come away defeated and discouraged. Spiritual authority is based on growth in spiritual life. The more maturity in spiritual life that a church experiences, the more spiritual authority the church wields. The gates of hell are there for the taking when the corporate body realizes its authority.

PUT YOUR EARS ON!

If you are old enough to remember the 1970s, you will recall everyone had CB radios. The most popular phrase was, "Hey good buddy, do you have ears on?"—meaning, is your CB radio on? God is still speaking today, and He wants to know if we have our spiritual ears on. "Whoever has ears, let them hear what the Spirit says to the churches" (Rev. 3:22).

In his book *The Hearing Ear* Larry Lea writes:

> Tides and currents are shifting. Dangerous shoals and treacherous reefs are lying in wait. New winds are blowing. If the church is to move forward in the flow of God, she must catch the fresh wind of the Spirit. The people of God must set their courses by the unwavering, sure revelation of the Holy Spirit. We must hear and obey what the Spirit is saying to the churches."[3]

There is a constant conflict between those who believe God speaks only through natural elements and those who believe God is still speaking today and is vitally connected to His people. There are many in the evangelical church world who believe you hear God only through preaching, teaching, and reading the Bible. They quickly discount any supernatural or spiritual intervention or direct communication with God. The foundation of their belief system is wrapped around the idea that when the Bible was complete, God put tape over His mouth and stopped talking. They live by the creed, "If it has anything to do with New Testament Christianity, let's leave it in the New Testament; it's certainly not for today!"

Those who argue against God's speaking today have the notion that we are talking about extrabiblical revelation or, in simple terms, adding to what God has already written. The Bible is very clear that we are not to add to or subtract from what has already been given in the Bible (Rev. 22:18–19). I would never suggest that we add anything to Scripture. What I am suggesting is that God is still giving revelation and illumination on what He has already written!

Yes, I believe God speaks through His Word, and I also believe that He still communicates through the voice of the Holy Spirit. No matter what the pragmatist and the doubters say, you *can* hear God's voice today. I am in no way suggesting we throw away the Bible or the teaching and preaching of the Word of God. I realize some would say since the Bible was not complete it was the only way God could communicate with His people.

I believe that it's possible to develop a "hearing ear." The first step is to believe it is God's will for you to hear His voice. One of the privileges belonging to every believer is the fact that you can hear His voice. Jesus said in John 10:4–5: "And when he brings out his own sheep, he goes before them; and the sheep follow him, for they know his voice. Yet they will by no means follow a stranger, but will flee from him, for they do not know the voice of strangers" (NKJV).

The Bible is filled with illustrations of God's speaking to His people. You don't have to read far or for very long to see how God communicated.

- God spoke to our first parents, Adam and Eve. They heard the sound and enjoyed communion with God. (See Genesis 2:16–17.)

- God personally instructed Noah. He heard the sound and saved his family and preserved future generations. (See Genesis 6:12–16.)

- God spoke to Abraham. He heard the sound and became the father of many nations. (See Genesis 12:1–3.)

- God spoke to Moses through the burning bush. He heard the sound and set the people free. (See Exodus 3:2–4, 7–8.)

- God spoke to His prophets. They heard the sound and declared the righteousness of God. (See Isaiah 6:8–9; Jeremiah 1:4–5).

There are many more examples in the Old Testament. I can hear someone saying now, "But are there any New Testament examples?" Yes, more than one.

After the Holy Spirit had been given and New Testament believers were baptized with the promise of the Holy Spirit, they became a powerful force to witness for Christ. The promise of Jesus was empowerment to do works greater than His (John 14:12). He had no intention of leaving His church then or now as orphans. As "King's kids" they went into all the world and preached the gospel under the anointing of the Holy Spirit to every creature. That mandate has never been rescinded. Here are just a few examples from the New Testament of God speaking to His people:

+ Jesus spoke directly to His disciples, who heard the sound and followed Him. (See John 10:27.)

+ God spoke to a deacon named Philip, who heard the sound and led the Ethiopian eunuch to Christ. An entire nation was affected. (See Acts 8:29–35.)

+ The Lord spoke specific directives to a man named Ananias, who heard the sound, laid hands on a man named Saul, and started a worldwide missionary movement. (See Acts 9:11–16.)

+ God sent an angel to speak to a man named Cornelius, who heard the sound and sent for a man named Peter. (See Acts 10:3–6.)

+ God spoke to the Apostle Paul, who heard the sound and turned in a different direction, exposing Europe to the gospel. (See Acts 16:6–7.)

Most would agree that God's Word, the Bible, was written to illuminate the person and work of Jesus. When we understand that, we will also understand that we have not only the written Word "on the outside" but also the living Word "on the inside." The indwelling Holy Spirit is not just our Comforter; He is also our guide. He is here to teach us how to hear and obey His voice. He wants to talk to us. And He wants us to listen and talk to Him too.

> Prayer is not monologue, but dialogue; God's voice is its most essential part. Listening to God's voice is the secret of the assurance that He will listen to mine.[4]
>
> —ANDREW MURRAY

AN OLD TESTAMENT PICTURE OF A NEW TESTAMENT TRUTH

In Numbers 10 we discover that the leaders of Israel communicated to the vast congregation of Israelites with the "sound" of a trumpet:

The LORD said to Moses: "Make two trumpets of hammered silver, and use them for calling the community together and for having the camps set out. When both are sounded, the whole community is to assemble before you at the entrance to the tent of meeting. If only one is sounded, the leaders—the heads of the clans of Israel— are to assemble before you. When a trumpet blast is sounded, the tribes camping on the east are to set out. At the sounding of a second blast, the camps on the south are to set out. The blast will be the signal for setting out. To gather the assembly, blow the trumpets, but not with the signal for setting out.

"The sons of Aaron, the priests, are to blow the trumpets. This is to be a lasting ordinance for you and the generations to come. When you go into battle in your own land against an enemy who is oppressing you, sound a blast on the trumpets. Then you will be remembered by the LORD your God and rescued from your enemies. Also at your times of rejoicing—your appointed festivals and New Moon feasts—you are to sound the trumpets over your burnt offerings and fellowship offerings, and they will be a memorial for you before your God. I am the LORD your God."

—NUMBERS 10:1–10

Numbers records the history of the Israelites' wandering after the Law was given on Mount Sinai. The Book covers a little more than thirty-nine years, but most of it deals with the end of that time. God wanted His people to be prepared to serve Him when they took possession of the Promised Land. His instructions were very specific and detailed so that the people could do exactly what God wanted.

What was in the "natural" to them becomes a "type" to us. I believe the trumpet is a picture of the current voice and leading of the Holy Spirit spoken in and through His anointed ministry. Those who have ears to hear know and recognize the sound of the prophetic voice speaking into this generation.

There were five reasons for blowing the trumpet in the camp of Israel. These five reasons are five distinct directions that God is speaking through His leadership today.

1. The sound of the trumpet: a call to unity

Make two trumpets of hammered silver, and use them for *calling the community together* and for having the camps set out.

—NUMBERS 10:1–3, EMPHASIS ADDED

Unity doesn't always come easily. Eugene Peterson observes, "The church is composed of equal parts mystery and mess. God is the mystery; we are the mess!"[5]

When the trumpets blew, the people were to gather. That meant all the people, not just those who weren't busy or who wanted to come.

Believers are not created to live solitary lives. Until we find fellowship with other believers, we are incomplete. Jesus modeled unity with His disciples. They united in a common purpose centered on their leader. Jesus had to constantly remind them they were brothers, not rivals. You read in the Gospel records that there was always some sort of tension among them. There was a competitive spirit trying to separate them; yet despite their bickering they banded together to transform the world.

David is the author of one of the best descriptions of unity found anywhere in the Bible:

> How good and pleasant it is when God's people live together in unity! It is like precious oil poured on the head, running down on the beard, running down on Aaron's beard, down on the collar of his robe. It is as if the dew of Hermon were falling on Mount Zion. For there the LORD bestows his blessing, even life forevermore.
> —PSALM 133:1–3

David certainly understood and appreciated the blessing of unity. Under God's anointing he united the twelve tribes of Israel. To form a united kingdom, all the Israelites had to put aside tribal differences and cooperate. With that unity David was able to establish the capital in Jerusalem and strengthen the nation against her enemies.

The "sound" of this generation is a call to lay aside our petty differences and realize we can be united for a common purpose. Paul said in Philippians 2:2, "Fulfill my joy by being like-minded, having the same love, being of one accord, of one mind" (NKJV). There is a huge difference between unity and uniformity. For many believers unity is all about what you wear, what you read (King James only), and where you go. That's not unity; that's uniformity.

A. W. Tozer wrote in *The Pursuit of God*:

> Has it ever occurred to you that one hundred pianos all tuned to the same fork are automatically tuned to each other? They are of one accord by being tuned, not to each other, but to another standard to which each one must individually bow. So one hundred

worshippers [meeting] together, each one looking away to Christ, are in heart nearer to each other than they could possibly be were they to become "unity" conscious and turn their eyes away from God to strive for closer fellowship.[6]

If a football team operated on the same principles of the modern church, scoring a touchdown would just be a figment of their imagination! To get the ball into the end zone requires a common purpose. When a play is called, the entire team has to be on the same page. If the right guard gets offended at the fullback and decides not to block, you have anarchy. If the quarterback refuses to call the play because he doesn't like the color of the uniform, you have rebellion. Whether dealing with anarchy, rebellion, or just not getting along, a football team will never be successful with that kind of attitude. A team player is one who says, "I don't care who gets the credit, just as long as we score!"

Oil

Psalm 133 contains two symbols that speak of unity: oil and dew. The first image describes the anointing. David gives the image of a large quantity of oil running down onto Aaron's beard and robe. The fragrance of the oil would cling to him. I believe that is the picture Paul gives in 2 Corinthians 2:14 when he says: "But thanks be to God, who always leads us as captives in Christ's triumphal procession and uses us to spread the aroma of the knowledge of him everywhere." Christians are to be an aroma of sweet perfume in a decaying world.

Oil has many uses. It softens the skin, makes things run smoothly (your car engine, for example), and can be used to heal wounds. Throughout Scripture oil is a symbol and type of God's presence and of the Holy Spirit. Individuals were set apart for service with the anointing of oil.

When the anointing oil flows through a church, it flows from the top down, Christ being the head (His very name means "The Anointed One"). If we ever hope to break down the walls of division among believers, we must start with a heavy dose of anointing oil.

Dew

Dew speaks of freshness and fertility. The higher the elevation, the heavier the dew. Israel is an arid country, so the early dew is important if plants are to grow. The dew fell on the loftiest peak, Mount Hermon, in the land of the northern tribes, as well as Mount Zion, a smaller peak in the land of the southern tribes. It was not unusual for travelers in the desert to stay alive by drinking the dew.

We must understand that the dew is necessary for us to flourish in our faith and cannot be attained by human effort. It is a gift produced by the Holy Spirit through the Lord Jesus Christ. He prayed in John 17:22, "I have given them the glory that you gave me, that they may be one as we are one."

Dew is a type and symbol of blessing:

+ Isaac blessed his son Jacob and said, "May God give you heaven's dew" (Gen. 27:28), meaning the resource of abundance.

+ In contrast Isaac told Esau that his "dwelling will be…away from the dew of heaven" (Gen. 27:39).

+ Moses prayed that his teachings would "descend like dew" (Deut. 32:2).

+ Proverbs describes the favor of a king "like dew on the grass" (Prov. 19:12).

+ Isaiah compares dew to the resurrection of our bodies (see Isaiah 26:19).

+ And God declares in Hosea, "I will be like the dew to Israel [which] will blossom like a lily" (Hosea 14:5).

Blessings descend to us, but we ought to receive them together. We are blessed individually and collectively. Both dew and oil are flowing down. They pour out on God's people from above.

Unity is a gift of grace, and life forevermore is the result. Living together in unity as God's people is just a glimpse of eternal life as part of God's forever family. If we are going to spend an eternity with fellow believers, it would be good to start living in unity with them now!

Ephesians 4:3 tells us unity is worth fighting for: "Make every effort to keep the unity of the Spirit through the bond of peace." (See Ron Phillips's book *Power of Agreement*, published by Charisma House.)

Charles Schulz may have hit home on this subject in one of his more famous *Peanuts* comic strips:

Lucy demanded that Linus change TV channels, threatening him with her fist if he didn't. "What makes you think you can walk right in here and take over?" asks Linus. "These five fingers," says Lucy. "Individually they're nothing but when I curl them together like this into a single unit, they form a weapon that is terrible to behold."

"Which channel do you want?" asks Linus. Turning away, he looks at his fingers and says, "Why can't you guys get organized like that?"[7]

2. The sound of the trumpet: gather the leadership

When summoned by the sound of the trumpet, the heads of the clans were gathered for a common purpose. "If only one is sounded, the leaders—the heads of the clans of Israel—are to assemble before you" (Num. 10:4).

The "sound" in our generation is calling leaders together! The day of the lone ranger is over. It is now time to put down the theological swords that we have been using to stab one another and realize we are on the same team.

The enemy is constantly driving wedges between the leaders. Of course, that is nothing new. This "civil war" has been raging in the church for centuries. Leaders preach change to their people, but unfortunately when it becomes personal to them, they resist it at all costs.

3. The sound of the trumpet: a call to advance

After the leadership and people were gathered and instruction was given, it was time to advance. Today the church needs to be careful not to give an "uncertain" sound. We must, in unity, sound the call in three ways: First, we must sound the call to advance; second, the call to warfare; and third, the call to worship.

> When a trumpet blast is sounded, the tribes camping on the east are to set out. At the sounding of a second blast, the camps on the south are to set out.
>
> —Numbers 10:5–6

When the cloud or the fire of God's presence moved, it was up to the leadership to blow the trumpet. Their responsibility was to alert the people that it was time to move with God's presence. In other words, when God moves, we must move with Him!

When the people heard the sound of the trumpet alerting them to pack up and move, they had a choice. They could obey and stay under the blessings, or they could choose to disobey and live on their own.

Psalm 105:37–45 describes the blessings the people enjoyed by obeying God and living under the cloud:

> He brought out Israel, laden with silver and gold, and from among their tribes no one faltered. Egypt was glad when they left, because dread of Israel had fallen on them. He spread out a cloud as a covering, and a fire to give light at night. They asked, and he brought them quail; he fed them well with the bread of heaven. He opened the rock, and water gushed out; it flowed like a river in the desert. For he remembered his holy promise given to his servant Abraham. He brought out his people with rejoicing, his chosen ones with shouts of joy; he gave them the lands of the nations, and they fell heir to what others had toiled for—that they might keep his precepts and observe his laws.

This passage points out six distinct blessings:

1. They enjoyed prosperity (v. 37)

2. There was none sick (v. 37)

3. God gave them victory over the enemy (v. 38)

4. All their needs were met (vv. 40–41)

5. Joy and gladness filled the camp (v. 43)

6. He gave them their inheritance (v. 44)

The sad thing is that God is moving forward today, but many people don't want to move. They are locked in the status quo and resist change at all costs.

What happened to the people who heard the sound of the trumpet and did not move? They were left behind to suffer the heat by day and the cold by night. God had supplied Israel with a supernatural cooling and heating system to withstand the harsh temperatures of the desert. The ones who refused to move, resisting change, not only exposed themselves to the horrific conditions of an arid climate, but also gave the enemy a free hand to destroy them.

> Instant obedience is the only kind of obedience there is; delayed obedience is disobedience. Whoever strives to withdraw from obedience, withdraws from Grace.[8]
>
> —Thomas à Kempis

The life of a believer is about change—moving with God. Given the choice, no one would intentionally choose the idea of losing the power and freshness of His presence. Tragically, that choice is being made on a daily basis when we refuse to follow after Him. There is an old saying: "You will never change what you're willing to tolerate." I believe it to be true! As long as mediocrity and inconsistent living are tolerated, nothing will ever change.

4. The sound of the trumpet: a call to war

> When you go into battle in your own land against an enemy who is oppressing you, sound a blast on the trumpets. Then you will be remembered by the LORD your God and rescued from your enemies.
>
> —NUMBERS 10:9

The Israelites faced many enemies. The enemies were fierce, unforgiving, and relentless in their dedication to keep God's people from inheriting their promises. This particular sound of the trumpet was an alarm to wake up an entire nation for the purpose of battle.

God's trumpet blast of warning is still being heard today! The present-day enemies are not flesh and blood, as some would suppose. The Scripture is clear that we have a common enemy: spiritual forces in high places aligned against the body of Christ.

In Ephesians 6:10–12 the Apostle Paul exposes exactly who the enemy is:

> Finally, be strong in the Lord and in his mighty power. Put on the full armor of God, so that you can take your stand against the devil's schemes. For our struggle is not against flesh and blood, but against the rulers, against the authorities, against the powers of this dark world and against the spiritual forces of evil in the heavenly realms.

Paul also makes it very clear in 2 Corinthians 10:3–5 that we have supernatural weapons to fight against the enemy:

> For though we live in the world, we do not wage war as the world does. The weapons we fight with are not the weapons of the world. On the contrary, they have divine power to demolish strongholds. We demolish arguments and every pretension that sets itself up

against the knowledge of God, and we take captive every thought
to make it obedient to Christ.

It is the responsibility of leaders not only to warn the people but also
to lead in battle. Too many of God's people have been taken captive by
the enemy because of a weakened leadership that refuses to recognize we
are in a war for the souls of men.

Instead of leading his army into battle, King David decided to stay
at home and let someone else take his place on the battlefield. The
tragic story of David and Bathsheba is a result of a leader abdicating his
responsibility and opening himself up to the attack of the enemy. We
may not like it, but we have a responsibility as leaders not just to warn
the people, but also to be actively involved in leading them to the battle-
front: "Again, if the trumpet does not sound a clear call, who will get
ready for battle?" (1 Cor. 14:8).

The modern church is filled with deserters because there is an uncertain sound coming from the pulpits. Some pulpits are sounding the
retreat, and others are sounding the charge.

In military situations specific musical sounds are used to relay specific
instructions to the soldiers:

- *Reveille.* Every morning when the trumpet would blow
  reveille, every soldier knew it was time to rise and meet in
  formation in the company street.

- *Retreat.* At 10:00 p.m. the trumpet would blow taps,
  which meant "lights out," the official end of the day.

- *Charge or Attack.* In battle it meant to charge or advance
  toward the enemy.

What do you suppose would happen if the bugler blew the retreat
when he was supposed to blow the charge? The army would not know
what to do. An uncertain sound can bring about the wrong actions and
results. If the soldiers do not recognize the sound then they will not
know what to do.

That is why there must never be an uncertain sound in the army of
the Lord. That is also why so many churches are not progressing into
spiritual battle with the enemy: they have been given an uncertain sound
and are not preparing themselves for battle. There is so much going on
in the church realm today that is giving out an uncertain sound.

Uncertain sounds are coming from every direction today. We certainly are getting them from Washington, DC; certainly from the news media—nearly every Christian publication is issuing an uncertain sound. Even a lot of churches are sending out an uncertain sound. May God give us leaders who will run to the sound of battle and not away from it!

> The desperate cries of women and children. The rapid bursts of machine gun fire. The deafening roar of a tsunami. Most people hear the sounds of chaos and run in the opposite direction. But there are a few who listen intently for these sounds not in the hopes of hearing them but to help rid the world of them. They are the few forged in the crucible of training to respond quickly and decisively in the midst of chaos and uncertainty. And when the time comes they are the first to move toward the sounds of tyranny, injustice, and despair. They are the first to move toward the sounds of chaos because the only things louder than the sounds of chaos are the sounds of the few moving toward them.[9]

> Blow the trumpet in Zion; sound the alarm on my holy hill. Let all who live in the land tremble, for the day of the LORD is coming. It is close at hand.
>
> —JOEL 2:1

> Proclaim this among the nations: Prepare for war! Rouse the warriors! Let all the fighting men draw near and attack. Beat your plowshares into swords and your pruning hooks into spears. Let the weakling say, "I am strong!"
>
> —JOEL 3:9–10

5. The sound of the trumpet: a call to the nation to praise and worship

> Also at your times of rejoicing—your appointed festivals and New Moon feasts—you are to sound the trumpets over your burnt offerings and fellowship offerings, and they will be a memorial for you before your God. I am the LORD your God.
>
> —NUMBERS 10:10

The call to the nation to offer praise and worship in Numbers 10 is the same call going out to this generation. Praise and worship did not start with them, nor will it end with this current generation! Somewhere along the line we have been given the impression that praise and worship is something new to our day.

For those of us who have been involved in the "worship wars," it might seem like a new phenomenon. I travel all over the country and preach in many different churches and denominations. I have witnessed firsthand the remains of those who tried to infuse praise and worship into a traditional music program. Churches have split over issues such as whether to use hymn books, video projectors, or no printed words for the music at all. The issue is not where the words are printed; the issue is a matter of the heart!

Real praise and worship cannot be forced or faked for very long. Jesus said in John 4:24, "God is a Spirit: and they that worship him must worship him in spirit and in truth" (KJV). Praise and worship is simply agreement with what He has already said and shown us about who He is.

The real purpose of praise and worship is to invite God into your current environment. God begins to work when praise is released. When He shows up, things change.

There are many benefits and blessings associated with praise and worship. Here are five that have been instrumental in changing my life:

1. Praise and worship creates an atmosphere of joy: "You make known to me the path of life; you will fill me with joy in your presence, with eternal pleasures at your right hand" (Ps. 16:11).

2. Praise and worship brings rest and peace: "Take my yoke upon you and learn from me, for I am gentle and humble in heart, and you will find rest for your souls" (Matt. 11:29).

3. Praise and worship will distinguish you and supernaturally attract the right people to you: "Then Moses said to him, 'If your Presence does not go with us, do not send us up from here. How will anyone know that you are pleased with me and with your people unless you go with us? What else will distinguish me and your people from all the other people on the face of the earth?'" (Exod. 33:15–16).

4. Praise and worship will release an abundance of blessings: "Blessed are those you choose and bring near to live

in your courts! We are filled with the good things of your
house, of your holy temple" (Ps. 65:4).

5. Praise and worship disarms the enemy: "Sing to the LORD
a new song, his praise in the assembly of his faithful
people. Let Israel rejoice in their Maker; let the people
of Zion be glad in their King. Let them praise his name
with dancing and make music to him with timbrel and
harp. For the LORD takes delight in his people; he crowns
the humble with victory. Let his faithful people rejoice in
this honor and sing for joy on their beds. May the praise
of God be in their mouths and a double-edged sword in
their hands, to inflict vengeance on the nations and punishment on the peoples, to bind their kings with fetters,
their nobles with shackles of iron, to carry out the sen-
tence written against them—this is the glory of all his
faithful people" (Ps. 149:1–9).

It's time to hear the sound of this generation!

> Shout it aloud, do not hold back. Raise your voice like a trumpet.
> Declare to my people their rebellion and to the descendants of
> Jacob their sins.
> —ISAIAH 58:1

> I appointed watchmen over you and said, "Listen to the sound of
> the trumpet!" But you said, "We will not listen."
> —JEREMIAH 6:17

There is a sound released into every generation. Those who have ears
to hear will hear it and respond. Abraham heard the sound and a nation
was born. The children of Israel heard the sound and the walls of Jericho
fell flat. Elijah heard the sound and rain poured from heaven. The twelve
disciples heard the sound and shook the world. Lazarus heard the sound
and walked out of a grave. The apostle John heard the sound on the Isle
of Patmos and gave us a revelation of the future.

What sound are you hearing?

THE ISRAELI CONNECTION FOR LAST-DAYS BLESSING

CHAPTER 3

THE KEY OF SUPPORTING ISRAEL

I

T IS SAID that one day in the late nineteenth century, Queen Victoria of England reportedly asked Prime Minister Benjamin Disraeli this question: "Mr. Prime Minister, what evidence can you give me of the existence of God?" Disraeli reportedly replied, "The Jew, your majesty."[1]

It was May 15, 1948, when the United Nations partitioned what was then called Palestine and declared a portion of the land to be named Israel. A nation was reborn in a day!

Israel became the only nation in history to die and be reborn. Three times the nation has been exiled and then returned to its homeland:

1. When famine swept the land in the time of Jacob, the nation went to Egypt to survive under the watchful and wise care of Joseph. Over the course of time they found themselves enslaved in Egypt, but Moses led them with a mighty hand to their Promised Land.

2. Under the rule of King Nebuchadnezzar, they were taken into captivity in Babylon, but they rebuilt their land.

3. In AD 70, when Israel was occupied by Rome, the Roman army swept into Jerusalem and razed it and sacked the land. A few years later Rome even changed the name of Jerusalem to *Aelia Capitolina* and forbade Jews to come within a furlong of the city. Israel appeared to be dead. But on May 15, 1948, the dry bones of a dead Israel came together. Today the nation lives!

This year Israel celebrated its sixty-seventh birthday. For many people—especially in Europe, where a nation's longevity is well known and taken for granted—that number would elicit a yawn and a shrug of the shoulders. But not in Israel's case.

How is it possible for a nation the size of New Jersey or Wales to defend itself against overwhelming forces that are determined to eliminate its very existence? Some considered this small piece of land a miracle of birth when in 1948 it planted the lone flag of democracy in the midst of its enemies!

THE REAL ISSUE

The real issue today is, how are we as Christians supposed to view the nation of Israel? When it comes to the gospel of Jesus Christ, are we supposed to witness to the Jews or leave them alone? I don't know of any subject that causes more controversy than that of how to treat the Jewish people when it comes to salvation.

In my research I have come to the conclusion that there are *three basic* views when it comes to this critical question:

+ Two-Covenant Theology

+ Replacement Theology

+ "One New Man" Theology

There are many good, godly men who differ on the subject. Every single view is backed up with Scripture along with valid points of argument. I will present each view, not for the purpose of name calling or mudslinging, but to try to make some sense out of a complicated issue.

TWO-COVENANT THEOLOGY

According to a Religious News Service article "two-covenant theology maintains that God's covenant with the Jews has never been abrogated and that Jewish people do not need to become Christians in order to attain salvation."[2] As hard as it is to believe, there are some who say the Holocaust demanded that Christians develop a new viewpoint toward the Jews. The belief was that the horrific event was nothing more than a new revelation of God equal to biblical revelation.

Through the years this position has gained acceptance in some of the most prestigious denominations. I have discovered that the Episcopal Church, the Presbyterian Church (USA), and the United Church of Christ all have fallen in line with similar theology.[3] They represent only a sampling of how entrenched this theology has become.

Many Christian and Jewish groups accept a teaching today that was first taught by Franz Rosenzweig (1886–1929) earlier this century. He taught that there are two separate but equal covenants, or ways to God.

He taught that the covenant in Moses and the covenant in Jesus are complementary to each other.

Rosenzweig's thought, as evidenced by the following quote, gives a brief glimpse into this perspective:

> The synagogue, which is immortal but stands with broken staff and bound eyes, must renounce all this work in the world, and muster all her strength to preserve her life and keep herself untainted by life. And so she leaves the work in the world to the church and recognizes the church as the salvation for all heathens in all time.[4]

Joseph P. Gudel wrote: "Concerning this, Rabbi Jakob J. Petuchowski stated, 'Rosenzweig conceded more than any Jew, while remaining a Jew, had conceded before him. He admitted the truth of John 14:6.' This is immediately qualified, though, by the assertion that 'the Jew does not have to come to the Father. He has been with the Father ever since Sinai.'"[5]

It would be virtually impossible to give a thorough survey of Jewish writers on this subject. Suffice it to say that the belief in two separate covenants is one of the most popular beliefs in the Jewish community today. Arthur Gilbert states: "Judaism allows for religious pluralism and does not consider it scandalous…We do not believe that God's plan for salvation requires your conversion to Judaism nor mine to Christianity. But it does require our cooperation, our concern for, our joint effort to repair the world."[6]

Not everyone agrees with this position.

Writing in the August 1, 2002, issue of *Christianity Today*, Kenneth A. Myers declares that the rejection of two-covenant theology by evangelicals "is based on much more than our understanding of Judaism. It is based on our understanding of theology itself and, in turn, on our understanding of the nature of God's revelation in Scripture."[7]

He goes on to say: "The essential theological agenda, as embodied in creeds, confessions and catechisms, is not altered by historical events, however momentous. Such events may cause the church to reexamine its theology but are not revelatory."[8]

According to Myers, two-covenant theology "not only calls into question Christian attempts to evangelize Jews; it seems to assume that the entire notion of salvation is misguided, perhaps rooted in the necessity of spiritualizing the kingdom of God. Hence, it is wrong to characterize two-covenant theology as saying that Judaism 'saves' Jews and Christianity 'saves' Christians. Almost none of the writers on this topic acknowledge the need for anyone to be saved."[9]

Myers concludes that "a new day in redemptive history dawned with the Resurrection, just as it did on Sinai. To reject it is to be cut off from the community of the prophesied new covenant. There is no other name [than Jesus] by which we are saved."[10]

> The devilish camel of universalism is trying to sneak into the camp of the church, and he has poked his nose into the Jewish tent first. If that camel of universalism comes into the camp, he will bring in a whole herd of camels, each one representing a different heresy, and then the church will have nothing but camels.[11]
>
> —MOISHE ROSEN (1932–2010)
> FOUNDER AND EXECUTIVE DIRECTOR OF JEWS FOR JESUS

Myers, Rosen, and others agree the claim that the Holocaust calls into question any attempt to evangelize and witness to the Jews is contrary to what Jesus taught. Jesus did not teach hatred of the Jews! Anti-Semitism was contrary to all He said and did. Anytime persecution is done in the name of Christ, you will find a demonic presence somewhere behind the scenes pulling the strings. The persecution of the Jews is not a valid reason to stop evangelizing; on the contrary, it is the perfect opportunity to share the gospel of the love of God in Christ.

Are there two roads leading to the same destination?

"And so, there are two ways of salvation, one for the Jewish people and another one for the Gentiles." This thought is found not only among Jewish writers, but also among numerous Christians who believe there are two roads leading to the same destination. Such views usually come from mainline denominations that do not hold a belief in the inerrancy and authority of Scripture. For example, Carl Braaten writes: "Christianity is the Judaizing of the pagans. The task of Christianity is to preach the gospel among the Gentiles...The task of Judaism meanwhile is to remind Christianity of its original biblical roots."[12]

Those who do not accept the full authority of Scripture are not the only ones who believe in the two-covenant theology. This view is also found among Christians who say they accept and believe in the inerrancy and authority of Scripture. For example, while George Sheridan was the East Coast regional director for the Southern Baptist department of

Interfaith Witness, he "asserted that God's bond with the Jewish people was never superseded with the coming of Jesus: 'The Jews of today, as ever, receive salvation through their having been chosen by God in covenant with Abraham, Moses, and the prophets...My position is that the Jews do not require evangelization.'"[13]

Is it true?

Space in this book does not allow us to examine and quote every theologian who holds the position of two covenants. But I do believe at this point it is important to return to the Bible and examine whether there is any biblical foundation for a belief system that allows for two separate but equal covenants. Just examining the example of Jesus, the actions of the apostles, and the practice of the Apostle Paul led me to believe there is not!

Consider the example of Jesus

- On numerous occasions we find that He came "to the Jew first." In John 1:11 we are told, "He came to that which was his own, but his own did not receive him."

- He ministered consistently to the Jewish people. (See Matthew 4:23–25; 9:35.)

- When Jesus sent out the twelve apostles, He told them: "Do not go among the Gentiles or enter any town of the Samaritans. Go rather to the lost sheep of Israel" (Matt. 10:5–6).

- Only under extraordinary circumstances did Jesus minister to Gentiles. The best examples are found with the Syrophoenician woman in Mark 7 and the Roman centurion's servant in Matthew 8.

Consider the actions of the apostles

After Jesus was resurrected, He commanded the apostles to deliver the message of salvation to the Jewish people. They were told to declare that Jesus was the true Messiah, but Jesus included an addendum to His command: they were to leave the confines of the Jewish people and declare to the Gentiles the message of salvation.

But you will receive power when the Holy Spirit comes on you;
and you will be my witnesses in Jerusalem, and in all Judea and
Samaria, and to the ends of the earth.

—Acts 1:8

From the very beginning we see the apostle Peter preaching the
good news in front of a Jewish audience (Acts 2:5). The same pattern of
preaching to the Jew first is found consistently throughout the Book of
Acts (Acts 3:11–26; 5:21). You have to read all the way to Acts 10 to find
any effort at taking the gospel to anyone other than the Jewish people.
Peter faced tremendous criticism for preaching the gospel of salvation to
Gentiles (Acts 11:1–2).

It took many years and a wave of persecution for the early church to
begin fulfilling Jesus's command to share the gospel with anyone other
than the Jews. Finally the Jerusalem Council decided for Paul, Barnabas,
and others to go and open the door of salvation for any and all who
would come in, which of course included the Gentiles (Acts 15).

Consider the practice of the Apostle Paul

Paul's normal practice was to declare the good news to the Jew first
before opening the door to the Gentiles. For example, Acts 14:1 states,
"At Iconium Paul and Barnabas went as usual into the Jewish synagogue."
Moreover we are told that they "spent considerable time there" (v. 3). It
is evident that from the very beginning of his ministry, Paul took the
gospel to the Jew first (Acts 9:20–22; 26–29). He established a pattern
that continued throughout his ministry.

When ministering to the Jews, Paul emphasized that apart from rec-
ognizing and accepting Jesus as their Messiah, they were cut off from
God and from their covenant with Him. In his second letter to the
Corinthians he wrote:

> We are not like Moses, who would put a veil over his face to keep
> the Israelites from seeing the end of what was passing away. But
> their minds were made dull, for to this day the same veil remains
> when the old covenant is read. It has not been removed, because
> only in Christ is it taken away. Even to this day when Moses is
> read, a veil covers their hearts. But whenever anyone turns to the
> Lord, the veil is taken away.
>
> —2 Corinthians 3:13–16

Paul never stopped asking for prayers for the Jewish people so that they might repent of their rejection of the Messiah and be restored back into a relationship with God. As he stated in Romans 9–11, the Jewish people were God's elect, yet they rejected all the types and shadows that pointed to the coming Messiah. God gave them covenants, the Law, promises—all to no avail.

I believe Paul summed up his feelings when he stated in Romans 10:1–2: "Brothers and sisters, my heart's desire and prayer to God for the Israelites is that they may be saved. For I can testify about them that they are zealous for God, but their zeal is not based on knowledge."

It is obvious to anyone with an open mind that Paul believed that although the Jews were cut off from God because of their rejection, God had not rejected the Jewish people.

It seems to me that Jesus, the early apostles, and Paul were not aware of a two-covenant theology! There is much more that I could say on the subject, but suffice it to say that throughout the New Testament the Jewish people are always referred to as a people who need to receive Jesus Christ just as the Gentiles do.

REPLACEMENT THEOLOGY

It's possible that you have never heard the term *replacement theology.* Whether you have or not, more than likely you have been exposed to all or part of its teaching. The teaching of replacement theology states that the church—the body of Christ—has replaced the nation of Israel regarding the plans, purpose, and promises of God.

Replacement theology goes on to say that most of the promises God made to Israel must be spiritualized. The covenants made with Israel are now fulfilled in the Christian church. For example:

+ The Christian church is now God's chosen people, not the Jewish people.

+ After the Day of Pentecost the term *Israel* referred to the church.

+ The new covenant (Luke 22:20) has replaced the Mosaic covenant (Exod. 20).

+ Circumcision of the heart (Rom. 2:29) has replaced physical circumcision.

+ The Jewish people are now no longer a "chosen people." In fact, they are no different from any other group such as the English, Hispanics, or Africans.

+ Apart from repentance, the new birth, and incorporation into the church, Jewish people have no future, no hope, and no calling in the plan of God. The same is true for every other nation and group.

Simply put, replacement theology places the church as the primary vehicle by which the world is blessed by God's work. While it is true that the church does replace Israel in some areas (representing God's Word on the earth, etc.), it is not scriptural to say that God is finished with Israel and the church is its replacement!

From its origins the church was deeply connected to its Jewish roots. Jesus did not intend for it to be any other way. Many are still shocked to discover that Jesus was Jewish, and the basis of all of His teaching is consistent with the Hebrew Scriptures. (See Matthew 5:17–18.)

The position of the early church fathers influences the church's view of Israel to this present day. All you have to do is scan a brief history of the first four centuries of Christianity and you will see a pattern of disdain and hatred toward Jews. This animosity continued in spite of the clear teaching of the New Testament. In the writings of the early church fathers, for example, we find the following:

+ Justin Martyr (circa AD 160), speaking to a Jew, said: "The Scriptures are not yours, but ours."[14]

+ Irenaeus, Bishop of Lyon (circa AD 177) declared: "Jews are disinherited from the grace of God."[15]

+ Tertullian (160–230), in his treatise against the Jews, announced that God had rejected the Jews in favor of the Christians.[16]

Early in the fourth century Eusebius declared that the promises of the Hebrew Scriptures were for Christians and not for Jews, and that the curses were for the Jews. He argued that the church was the continuation of the Old Testament and thus superseded Judaism.

The young church declared itself to be the true Israel, or "Israel according to the Spirit"; heir to the divine promises. They found it essential to discredit "Israel according to the flesh" in order to prove that God had cast away His people and transferred His love to Christians.

Backed up by more than four hundred years of teaching and preaching hatred against the Jews, the results were inevitable:

+ The Crusades

+ The forced wearing of distinguishing marks to ostracize Jews

+ The Inquisition

+ Separation of entire Jewish communities into ghettos

+ Destruction of Jewish literature and synagogues

+ Physical, mental, and emotional persecution that included execution

+ The Holocaust: the systematic extermination of more than 6 million Jews in so-called Christian Europe

Clarence H. Wagner Jr. writes:

> Had the Church understood the clear message of being grafted into the Olive Tree from the beginning, then the sad legacy of anti-Semitic hatred from the Church may have been avoided. The error of Replacement Theology is like a cancer in the Church that has not only caused it to violate God's Word concerning the Jewish people and Israel, but it made us into instruments of hate, not love in God's Name.[17]

Is anti-Semitism taught in the New Testament? Was it the intent of New Testament writers for the church to treat the Jewish people with scorn and contempt? The answer is, *absolutely not!*

It is clear.

The clear teaching of the New Testament is that the church was and is to love and honor the Jewish people. In Ephesians 2:11–18 we are told that by the blood of Messiah we Gentiles are "brought near" to the commonwealth of Israel, or the covenants, promises, and hopes given to Israel. In Romans 11:11–12, 25 we are told that "blindness in part" (KJV) has come to the Jews so that the message will be forced out into the nations. Nevertheless, we are told that a time will come when "all

Israel will be saved" (v. 26) because the gifts and callings of God toward
Israel and the Jewish people were given "without repentance" (v. 29, KJV).
God's relationship with Israel and the Jewish people is everlasting.

We Gentile Christians are told that the Jews are "beloved" for the
sake of the patriarchs (Rom. 11:28, KJV). They are a chosen people who
fulfilled their calling and brought the gospel to the world.

The church has a choice. It can try to replace Israel, or it can relate
to Israel. The church cannot have it both ways—teaching a replacement
theology while at the same time blessing Israel and praying for the peace
of Jerusalem. No wonder the average pew sitter is confused!

I am convinced that the role of the church is to take its place in God's
reconciliation plan for the world while understanding and appreci-
ating God's ongoing covenant with and love for the Jewish people. We
Christians are much better off when we show respect, love, and honor to
God's chosen people.

The danger of replacement theology is that it causes a violation of
God's Word about the nation of Israel in general and the Jewish people
in particular. The church's legacy of hate and anti-Semitism could have
been avoided had we understood the clear biblical message from the
beginning. The gospel of Jesus Christ is good news for all people. It is a
message of love, not hate!

"ONE NEW MAN" THEOLOGY

The "one new man" viewpoint does not teach that there are two separate ways of salvation—one for the Jews and one for the Gentiles. It
teaches that all people, whether Jew or Gentile, must come the same
way—through faith in Christ crucified, buried, and resurrected. The
Scripture is clear: "There is no other name under heaven given among
men by which we must be saved" (Acts 4:12, NKJV). Jew and Gentile
alike find salvation, reconciliation, and unity through the shed blood
of Christ.

When we examine Paul's message to the Ephesian believers, especially
the latter part of Ephesians 2, we get a clear meaning of the one new
man viewpoint:

> Therefore, remember that formerly you who are Gentiles by birth
> and called "uncircumcised" by those who call themselves "the
> circumcision" (which is done in the body by human hands)—
> remember that at that time you were separate from Christ,

excluded from citizenship in Israel and foreigners to the covenants of the promise, without hope and without God in the world. But now in Christ Jesus you who once were far away have been brought near by the blood of Christ.

For he himself is our peace, who has made the two groups one and has destroyed the barrier, the dividing wall of hostility, by setting aside in his flesh the law with its commands and regulations. His purpose was to create in himself one new humanity out of the two, thus making peace, and in one body to reconcile both of them to God through the cross, by which he put to death their hostility. He came and preached peace to you who were far away and peace to those who were near.

—EPHESIANS 2:11–17

Writing under the inspiration of the Holy Spirit, the Apostle Paul gives us the clearest view of what it really means to be "one new man." The first thing he does is remind the Gentile believers of what took place before they came to salvation in Christ. Paul draws a comparison between what they were and what they are now as a result of being in Christ. It's always good to remember how far we have come.

+ *They were uncircumcised* (v. 11). They were excluded because they did not give evidence of the sign of God's covenant: circumcision. Judaism saw that circumcision was the primary symbol of obedience to the Torah, of belonging to the family of God. The Jews held contempt for the Gentiles for this and many other practices commanded by the law. The attitude of the Gentiles toward the Jews was no better.

+ *They were Christless* (v. 12). The Gentiles were alienated from the Jews due to their alienation from Christ, the Messiah. The Gentiles did not have sacrifices that promised redemption and forgiveness of sins. Their best hope was to please their gods any way possible.

+ *They were stateless* (v. 12). Pointing out their exclusion from citizenship was ironic, for to the Greek few things were more important than having the rights of a citizen. To be excluded from citizenship was to be a barbarian; it was to suffer the worst kind of oppression.

- *They were hopeless* (v. 12). They had no hope in the future because sin alienated them from God. They had no sense of community, a Savior, or a family. Because "hope deferred makes the heart sick" (Prov. 13:12), the Gentiles were literally a sick people group.

- *They were Godless* (v. 12). They had plenty of gods, and in their view they were not lacking in spirituality. To say they were godless appears to be ridiculous. They were missing the key element, however—a personal knowledge of the true and living God, and His mercy and grace.

But God had an answer for their alienation—and ours!

The alienation is gone. How? It was accomplished not by religious activity nor by making certain appeasements to the gods. Paul's simple statement provides us with the answer: "But now in Christ Jesus" (v. 13)!

Alienation is eradicated by Christ's death. Because of His sacrifice, alienation and hostility are replaced by His peace! Christ does not just bring peace; He is our peace. To speak of peace is to speak of Christ. There is an echo here of Micah 5:5, in which the shepherd from Bethlehem will come to lead His people and "He will be [their] peace."

Paul describes the establishment of peace like the destruction of a barricade. Some Bible scholars believe that Paul's description referred to the literal wall in the Jerusalem temple.

> What Paul most likely is referring to here is a literal wall in the Jerusalem Temple. The Jewish Temple was comprised of a series of concentric courts. At the center was the Holy of Holies where the High Priest entered just once each year. Then the Holy Place, where the priests did their daily work. Beyond that Jewish men could gather to worship. Beyond that, the Jewish women could gather. At the edge of that court there was a five-foot-high barricade separating the Court of Women from the furthest circle, the Court of the Gentiles. Several years ago archaeologists discovered plaques cautioning Gentiles from stepping over the line: "No foreigner may enter within the barricade which surrounds the sanctuary and enclosure. Anyone who is caught doing so will have himself to blame for his ensuing death."
>
> Paul likewise draws a comparison between this physical wall and the law, that in Christ the distinction between Jew and Gentile has been destroyed by abolishing the law.[18]

Paul declares God's purpose in all of this. Two completely divergent groups are created into "one new man." He is not suggesting that Gentiles should become Jews in order to be accepted by God. God has created something new and different.

ONE NEW MAN EQUALS A NEW CREATION

Therefore, if anyone is in Christ, the new creation has come: The old has gone, the new is here!

—2 CORINTHIANS 5:17

In the New Testament two Greek words are translated "new," although they have different meanings. It is crucial to understand the difference.

The first word, *neos*, means "numerically new," but not "different." For instance, if you buy a brand-new microwave of a certain make and model, you have a new microwave; but there are thousands more just like it all over the world. It's new to you, but it's not different.

The second word for new is *kainos*, which means not only "numerically new" but also "quantitatively new." For example, a car manufactured in 1910 will be different from a car manufactured today. Not only is this numerically new, but it is also quantitatively new because it is different. We all would agree that a Ford Model T automobile and a Ferrari are radically different!

In 2 Corinthians 5:17 the word *kainos* is used. We are not just replicas or duplications of something else, which would require the word to be *neos*. We are new and, in a sense of being different, *kainos*. In Christ we are qualitatively new—new creations, brand-new in kind and quality. To be born again by the Spirit of God does not mean we are just the same people with a few changes made to us. *No!* A thousand times *no!*

God has put a different nature in us and transformed us by the power of the Holy Spirit. The word *kainos* does not simply mean new in point of time, but new in the sense that it brings into the world a new kind of thing, a new quality of thing, that did not exist before. What is that new thing? This "new man" is a new race altogether. We can now be at peace with one another because we are reconciled to God.

It's time to stop the madness! For generations we have been like the proverbial man who said, "Don't confuse me with the facts; my mind is made up." My purpose in this chapter has not been to add to the confusion but simply to point out that so-called theologians have for generations propagated "another gospel."

While it is true that many good and decent people can disagree on the finer points of theology, make no mistake that there is one thing we must all agree on: Christ is the *only* way to the Father. Whether Jew or Gentile, we can only enter into the community of peace one way, and that is through the shed blood of Jesus Christ!

> The church is not a theological classroom. It is a conversion, confession, repentance, reconciliation, forgiveness and sanctification center, where flawed people place their faith in Christ, gather to know and love Him better, and learn to love others as He designed.[19]

The evidence is clear. There is only one way into the body of Christ. Next we will see what God thinks about Jerusalem in particular.

CHAPTER 4

JERUSALEM, ISRAEL'S CAPITAL

*The view of Jerusalem is the history of the world; it is
more; it is the history of heaven and earth.*[1]
—BENJAMIN DISRAELI
FORMER PRIME MINISTER OF ENGLAND

JERUSALEM STANDS ALONE as the positive pole of God's plan for His creation. It is the city God selected as His dwelling place, the capital of God's kingdom on Earth. It is the city where God's Son died for the sins of the world. Jerusalem may well be the capital city of the universe!

Jerusalem is a port city on the shore of eternity.[2]
—YEHUDA AMICHAI
ISRAELI POET

After exhaustive research I have discovered the city is mentioned 881 Times in Scripture—667 times in the Old Testament and 144 in the New Testament. No city on Earth has seen more and experienced more than this ancient city. Not a day, week, or month goes by that Jerusalem is not the focus of world attention.

The LORD, who stretches out the heavens, who lays the foundation of the earth, and who forms the human spirit within a person, declares: "I am going to make Jerusalem a cup that sends all the surrounding peoples reeling. Judah will be besieged as well as Jerusalem. On that day, when all the nations of the earth are gathered against her, I will make Jerusalem an immovable rock for all the nations. All who try to move it will injure themselves.
—ZECHARIAH 12:1–3

JERUSALEM: THE BEGINNING

In Genesis 14 Moses introduces Jerusalem (Salem) as a part of the story of Abram, whom God later renamed Abraham. God promised to make

Abraham's name great, as long as he obeyed Him. As long as Abraham's descendants gave glory to God, Jerusalem would flourish.

Abraham obeyed God's call and moved his family to Canaan, the land God promised him. The land of promise became a land of testing and struggle. Abraham faced many obstacles, including famine, invasion from without, and family strife from within.

Genesis 14 also describes an attack by an alliance of four kings from the East. The attack was against five kings who lived in the land of promise. As was so often the case, Abraham found himself right in the middle of the threat. The four kings from the East were Amraphel, king of Shinar (Babylon); Arioch, king of Ellasar (an ancient city about ten miles north of Ur); Kedorlaomer, king of Elam (Persia, modern Iran); and Tidal, king of Goiim (a group of tribes). All four of these kings were from the region of southern Mesopotamia.

I'm sure there were those in Abraham's camp wondering how this could be called a land of promise when invading armies could come in and devastate everything in their path.

Even though the situation looked hopeless, Abraham had a promise to stand on in the midst of darkness:

> I will make you into a great nation, and I will bless you; I will make your name great, and you will be a blessing. I will bless those who bless you, and whoever curses you I will curse; and all peoples on earth will be blessed through you.
>
> —GENESIS 12:2–3

Charles H. Dyer writes in *The Rise of Babylon*:

> Here was the first great test of God's promise and Abram's faith. The situation looked hopeless, but when the four kings left to carry the spoils of conquest back to Mesopotamia, Abram, trusting in God's promise, pursued and defeated them. Melchizedek, king of Salem, proclaimed the source of Abram's victory: Blessed be God Most High, who delivered your enemies into your hand.[3]

Salem (Jerusalem) was the city of Melchizedek, a king-priest who ruled the city. Many scholars believe that he stands as a type of Christ, a picture of the Messiah who was to come.

This Melchizedek was king of Salem and priest of God Most High. He met Abraham returning from the defeat of the kings and blessed him, and Abraham gave him a tenth of everything. The name *Melchizedek* means "king of righteousness," and *king of Salem* means "king of peace." (See Hebrews 7:1–2.)

Who was this mystery King?

It appears that although he was not a Jew, Melchizedek did worship the one true and living God. We see him blessing Abraham after Abraham rescued his nephew Lot from enemy captivity. Abraham expressed honor by giving Melchizedek a tithe of the spoils of battle. Abraham received disdain from the king of Sodom, but he received blessing and honor from Melchizedek, the king of Salem.

It was a rare thing in the ancient world to worship only one God. Idol worship (the worship of many gods) was the religion of the day. Yet at some point God had revealed Himself to Melchizedek, just as He did to Abraham.

The act of presenting "bread and wine" to Abraham is a symbol of Melchizedek's holiness. It led many Bible scholars to ascribe these qualities as a picture of Jesus Christ revealed in the Old Testament. With no genealogical background and no record of father or mother, the "type" of Christ is certainly appropriate.

Melchizedek is mentioned several times in the Book of Hebrews. One of the key points of the book is understanding Jesus's status as our High Priest. The writer points out that just as Melchizedek was not born into Levitical priesthood but was appointed by God, so Jesus was named our eternal High Priest, interceding on our behalf:

> Son though he was, he learned obedience from what he suffered and, once made perfect, he became the source of eternal salvation for all who obey him and was designated by God to be high priest in the order of Melchizedek.
>
> —HEBREWS 5:8–10

> If perfection could have been attained through the Levitical priesthood—and indeed the law given to the people established that priesthood—why was there still need for another priest to come, one in the order of Melchizedek, not in the order of Aaron?
>
> —HEBREWS 7:11

> And what we have said is even more clear if another priest like Melchizedek appears, one who has become a priest not on the basis of a regulation as to his ancestry but on the basis of the power of

an indestructible life. For it is declared: "You are a priest forever, in the order of Melchizedek."

—HEBREWS 7:15–17

It is true that we may never know all the details about this mystery king. One thing most can agree on is this: he paints an Old Testament picture of the final King, the Priest of Jerusalem, who will rule in righteousness. He is Jesus Christ!

Psalm 110 pictures the Messiah as both victorious King and a Priest forever in the order of Melchizedek:

> The LORD says to my lord: "Sit at my right hand until I make your enemies a footstool for your feet." The LORD will extend your mighty scepter from Zion, saying, "Rule in the midst of your enemies!" Your troops will be willing on your day of battle. Arrayed in holy splendor, your young men will come to you like dew from the morning's womb. The LORD has sworn and will not change his mind: "You are a priest forever, in the order of Melchizedek."
>
> —PSALM 110:1–4

Later in history Salem came to be called *Jebus*, the stronghold of the Jebusites. David was commanded by God to conquer that city. First Chronicles 11:4 records: "And David and all Israel went to Jerusalem, which is Jebus; where the Jebusites were, the inhabitants of the land" (KJV). Thereafter, David called the name of the city *Jerusalem*, which means "foundation of peace."

The claim of God on this city is eternal. He chose the city as His own! Jerusalem is necessary for the outworking of God's plan, and no matter what comes against the city, the apple of God's eye will not be destroyed.

God calls Jerusalem

+ "My city" in Isaiah 45:13: "I will raise up Cyrus in my righteousness: I will make all his ways straight. He will rebuild *my city* and set my exiles free, but not for a price or reward, says the LORD Almighty" (emphasis added);

+ "My holy mountain" in Isaiah 11:9: "They will neither harm nor destroy on all *my holy mountain*, for the earth will be filled with the knowledge of the LORD as the waters cover the sea" (emphasis added);

+ "The holy city" in Nehemiah 11:1: "Now the leaders of the people settled in Jerusalem. The rest of the people cast lots to bring one out of every ten of them to live in Jerusalem, *the holy city*, while the remaining nine were to stay in their own towns" (emphasis added).

Jerusalem was also where David first established worship, and where Solomon built the temple. Jerusalem is where Jesus died on the cross and rose from the grave. And Jerusalem is where Jesus will return!

JERUSALEM: THE BURDEN

Through the centuries Jerusalem has experienced every form of misery and heartache. It has experienced siege, war, and destruction. Ezra, Nehemiah, and later Herod had the job of rebuilding the city at different times in its history.

After the Romans destroyed the city, Emperor Hadrian changed the name again to *Aelia Capitolina*. After Rome's war against the Jews in AD 70, the Romans destroyed the second temple. It was a devastating loss for the Jewish people. The Romans also laid waste to Herod's palace and all the mansions in the upper city.

In AD 130 Hadrian determined to rebuild Jerusalem as a gift to the Jewish people. It was not going to be as simple as it sounded. His plans included building temples to pagan gods in the center of Jerusalem, as well as erecting a temple to Jupiter on the Temple Mount.

His plan elicited hatred from the Jewish people, who staged a doomed revolt led by the warrior Bar Kochba. As punishment, Hadrian exiled all Jews from Jerusalem and at the same time brought a wide variety of people from other parts of the known world. For centuries *Aelia Capitolina* was the only name for Jerusalem that most people could remember.

During the Crusades the Muslims called it *Al-Quds*, or "The Holy." To this day Muslims still refer to Jerusalem by that name. At the present hour the explicit goal of militant Islam is to seize control of all of Jerusalem. Many efforts have been made to reconcile the problems in Israel and the Palestinian territories, but at the time of this writing the hatred against Jerusalem is a ticking time bomb that could explode and plunge the world into a conflagration at any moment.

Although Jerusalem was founded as a city of peace and blessing, she has known centuries of war. Armies from many nations have marched across the landscape of Jerusalem: Pharaoh and Egypt, Assyria and Babylon, Alexander the Great of Greece, the powerful Roman legions, the Ottoman Empire, and the armies of Great Britain, to name a few:

> Throughout the bloodiest pages of history, the people of Jerusalem have been betrayed time and time again. The three-thousand-year chronicle of this ancient capital is an ageless story of victory and defeat, conquest and carnage, bloodshed and betrayal. The City of David has changed hands twenty-six times and has been leveled to the ground on five separate occasions. And still, it remains today one of the most coveted pieces of real estate on earth and the one city most ardently sought after by the enemies of God. For decades Jerusalem has been a bone in the throat of the architects of the new world order.[4]

Since her birth in 1948 Israel has known continuous conflict:

+ 1948—War of Independence

+ 1967—Six-Day War

+ 1973—Yom Kippur War

+ 1987—The First Intifada

The conflict continues to this day! Jerusalem is restored, but it is still a divided city. On the western end of the Temple Mount stands the third holiest site of Islam, the Dome of the Rock. A short distance away is the Al-Aqsa Mosque, which towers above the ancient Western Wall of Solomon's Temple, also known as the Wailing Wall.

Not only do you find some of the holiest places of Islam located in Jerusalem, but also Christianity's greatest treasures are there as well:

+ Bethlehem, the city of Christ's birth, is a suburb of Jerusalem.

+ The Temple Mount is the place where Jesus astonished the great teachers when He was only twelve years old.

+ The Via Dolorosa, "the way of the cross," is a cherished landmark.

+ Golgotha, "the place of the skull" and the site of the Crucifixion, is located in the city.

◆ The Garden Tomb and the Mount of Olives are among the special places where Jesus walked, talked, and taught within the great city of Jerusalem.

JERUSALEM: THE BLESSING

I have made many trips to the Middle East. I have visited Israel, Egypt, Jordan, and Lebanon. But there is one city that has a special place in my heart: Jerusalem. I can still recall the emotions that swept over my soul the last time I stood in the ancient city. I never tire of going to Jerusalem and walking through the streets where Jesus once walked.

When you enter the part of Jerusalem called the Old City, you find some of the same types of vendors that sold their wares in Jesus's day. They still have the spices and foodstuffs out in open stalls.

Along with the old, you can look around from that place and see tall, modern buildings as well. You see a city that has swept out of those ancient walls and is now reaching into the heels of Judea. You look at it and wonder, "Could anything be more beautiful on the face of the earth?"—especially considering what God did here?

God clearly loves this city! Psalm 87:1–2 says, "His foundation is in the holy mountains. The LORD loves the gates of Zion more than all the dwellings of Jacob" (NKJV).

David Ben-Gurion, the first prime minister of Israel, said, "No city in the world, not even Athens or Rome, ever played as great a role in the life of a nation for so long a time, as Jerusalem has done in the life of the Jewish people."[5]

Jerusalem will be the last and final city to rule the world. God will cause this earthly city to survive. Our task today is to support it. Isaiah 40:1–2 says, "Comfort, comfort my people, says your God. Speak tenderly to Jerusalem, and proclaim to her that her hard service has been completed, that her sin has been paid for, that she has received from the LORD's hand double for all her sins."

One day God will establish a New Jerusalem. What a stunning sight it will be when the heavenly city descends! The traveling city, set up in stationary orbit, will drift over earthly Jerusalem!

> And he carried me away in the Spirit to a mountain great and high, and showed me the Holy City, Jerusalem, coming down out of heaven from God. It shone with the glory of God, and its brilliance was like that of a very precious jewel, like a jasper, clear as

crystal. It had a great, high wall with twelve gates, and with twelve angels at the gates. On the gates were written the names of the twelve tribes of Israel.

—REVELATION 21:10–12

But you have come to Mount Zion, to the city of the living God, the heavenly Jerusalem. You have come to thousands upon thousands of angels in joyful assembly, to the church of the firstborn, whose names are written in heaven. You have come to God, the Judge of all, to the spirits of the righteous made perfect, to Jesus the mediator of a new covenant, and to the sprinkled blood that speaks a better word than the blood of Abel.

—HEBREWS 12:22–24

Richard F. Ames wrote an amazing article in *Tomorrow's World* magazine titled "The Future of Jerusalem." It is a rather lengthy article, but one worth noting. In it he writes:

Disputes over Jerusalem are constantly in the news. Arabs and Israelis are fighting over its future, but God has an amazing plan for this long-troubled city. Will Jerusalem ever see peace? The answer may surprise you!

Today, Jerusalem faces ongoing violence and the threat of all-out war. But your Bible reveals that this historic city will soon be the capital of the world!

Jerusalem is a focal point of conflict in the Middle East. Across the Arab world, millions oppose Israel's hold on this historic city. Around the globe, millions of Muslims hope the day will come when Jerusalem is no longer under Israel's control…

Since 1967, Jerusalem has remained under Israeli administration. Yet tensions persist in this densely peopled city, with an estimated population above 700,000. About 32 percent of the city's population are Arab Muslims, who often find themselves in conflict with the 65 percent of the population who are Jewish.

THREE RELIGIONS, ONE CITY

Can Israel and the Arab states find peace while Jerusalem remains a source of conflict? Will the city ever be the capital of a Palestinian state? Will it come under international control? Your Bible shows that the conflict over Jerusalem will be a central focus of end-time events.

Jerusalem today is a city of many faiths; one survey in 2006 identified 1,200 synagogues, 150 churches and 70 mosques within its boundaries.

Jews look to Jerusalem as the city of the great prophets, and as the capital of the Kingdom of Israel and Judah under King David and his son King Solomon. Ancient Israel's first and second temples, in Jerusalem, were the center of Jewish worship until the Romans destroyed the city in 70 AD. Today, Jews worship at the Western Wall, or Wailing Wall, which they believe is the only surviving element of the Second Temple now accessible to Jewish worshipers.

Jerusalem is also the third most holy city of Islam, after Mecca and Medina. Today, the Mosque of Omar, also called the Dome of the Rock, dominates the Temple Mount. The Arabic term for the Temple Mount is al-Haram as-Sharif, which means "The Noble Sanctuary." Muslims believe that Muhammad ascended to heaven from there.

Christians remember Jerusalem as the place where the Savior was crucified, and where He taught in the Temple—and as the place to which He will return to establish His kingdom, with Jerusalem as world capital.

MILITARY MOVEMENTS PROPHESIED

What does Bible prophecy reveal will happen to Jerusalem? Eventually, this ancient city will be the capital of the whole world. But before that time, dramatic military movements will affect Jerusalem. A time will come, near the end of the age, when enemy armies will invade the Holy Land and surround the city of Jerusalem. As Jesus Christ Himself warned, "But when you see Jerusalem surrounded by armies, then know that its desolation is near" (Luke 21:20).[6]

Ames concludes his article by saying:

PEACE IS COMING

Today we live in a world of war and terrorism. Nations strive for peace. But, as the Apostle Paul cautioned us, "As it is written: 'There is none righteous, no, not one; there is none who understands; there is none who seeks after God'" (Romans 3:10–11). He continues: "Their feet are swift to shed blood; destruction and misery are in their ways; and the way of peace they have not known. There is no fear of God before their eyes" (vv. 15–18).

The only one who will bring us world peace, is the Messiah, Jesus Christ. He is coming back as King of kings, and Lord of lords, as it tells us in Revelation 19:16. And Scripture tells us the exact location to which He will return: "Then the Lord will go forth and fight against those nations, as He fights in the day of battle. And in that day His feet will stand on the Mount of Olives, which faces Jerusalem on the east" (Zechariah 14:3–4). The Mount of Olives is just east of the Temple Mount in Jerusalem, across the Kidron Valley.

Jerusalem will be prosperous and flourishing when the Messiah rules the world from Jerusalem. Notice this description: "And in that day it shall be that living waters shall flow from Jerusalem, half of them toward the eastern sea and half of them toward the western sea; in both summer and winter it shall occur. And the Lord shall be King over all the earth. In that day it shall be—'The Lord is one,' and His name one" (Zechariah 14:8–9).

I hope you are looking forward to that day foretold by the prophet Isaiah. "O Zion, you who bring good tidings, get up into the high mountain; O Jerusalem, you who bring good tidings, lift up your voice with strength, lift it up, be not afraid; say to the cities of Judah, 'Behold your God!'" (Isaiah 40:9).

Yes, as we have seen, the Messiah is coming to Jerusalem! The whole world will soon understand, that the God of Abraham, Isaac, and Jacob is the Messiah. Remember the Rock of Israel? Speaking of ancient Israel, the Apostle Paul writes, "Moreover, brethren, I do not want you to be unaware that all our fathers were under the cloud, all passed through the sea, all were baptized into Moses in the cloud and in the sea, all ate the same spiritual food, and all drank the same spiritual drink. For they drank of that spiritual Rock that followed them, and that Rock was Christ" (1 Corinthians 10:1–4). Yes, that Rock was the Messiah—and He will soon return!

As Isaiah wrote: "Behold, the Lord God shall come with a strong hand, and His arm shall rule for Him; behold, His reward is with Him, and His work before Him. He will feed His flock like a shepherd; He will gather the lambs with His arm, and carry them in His bosom, and gently lead those who are with young" (Isaiah 40:10–11).

Yes, the Lord will save His people, and He will educate and wisely rule over all nations. Notice this prophecy concerning Jerusalem. "The word that Isaiah the son of Amoz saw concerning Judah and Jerusalem. Now it shall come to pass in the latter days that the mountain of the Lord's house shall be established on the top of the mountains, and shall be exalted above the hills; and all nations shall flow to it" (Isaiah 2:1–2).

PEACEFUL WORLD GOVERNMENT AHEAD

Mountains are a biblical symbol for a kingdom or government. Isaiah states plainly that the Lord's kingdom will be established in Jerusalem. All nations will submit to the new world government. This will not be government in the hands of selfish human beings. The new government will be a world-ruling divine Kingdom—the Kingdom of God. This world-ruling kingdom will be governed by the Messiah, the King of kings, Jesus Christ! That is the good news we all look forward to. I hope that you are looking forward to that time of world peace! I hope that you are yearning for the Kingdom to come! I hope you are praying for the Kingdom to come, as we are taught to pray in Matthew 6:10!

Notice this beautiful description of future life in Jerusalem: "Thus says the Lord: 'I will return to Zion, and dwell in the midst of Jerusalem. Jerusalem shall be called the City of Truth, The Mountain of the Lord of hosts, The Holy Mountain.' Thus says the Lord of hosts: 'Old men and old women shall again sit in the streets of Jerusalem, each one with his staff in his hand because of great age. The streets of the city shall be full of boys and girls playing in its streets'" (Zechariah 8:3–5).

The city of Jerusalem will finally live up to its name, "City of Peace," because the Messiah, Jesus Christ will actually dwell there. Only then will the whole world begin to experience genuine peace.

Jerusalem will be the capital of planet earth, and you can have a part in the glorious Kingdom ruled from that capital. Tomorrow's world will be here sooner than you realize. As events move toward this wonderful climax, be sure you are watching world news in the light of Bible prophecy!"[7]

Until then, we must continually pray for the peace and safety of Jerusalem!

> Pray for the peace of Jerusalem: "May those who love you be secure. May there be peace within your walls and security within your citadels." For the sake of my family and friends, I will say, "Peace be within you."
>
> —PSALM 122:6–8

CHAPTER 5

THE LATTER RAIN AND ISRAEL

T HOUGH ONLY MENTIONED a few times in Scripture, the "latter rain" serves as a significant marker of the last days. Admittedly there has been some difficulty and disagreement on what the term signifies.

In the natural order of things the latter rain was the second of two necessary rains to produce food, oil, and wine. The "early" or "former" rain prepared the ground and nourished the seeds, planting trees and vines. This early rain was a season or a special time.

The latter rain came in two waves. The first watered the wheat crop, causing the grain to mature. This season also prepared the olive groves and vineyard for the early fall harvest.

PROPHETIC SIGNIFICANCE

The latter rain, as all seasoned activity in Israel, had prophetic significance. We find allusion to the latter rain early in Scripture as well as toward the end of it.

To understand any concept in Scripture, there are immutable laws of interpretation. One of them is the law of first mention. The first mention of anything in Scripture sets its primary meaning for every other time it is mentioned. This is especially important for Israel and for those of us living in these last days.

Latter rain is first mentioned in Deuteronomy. Before we look at that mention and note its significance, let me give some introduction to this part of Scripture.

Deuteronomy means "second law." This book was the part of sacred Scripture most quoted by Jesus in His earthly ministry. Furthermore, Deuteronomy drops prophetic clues regarding Israel in the last days all through its pages.

For example, look at two verses:

> When you are in distress, and all these things come upon you in
> the latter days, when you turn to the Lord your God and obey
> His voice.
> —Deuteronomy 4:30, nkjv

This was a word to Israel about their troubles, including the
Tribulation of the last days.

> Who fed you in the wilderness with manna, which your fathers did
> not know, that He might humble you and that He might test you,
> to do you good in the end.
> —Deuteronomy 8:16, nkjv

This was God's promise to prosper Israel in the last days.
Understanding this, let's look at the first mention of the latter rain:

> But the land which you cross over to possess is a land of hills and val-
> leys, which drinks water from the rain of heaven, a land for which the
> Lord your God cares; the eyes of the Lord your God are always on
> it, from the beginning of the year to the very end of the year. And it
> shall be that if you earnestly obey My commandments which I com-
> mand you today, to love the Lord your God and serve Him with all
> your heart and with all your soul, then I will give you the rain for
> your land in its season, the early rain and the latter rain, that you may
> gather in your grain, your new wine, and your oil.
> —Deuteronomy 11:11–14, nkjv

This is God's first mention of the latter rain. Notice that the latter
rain is inextricably bound to Israel's possession of the land. Also, Yahweh
expresses His deep affection not just for the people but also for the land.
Clearly God cares for that small piece of real estate called Israel.

Later these rains were part of Israel's three seasons of feasts. The
word for season is *bitayth* in Hebrew and *kairos* in Greek. It means "a
special limited time"!

Now let us unpack these signposts of the last days.

THE LATTER RAIN AND ISRAEL

As I have mentioned—and its importance will intensify—the latter rain
is always connected to Israel's possession of the land. Let's look back
to Deuteronomy just before the rain is first mentioned and read some
verses on possession of the land:

> Therefore you shall keep every commandment which I command you today, that you may be strong, and go in and possess the land which you cross over to possess, and that you may prolong your days in the land which the LORD swore to give your fathers, to them and their descendants, "a land flowing with milk and honey."
> —DEUTERONOMY 11:8–9, NKJV

The rain that is called "the rain of heaven" two verses later in Deuteronomy 11:11 comes to land that has been claimed and possessed. Look back at another passage:

> For the land which you go to possess is not like the land of Egypt from which you have come, where you sowed your seed and watered it by foot, as a vegetable garden; but the land which you cross over to possess is a land of hills and valleys, which drinks water from the rain of heaven, a land for which the LORD your God cares; the eyes of the LORD your God are always on it, from the beginning of the year to the very end of the year.
> —DEUTERONOMY 11:10–12, NKJV

Here Israel was viewed as distinct from Egypt, receiving rain from heaven, and a land for which God cares! Israel was viewed as sacred, special, and separated from other lands. This land was also supplied with all it needed to furnish the people:

> Then I will give you the rain for your land in its season, the early rain and the latter rain, that you may gather in your grain, your new wine, and your oil.
> —DEUTERONOMY 11:14, NKJV

Later the prophet Ezekiel—knowing that captive Israel was a valley of dry bones, indeed a dead nation—prophesied:

> I will make them and the places all around My hill a blessing; and I will cause showers to come down in their season; there shall be showers of blessing. Then the trees of the field shall yield their fruit, and the earth shall yield her increase. They shall be safe in their land; and they shall know that I am the LORD, when I have broken the bands of their yoke and delivered them from the hand of those who enslaved them. And they shall no longer be a prey for the nations, nor shall beasts of the land

devour them; but they shall dwell safely, and no one shall make
them afraid.

—EZEKIEL 34:26–28, NKJV

Here the latter rain again was a connection to Israel's return to their land.

THE BLESSING PRINCIPLE

I need to quickly add (and you will see clear historical proof of this
later) that the Latter Rain movements in these last days are for those
who support Israel's right to possess the land. The following promise to
Abraham still holds true:

I will bless those who bless you, and I will curse him who curses
you; and in you all the families of the earth shall be blessed.

—GENESIS 12:3, NKJV

THE LATTER RAIN IN WORLD HISTORY

There have been two distinct revival periods labeled as "Latter Rain."
From around 1886 to 1907, give or take a few years, there was the Latter
Rain movement. Men such as Richard Spurling and A. J. Tomlinson
came out of various denominational groups in a mighty move of
Pentecostal awakening. This wave affected all of the Southern United
States and would eventually impact the world. Some believe that the
Church of God of Cleveland came out of this movement.

It is interesting that at the exact same time, Zionism, the national
movement to bring Jews home to Israel, began. Theodor Herzl wrote his
book *Der Judenstaat*, which means "The Jew State," in 1896—right in
the middle of the first Latter Rain movement.

Note that the Latter Rain movement occurred when the issue of
Israel and its homeland was in place.

SECOND LATTER RAIN MOVEMENT

From 1948 to around 1969 there was a second Latter Rain revival.
Associated with this awakening were Oral Roberts, William Branham,
Jack Coe, and A. A. Allen

Notice again the dates! On May 15, 1948, Israel became a state for
the first time in two thousand years. Harry S. Truman, the US pres-
ident, recognized the state of Israel fifteen minutes after David Ben-
Gurion's announcement by wire. America exploded in growth, blessing,
and prosperity because of our connection with Israel.

Notice that every time the Latter Rain revivals have broken out, Israel has been contesting for her land! This is significant for today. There is again an unprecedented attack on the Jews, and serious dispute about the land and Israel's right to a homeland. More on this at the end of the chapter.

WHAT IS THE LATTER RAIN PROPHETICALLY?

Latter rain represents an outpouring of the Word of God and the Spirit of God at the same time. True renewal and awakening always represent a return to Scripture and an outbreak of passion and power! The Word of God will not be bound, and the Holy Spirit of God cannot be caged or managed by anyone or any group!

The latter rain of the last days is marked by a fresh revelation of God's Word. This final latter rain revival must happen before Christ's return:

> Repent therefore and be converted, that your sins may be blotted out, so that times of refreshing may come from the presence of the Lord, and that He may send Jesus Christ, who was preached to you before, whom heaven must receive until the times of restoration of all things, which God has spoken by the mouth of all His holy prophets since the world began.
> —ACTS 3:19–21, NKJV

Notice that the "times of refreshing" precede the return of Jesus. This refreshing centers on the Word of God falling like rain all over the world. The prophet Isaiah describes this latter rain as God's Word:

> For as the rain comes down, and the snow from heaven, and do not return there, but water the earth, and make it bring forth and bud, that it may give seed to the sower and bread to the eater, so shall My word be that goes forth from My mouth; it shall not return to Me void, but it shall accomplish what I please, and it shall prosper in the thing for which I sent it. For you shall go out with joy, and be led out with peace; the mountains and the hills shall break forth into singing before you, and all the trees of the field shall clap their hands. Instead of the thorn shall come up the cypress tree, and instead of the brier shall come up the myrtle tree; and it shall be to the LORD for a name, for an everlasting sign that shall not be cut off.
> —ISAIAH 55:10–13, NKJV

Wow! What a promise to all who hold fast the Word of God. For us rain falls, God promises, in the form of His Word (v. 11). Sometimes the Word is viewed as seed and sometimes as rain. Here the great prophet sees both at the same time.

Lift up your head and heart. God's provision will come down before the Rapture. The greatest revival is yet to be.

THE LATTER RAIN AND THE COMING OF CHRIST

Some would immediately respond, "That is the Old Testament. Is there anything in the New Testament about the latter rain?" The answer is an astounding yes! Perhaps the most neglected Scripture passage on signs of the end is the Book of James:

> Therefore be patient, brethren, until the coming of the Lord. See how the farmer waits for the precious fruit of the earth, waiting patiently for it until it receives the early and latter rain.
>
> —JAMES 5:7, NKJV

Here James clearly speaks of a latter rain revival before the return of our Lord Jesus. Now let us take a look at that verse in the context of this chapter and see what it says to us.

1. This chapter speaks to the Jews already scattered.

> James, a bondservant of God and of the Lord Jesus Christ, to the twelve tribes which are scattered abroad: Greetings.
>
> —JAMES 1:1, NKJV

When James wrote this letter, Jews were already scattered, though some would remain in the land for a season longer. The word *scattered* is the Greek word *diaspora. Dia* means "through and through." *Spora* means "seed"! The Jews were scattered, but like seeds, they had life!

2. The end times would be a time of great wealth and financial oppression.

> Come now, you rich, weep and howl for your miseries that are coming upon you! Your riches are corrupted, and your garments are moth-eaten. Your gold and silver are corroded, and their corrosion will be a witness against you and will eat your flesh like fire. You have heaped

up treasure in the last days. Indeed the wages of the laborers who
mowed your fields, which you kept back by fraud, cry out; and the
cries of the reapers have reached the ears of the Lord of Sabaoth.

—JAMES 5:1–4, NKJV

Worldwide, the elite will hoard great wealth, including gold and
silver, while the middle and lower classes will be robbed of proper pay
and benefits. Is it not interesting that gold and silver have become such
end-times commodities today. You can hardly watch television without
seeing a pitch for gold and silver. God says that money and wealth will
not be enough at the end.

**3. Notice also that these days are marked by injustice, white-collar
crime, and mistreatment of believers (the just).**

Indeed the wages of the laborers who mowed your fields, which
you kept back by fraud, cry out; and the cries of the reapers have
reached the ears of the Lord of Sabaoth. You have lived on the
earth in pleasure and luxury; you have fattened your hearts as in a
day of slaughter. You have condemned, you have murdered the just;
he does not resist you.

—JAMES 5:4–6, NKJV

**4. There is hope for those who are "patient" in the last days. *Patient*
in Greek is "endurance." Take note of the following promises to the
end-times church from James 5:**

+ Our harvest is coming.
    "Therefore be patient, brethren, until the coming of the
    Lord. See how the farmer waits for the precious fruit of
    the earth, waiting patiently for it until it receives the early
    and latter rain" (v. 7, NKJV).
    The latter rain will fall, and we will be blessed—even
    with end-time troubles all around us.

+ Our Lord is coming.
    "You also be patient. Establish your hearts, for the
    coming of the Lord is at hand" (v. 8, NKJV).
    This final latter rain will herald the coming of our King.

+ Our attitude needs to be right.
    "Do not grumble against one another, brethren, lest you

be condemned. Behold, the Judge is standing at the door!" (v. 9, NKJV).

We need to stop grumbling and rest our case with the Lord who is the judge and final arbiter!

+ Our end will be greater than our beginning.

"My brethren, take the prophets, who spoke in the name of the Lord, as an example of suffering and patience. Indeed we count them blessed who endure. You have heard of the perseverance of Job and seen the end intended by the Lord—that the Lord is very compassionate and merciful" (vv. 10–11, NKJV).

If we endure like Job, God will give us a double portion for all Satan has stolen from us.

+ Our prayers and worship matter.

"Is anyone among you suffering? Let him pray. Is anyone cheerful? Let him sing psalms. Is anyone among you sick? Let him call for the elders of the church, and let them pray over him, anointing him with oil in the name of the Lord. And the prayer of faith will save the sick, and the Lord will raise him up. And if he has committed sins, he will be forgiven. Confess your trespasses to one another, and pray for one another, that you may be healed. The effective, fervent prayer of a righteous man avails much" (vv. 13–16, NKJV).

Look at these promises. Our praise can restore joy. Our prayers can heal the sick. Our faith can release miracles. Our community can forgive and restore the fallen and those who wander away.

WHAT CAN WE DO?

Elijah was a man with a nature like ours, and he prayed earnestly that it would not rain; and it did not rain on the land for three years and six months. And he prayed again, and the heaven gave rain, and the earth produced its fruit.

—JAMES 5:17–18, NKJV

Like Elijah, we can pray for rain, for an outpouring from heaven.

Hosea the prophet spoke of rain in a wonderful prophecy:

> Come, and let us return to the LORD; for He has torn, but He
> will heal us; He has stricken, but He will bind us up. After two
> days He will revive us; on the third day He will raise us up, that
> we may live in His sight. Let us know, let us pursue the knowl-
> edge of the LORD. His going forth is established as the morning;
> He will come to us like the rain, like the latter and former rain
> to the earth.
>
> —HOSEA 6:1–3, NKJV

Notice that Hosea speaks of a first and second day. Could it be that
day one was the Latter Rain Movement of 1886–1907? Could it be that
the second day was the Latter Rain Movement of 1948–1969? Hosea
says that "after two days He will revive us." That is exactly what happened in those two movements.

THE THIRD DAY

Could it be that the third day is our day? "On the third day He will raise
us up" (Hosea 6:2, NKJV). He will raise us to live in His sight. Glory!
Hallelujah! Thank God for the previous latter rain outpouring; but the
next one will exalt the church to life and at last will herald the coming of
Jesus.

What are we to do? We must position and prepare for this moment
by living by God's Word, being filled with the Spirit, and being connected to an end-times church. Above all, we can pray! Listen to the
prophet Zechariah:

> Ask the LORD for rain in the time of the latter rain. The LORD will
> make flashing clouds; He will give them showers of rain, grass in
> the field for everyone.
>
> —ZECHARIAH 10:1, NKJV

We must pray for rain at the time of the latter rain. Yes, we must ask
for the showers of blessing! Let the rain fall, O God! The drought is
almost over; the raindrops are beginning to fall!

CHAPTER 6

KNOW THE END-TIMES ENEMY

WE ARE AT war! The war has been raging for thousands of years. On the surface it appears the war is for material things: oil, land, possessions, wealth, and even entire cultures. But underneath there is far more at stake—the souls of men hang in the balance.

The battle today stretches beyond the sands of Iraq, the mountains of Afghanistan, and the streets of Jerusalem. This war reaches into the invisible realm Scripture calls "the heavenlies."

According to Dr. Muhammed Ibrahim Madi, delivering the main Friday sermon on Palestinian TV on April 13, 2001, the *Hadith* states:

> The Day of Resurrection will not arrive until the Moslems make war against the Jews and kill them, and until a Jew hiding behind a rock and tree, and the rock and tree will say: "Oh Moslem, Oh servant of Allah, there is a Jew behind me, come and kill him!"[1]

While our national leaders fight with weapons of the flesh, we must understand that the battle must be won in the spiritual realm.

Only in the last century was the powerful Ottoman Empire finally defeated and the Holy Land freed. The Turks left Israel, but Muslims remained opposed to the resettling of the land by the Jews. Also, the Palestinian Islamic Order supported Hitler and his program of systematic elimination of the Jews. Four times the Arab populations declared war on Israel, and they lost at every turn.

THE ENEMY EXPOSED

The prophet Ezekiel gives us a remarkable outline of end-time events in chapters 35–39. As we look at these chapters, they become contemporary and read like the morning newspaper!

> The word of the LORD came to me: "Son of man, set your face against Mount Seir; prophesy against it and say: 'This is what the Sovereign LORD says: I am against you, Mount Seir, and I will

stretch out my hand against you and make you a desolate waste. I
will turn your towns into ruins and you will be desolate. Then you
will know that I am the LORD.

'Because you harbored an ancient hostility and delivered the
Israelites over to the sword at the time of their calamity, the time
their punishment reached its climax, therefore as surely as I live,
declares the Sovereign LORD, I will give you over to bloodshed and
it will pursue you. Since you did not hate bloodshed, bloodshed
will pursue you.'"

—EZEKIEL 35:1–6

Mount Seir represents the Arab nations that have pursued an ancient
hatred of Israel that dates back to the tents of Abraham. It is clear from
Scripture that God has an everlasting covenant with Israel whereby it
was given the land that is now in dispute. It is also clear that the possession of the land was dependent on their obedience to the Word of God.
Periodically they would be dispossessed for a season, but God always
brought them back.

Daniel heard the testimony of Michael the archangel, of how he fought
the principality (a demon of power) in Persia for two weeks. Satan will
go to any lengths to receive worship from the people blinded by Islam.
Strong spiritual forces are arrayed against the church and against Israel.

Mitchell Bard stated the following in an article titled "A Guide to the
Arab-Israeli Conflict":

The desire for peaceful relations between Jews and Arabs sometimes leads people to overlook public comments by Arab officials
and media publications that are often incendiary and sometimes
outright anti-Semitic. Frequently, more moderate tones are
adopted when speaking to Western audiences, but more accurate and heartfelt views are expressed in Arabic to the speaker's
constituents.

The following is just a tiny sample of some of the remarks that
have been made regarding Israel and the Jews. They are included
here because they demonstrate the level of hostility and true
beliefs of many Arabs and Muslims. Of course, *not all* Arabs
and Muslims subscribe to these views, but the examples are not
random, they are beliefs held by important officials and dissemi-
nated by major media. They are also included because one of the
lessons of the Holocaust was that people of good will are often

unwilling to believe that people who threaten evil will in fact carry
out their malevolent intentions...[2]

Here are a few examples of voices that echo this ancient hatred today:[3]

The Jewish nation, it is known, from the dawn of history, from the
time Allah created them, lives by scheme and deceit.
—PA COMMUNICATIONS MINISTER IMUD FALOUJI
PALESTINIAN TELEVISION, AUGUST 8, 2002

We know that the Jews have manipulated the Sept. 11 inci-
dents and turned American public opinion against Arabs and
Muslims...We still ask ourselves: Who has benefited from Sept.
11 attacks? I think they (the Jews) were the protagonists of such
attacks.
—SAUDI INTERIOR MINISTER
PRINCE NAYEF IN ASSYASAH (KUWAIT)
TRANSLATION FROM SAUDI MAGAZINE
'AIN-AL-YAQIN, NOVEMBER 29, 2002

The Jews are the cancer spreading all over the world...the Jews are
a virus like AIDS hitting humankind...Jews are responsible for all
wars and conflicts.
—SERMON BY SHEIK IBRAHIM MUDEIRIS
PALESTINE AUTHORITY TV, MAY 13, 2005

Jews subscribe to a belief in racial superiority...Their religion even
teaches them to call down curses upon the worship places on non-
Jews whenever they pass by them! They arrogantly refer to anyone
who is not Jewish as "gentiles," equating them with sin.
—WHAT ISLAM IS ALL ABOUT TEXTBOOK
IBTS, PG. 188, TARGET READERS: GRADES 3–6

We will never recognize Israel or cease to fight for our land. Our
battle against Israel is one of resistance to occupation.
—HAMAS POLITICAL CHIEF KHALID MASHAAL
ADDRESS TO THE DECLINE OF
THE ZIONIST REGIME CONFERENCE
TEHRAN UNIVERSITY, TEHRAN TIMES, MAY 27, 2008

IT'S TIME TO WAKE UP!

Paul made it very clear in his message to the church at Corinth that believers must not be ignorant of Satan's schemes (devices). He warned the believers that it is possible for Satan to take advantage of them: "In order that Satan might not outwit us. For we are not unaware of his schemes" (2 Cor. 2:11).

Informed Christians, however, need not be in a position to be caught off guard. Satan can take advantage only if we are "ignorant of his tricks." If we are aware of his methods and message, we can resist him successfully!

Ephesians 6 makes it clear that Satan has ranks of warriors, including principalities, powers, and rulers of the dark forces of evil. These ranks are organized to take the planet. They operate in the religious realm.

Satan was the high angel of worship in heaven before his fall. He was anointed as a worshipper to cover the earth with the glory of God. But he turned from God and fell to the earth along with one-third of the angels. Satan's goal is to deflect the worship of the Lord Jesus Christ to himself—to rob God of His glory!

Radical Islam is a religion of demonic origin and satanic terror. As you read through historical records, you uncover the fact that the leader of this religion, Muhammad, was known for a life and a sword stained with the blood of the innocent. Islam's record is a *river of blood* shed violently in order to obtain more territory. Radical Muslims are dangerous. Their goal is not just to terrorize us but also to annihilate us:

> Muslim terrorists are a faceless enemy; they wear no uniform and they fight dirty. They walk among us with equality and they are gaining a preferred status! They have more protection and special rights than you or I have as Christians! For example Attorney General Eric Holder's Justice Department filed suit against the Berkeley School District in Illinois for denying a request for a 19-day leave of absence in the middle of the semester by a Muslim computer lab teacher who wanted to make a pilgrimage to Mecca. The Justice Department wants a federal court to grant Safoorah Khan back pay with interest, reinstatement, and award damages "to fully compensate her for pain and suffering" caused by the resignation because the school district forced her "to choose between her job and her faith."[4]

The Islamic worldview is slowly but surely encroaching into countries around the world. Even in America the number of mosques has increased significantly. According to an article in *USA Today*, there was a 74 percent increase in the number of Islamic houses of worship, from 1,209 in the year 2002 to 2,106 in 2010.[5]

Don't be ignorant of their vocabulary.

Words are powerful. Islam, like most religions, has a vocabulary to describe what it believes. It's nearly impossible to understand what someone believes if you don't know the meaning of his or her words.

Below is just a sample:

+ *Islam.* Arabic meaning "submission." Islam is based on the revelations and teachings of Muhammad. It is a system of religious beliefs and practices.

+ *Muslim.* The name given to one who adheres to the religion of Islam.

+ *Allah.* Arabic term for God. "Allah was then known as the Moon God, who had three daughters who were viewed as intercessors for the people into Allah....Mohammed drove the other idols away; he made one god now the only god and he was its messenger....Muhammad used the name Allah which was formerly the name of a specific idol without ever distinguishing it from the idol the Meccan's were already worshipping. These names show the devotion of Mohammed's pagan roots, and also prove that Allah was part of a polytheistic system of worship before Allah was made the supreme and only god from the other gods.... The crescent moon was the symbol of the moon God Allah (Hubal) and is still used as a symbol of Islam today."[6]

+ *Quran.* Arabic for "the recitation"; refers to the collection of revelations supposedly given to Muhammad by Allah through his archangel. Muslims believe in the Law of Moses, the Psalms of David, and even the gospel of Jesus Christ; however, they believe that the Quran, as given by Muhammad, is superior and supersedes all other Scripture. If the Bible contradicts Islam, the Muslim says the Bible is wrong.

+ *The Hadith*. Arabic for the "collected traditions." These are supposed words and deeds of Muhammad, and are used to provide the basics of Islamic law and practice.

+ *Jihad*. This term refers to a Muslim holy war, or "spiritual struggle against infidels." This teaching calls on Muslims to wage war against the enemies of Islam. Muslims who die in combat for jihad become martyrs and are guaranteed a place in paradise.

Don't be ignorant of their leader.

Muhammad ibn Abdullah, or simply the prophet Muhammad, was born around AD 570 in the city of Mecca, which is now located in Saudi Arabia. Tradition says he was raised by his grandfather and uncle. At about age forty, Muhammad is said to have begun to see visions and receive revelations.

Muhammad was clearly a great military leader. He also considered himself to be the prophet of Allah, and as such, he founded Islam, which he taught was a return to the pure worship of the one true God of Abraham. Muhammad believed that God's true path came from Ishmael, the first son born of Hagar to Abraham, when Abraham disobeyed God's command to wait for a child to be born of his aging wife, Sarah (Gen. 16:11–12.)

This connection is crucial to understanding the Islamic religion. Muhammad believed the Kaaba, which was the central shrine of Arabs in Mecca, was built by Abraham as a place of worship to God. Muhammad considered Abraham to be his father; thus the religion he founded was to be not so much a new thing as a return to the worship of the one true God of his father.

It is important to note, however, that the name given to god by Muhammad, Allah, does not find its roots in the true worship of Abraham. It is rather from pagan traditions. "Allah corresponded to the Babylonian god Baal, and Arabs knew of him long before Mohammed worshipped him as the supreme God....Allah was the god of the local Quarish tribe which was Mohammed's tribe before he invented Islam to lead his people out of their polytheism."[7]

The church was established more than six hundred years before the rise of Islam. It seems as though Muhammad's interest in establishing Islam was entirely driven by a desire for unrestrained power using religion as the central core.

Don't be ignorant of what they believe.

Muslims believe salvation is dependent on man, not God. Because of that, the Quran—doctrine revealed to Muhammad by what is no doubt a demonic entity—is the Islamic "bible." It is highly memorized and revered as the means by which a person learns what Allah requires of him. Allah lends his guidance and offers salvation to those who deserve it. This is why so many Muslims are willing to prove their devotion and loyalty even unto death—because that will assure their salvation.

Islam has five primary obligations, or pillars of faith, that each Muslim must fulfill in his or her lifetime. They are as follows:

> **Shahadah,** profession of faith, is the first pillar of Islam. Muslims bear witness to the oneness of God by reciting the creed "There is no God but God and Muhammad is the Messenger of God." This simple yet profound statement expresses a Muslim's complete acceptance of and total commitment to Islam.

> **Salah,** prayer, is the second pillar. The Islamic faith is based on the belief that individuals have a direct relationship with God. The world's Muslims turn individually and collectively to Makkah, Islam's holiest city, to offer five daily prayers at dawn, noon, mid-afternoon, sunset and evening. In addition, Friday congregational service is also required.

> **Zakat,** almsgiving, is the third pillar. Social responsibility is considered part of one's service to God; the obligatory act of *zakat* enshrines this duty. Zakat prescribes payment of fixed proportions of a Muslim's possessions for the welfare of the entire community and in particular for its neediest members. It is equal to 2.5 percent of an individual's total net worth, excluding obligations and family expenses.

> **Sawm,** fasting during the holy month of *Ramadan,* is the fourth pillar of Islam. Ordained in the…*Qur'an,* the fast is an act of deep personal worship in which Muslims seek a richer perception of God. Fasting is also an exercise in self-control whereby one's sensitivity is heightened to the sufferings of the poor. *Ramadan,* the month during which the…*Qur'an* was revealed to the Prophet Muhammad, begins with the sighting of the new moon, after which abstention from eating, drinking and other sensual pleasures is obligatory from dawn to sunset.

Hajj, the pilgrimage to Makkah, is the fifth pillar and the most significant manifestation of Islamic faith and unity in the world. For those Muslims who are physically and financially able to make the journey to Makkah, the *Hajj* is a once in a lifetime duty that is the peak of their religious life.[8]

William M. Miller wrote in *A Christian's Response to Islam*:

Originally and still for some Muslims the first two pillars are combined and the last pillar of Islam is the jihad or holy war. Today it is often referred to as the sixth pillar of Islam. A revelation came to Muhammad (Sura 9:5) that he should make war on idolaters and force them to submit and become Muslims, and so he did. Muslims see the world divided into two hostile camps, that of Muslim believers and that of Infidels and there must be war till Allah's army prevails. Some modern Muslims take jihad as a personal struggle for the cause of God and are more in favor of missionary efforts other than the sword.[9]

Don't be ignorant of their goal.

It's time to wake up and realize that radical Islamists have a twofold agenda for America, Israel, and any other country that does not submit to their agenda.

1. Terrorism

Islam demands its adherents' absolute and ultimate loyalty, even if it requires that an individual betray his own country. Its goal is to rule the whole world through terror and fear.

Radical Islam's kinship with terrorism, and its willingness to use violence as a means to its ultimate ends, is clearly spelled out in a training manual produced by the radical Islamist terror group al Qaeda, whose operatives carried out the 9/11 attacks. This publication candidly says:

"[An] Islamic government would never be established except by the bomb and rifle. Islam does not coincide or make a truce with unbelief, but rather confronts it. The confrontation that Islam calls for with these godless and apostate regimes, does not know Socratic debates, Platonic ideals nor Aristotelian diplomacy. But it knows the dialogue of bullets, the ideals of assassination, bombing, and destruction, and the diplomacy of the cannon and machine-gun.

The young came to prepare themselves for Jihad [holy war], commanded by the majestic Allah's order in the holy Koran."[10]

Islamic terrorism is a form of religious terrorism committed by Muslims to achieve varying political ends in the name of religion. Islamic terrorism has occurred in the Middle East, Africa, Europe, Southeast Asia, South Asia, and North America. Islamic terrorist organizations have been known to engage in tactics that include suicide attacks, hijackings, kidnapping, and recruiting new members through the Internet.

Space would not permit me to list even a sample of acts or attempted acts of terrorism committed by Islamic extremists. Suffice it to say the goal of achieving political or religious ends has resulted in thousands of deaths.

Commenting on the 2001 terrorist attacks committed against the United States, Franklin Graham, the son of Billy Graham, said the following of Islam:

> I don't believe this is a wonderful, peaceful religion. When you read the Koran and you read the verses from the Koran, it instructs the killing of the infidel, or those that are non-Muslim.[11]

He went on to say:

> It wasn't Methodists flying into those buildings, it wasn't Lutherans. It was an attack on this country by people of the Islamic faith.[12]

Washington Post syndicated columnist Charles Krauthammer states:

> We're now at the dawn of an era in which an extreme and fanatical religious ideology, undeterred by the usual calculations of prudence and self-preservation, is wielding state power and will soon be wielding nuclear power.[13]

The goal of Islamic extremists is best summed up using their own words. It would take volumes to list the quotes of hatred just from the last decade. Time and space would not allow me to list them here. A simple Google search will reveal hundreds of quotes from Muslim clerics declaring the destruction of Israel and the Western way of life.

2. Islamization
Islamization is a slow, incremental process. The goal is to push whatever country Muslims are living in toward Islam. The word *Islamization*

was originally coined by Muslims to describe the conversion of a *kufr* ("infidel") society to an enlightened Islamic society. Islamization is a phenomenon that has existed since the Prophet Muhammad lived 1,400 years ago. Islamization has been effective, since Islam is now the main religion in fifty-seven countries.[14] The Association of Islamic countries, OIC, is the world's largest supranational organization, surpassed only by the United Nations.

The agenda is threefold:

1. *All non-Islamic traditions and symbols must be removed.* This is done to avoid offending Muslims. The goal is to reduce competition from the country's original religion (Christianity in America, for example) and culture in order to gain a better foothold for the goal of Islamization. For example, the Red Cross fell into the trap by refusing to decorate its stores for Christmas. Also, a number of banks no longer give out piggy banks to their customers' kids because pigs are unclean in Islam!

   These situations and others only highlight the fact that our culture is moving toward the idea of political correctness to the extreme and is becoming especially sensitive not to offend Muslims for fear of losing Muslim customers.

2. *Islamic traditions and rules are made part of non-Islamic societies and cultures.* Examples are seen in the reconstruction of public sports facilities to cater for Muslims' inhibited views on nudity and contact between the sexes and the imposition of time off for Islamic holidays.

3. *Certain areas or neighborhoods acquire such a high proportion of Muslims that the region's indigenous culture and people are pushed out.* One example is when non-Islamic authorities such as local police and fire departments are met with disrespect and sometimes even threats and violence while imams, Muslim fathers' groups, homemade Sharia courts, and Islamic mediation meetings are free to exercise their power. Another example is when Jewish men cannot wear yarmulkes or girls cannot wear miniskirts in Muslim-dominated areas at the risk of being attacked.

Ramesh R. Desai stated the following in an excellent article, "Islamization of the World by the Year 2501: Is It Possible?":

> Islamization means conversion of a country or a state or a region's legal system to Islamic (or Quaranic or Sharia) law. Islamization of the world means 50% of the world population living under Sharia law. Once a region is muslimised, Muslims demand for a separate country or a region for themselves, e.g. Pakistan and Bangladesh and now a demand for independent Kashmir. Once a country is muslimised, Islamists demand for Islamic or Quranic or Sharia law.[15]

Islam is on the rise. It is the second-largest religion in the world after Christianity. Remember, Islam is not simply a religion. In its fullest form, it is a 100 percent, total, complete, personal and national system for life. Islam has religious, legal, political, economic, social, and military components. The religious component is a springboard for its other components.

Chris Surber shares Nigerian Bishop E. C. Okoye of Nigeria thoughts on why Islam is on the rise today:

> In Nigeria and elsewhere, the reason Islam grows is because they are very proactive in their missionary efforts. Islam in Africa receives support from Muslims in oil-rich Islamic nations for the building of schools, roads, and hospitals. When you are poor and Islam built the school you attend and the hospital that cares for you it is easy to trust in Allah.[16]

THE ENEMY ENGAGED

There is a common but erroneous belief that Muslims cannot be reached with the love of God. Christians have buried their heads in the sand when it comes to the idea that Islam can be overcome with the gospel of Jesus Christ.

Many Muslim converts to Christianity have said that many of their unconverted brethren have a deep spiritual hunger that has yet to be satisfied. There are many who desire to know God on an intimate basis, and to be assured of His love, forgiveness, and acceptance. Only by touching the hearts of Muslims with that love can we begin to overcome the seemingly insurmountable barriers to conversion.

BUT LET'S BE CLEAR

The majority of Muslims in the United States and around the world are conservative, peaceful people. They don't walk around with explosives wrapped around their bodies and have no intention of becoming terrorists. They don't believe in jihad. They, like most of us, want good things for their kids, a good place to work, and the right to practice their faith. As more horrific events unfold around the world, more and more courageous Muslims are speaking out against the extremists of their religion. Many of them risk their very lives in order to pull away the ugly mask of terror.

What are we to do? Run away and hide? Sit in our comfortable pews on Sunday morning and hope the growing danger will go away? No!

It's time for the body of Christ to hear the "sound" being released by the Holy Spirit and engage the enemy. And remember, the enemy is not flesh and blood but a demonic system of beliefs that has ensnared millions of people.

What is the best way to engage? It is summed up in one word: love. The God of the Bible is love personified.

One hundred years ago the missionary Samuel Zwemer was known as the Apostle to Islam. His whole approach could be summarized with the phrase "a ministry of friendship." He once said that you can say anything to a Muslim, provided you say it in love and with a smile.[17]

Using the word *love* as an acrostic, here are some simple steps to communicating your faith:

L: Learn

The level of ignorance displayed by Christians concerning the Islamic faith is astounding. To effectively communicate your faith will require knowledge, wisdom, and a commitment to study and learn. It is almost impossible to witness to a person of another faith if you don't know what they believe. Finding information about the Islamic faith is as easy as a keystroke on your computer or a trip to your nearest library.

> Do your best to present yourself to God as one approved, a worker who does not need to be ashamed and who correctly handles the word of truth.
>
> —2 TIMOTHY 2:15

O: Observe

Observe the very basic guidelines for witnessing to any nonbeliever. A Muslim is not an enemy to be conquered but a friend with whom to share the love of God.

+ Always avoid arguments.

+ Never display a judgmental attitude.

+ Be respectful even if you don't agree.

+ Develop a friendship, even if your first attempt fails.

+ Be open about your relationship with Jesus Christ.

+ Most importantly, pray for them.

> I am sending you out like sheep among wolves. Therefore be as shrewd as snakes and as innocent as doves.
> —MATTHEW 10:16

V: Vocalize

Be prepared to answer questions. There is no such thing as a silent witness for Christ. Don't be afraid to be open about what Jesus has done in your life. Be bold and talk openly and honestly about where you came from and what God has done for you personally. Share your experiences of God's mercy, grace, and forgiveness.

> But in your hearts revere Christ as Lord. Always be prepared to give an answer to everyone who asks you to give the reason for the hope that you have. But do this with gentleness and respect.
> —1 PETER 3:15

E: Exemplify

To exemplify the Christian faith is the best way to reach a Muslim. To Muslims, religion is not just an acceptance of a doctrine; it involves a way of life. To be an effective witness for Christ, our walk and our talk must match. It is much easier to witness when our lives demonstrate the reality of Christ's presence and power. Effective witness comes from a Christian who lives a Christ-centered life, not a once-a-week Christianity compromised by a loose lifestyle.

Join together in following my example, brothers and sisters, and just as you have us as a model, keep your eyes on those who live as we do.

—PHILIPPIANS 3:17

REMEMBER...

God so loved the world—including the Muslim world—that He gave His one and only Son, that whoever believes in Him should not perish but have everlasting life (John 3:16). Reaching Muslims with the life-changing gospel message of Jesus Christ will be difficult. Mighty mountains are blocking the advance of the good news not only in Muslim lands, but also in Muslim hearts and minds. All seems lost to the natural man, but not to God. All things are possible with God if we will only believe (Mark 9:23).

The only river of blood that is effective enough to meet and challenge the growing threat of radical Islam is not found on the streets of Jerusalem or in the ashes of the Twin Towers. Let the words of the great hymn writer William Cowper (1731–1800) speak:

> There is a fountain filled with blood
> Drawn from Emmanuel's veins;
> And sinners plunged beneath that flood
> Lose all their guilty stains.
> Lose all their guilty stains,
> Lose all their guilty stains;
> And sinners plunged beneath that flood
> Lose all their guilty stains.
>
> The dying thief rejoiced to see
> That fountain in his day;
> And there may I, though vile as he,
> Wash all my sins away.
> Wash all my sins away,
> Wash all my sins away;
> And there may I, though vile as he,
> Wash all my sins away.[18]

CHAPTER 7

IS THERE A FUTURE IN ISRAEL'S HOPE?

*Some people like Jews and some do not; but no thoughtful man can
doubt the fact that they are beyond all question the most formidable
and the most remarkable race which has ever appeared in the world.*[1]
—SIR WINSTON CHURCHILL

How IS IT that a small sliver of land in the Middle East called Israel could become a geopolitical focus of the whole world? How can we explain the continued existence of the Jewish people despite facing millennia of hatred, opposition, and persecution? The survival of the Jewish race is nothing short of a miracle! They have been scattered among the nations, despised and persecuted by kings and emperors, yet they have endured as a people. It took the horrors of the Holocaust to alarm the world and at long last give Israel her homeland. The Jews are a "miracle people," a tiny ethnic remnant in a world of 7.3 billion people.

The Jews exist not only in Israel but also in nearly every nation on Earth. Some people find it appalling that the Jewish people have an importance that far exceeds their numbers; yet the way I see it, it is part of the blessing of God on His chosen people.

Author Walter B. Knight wrote, "Through the centuries, the Jew has maintained his racial identity. Like Jonah in the belly of the great fish—undigested, unassimilated—the Jew has remained unassimilated, una-malgamated, undigested though he has wandered among all nations."[2]

For centuries people have been more than puzzled by the Jewish nation. Although recognized by the Roman government, the Jewish religion was still called the *secta nefaria*, "a nefarious sect." Arnold Toynbee classified Israel as "fossil civilization" and did not know what to do with it. For some reason, the nation did not fit into his historical theories.

THE PROPHECY OF ISRAEL'S BANISHMENT

Ezekiel was a prophet to the Israelites during their exile to Babylon—a time of judgment on the nation for its idolatry. The final chapters of the Book of Ezekiel describe the future of Israel and the alignment of nations even until this very hour.

Israel became a possession of other nations.

In AD 70 Israel was destroyed and its people were scattered across the face of the earth, just as the Bible predicted:

> This is what the Sovereign LORD says: The enemy said of you, "Aha! The ancient heights have become our possession." Therefore prophesy and say, "This is what the Sovereign LORD says: Because they ravaged and crushed you from every side so that you became the possession of the rest of the nations and the object of people's malicious talk and slander, therefore, mountains of Israel, hear the word of the Sovereign LORD: This is what the Sovereign LORD says to the mountains and hills, to the ravines and valleys, to the desolate ruins and the deserted towns that have been plundered and ridiculed by the rest of the nations around you—this is what the Sovereign Lord says: In my burning zeal I have spoken against the rest of the nations, and against all Edom, for with glee and with malice in their hearts they made my land their own possession so that they might plunder its pastureland."
>
> —EZEKIEL 36:2–5

Israel became the plunder of other nations.

The little state of Israel has been invaded and possessed by the Romans, the Ottomans, the armies of the Crusades, the British, and the Arabs.

> Therefore, mountains of Israel, hear the word of the Sovereign LORD: This is what the Sovereign LORD says to the mountains and hills, to the ravines and valleys, to the desolate ruins and the deserted towns that have been plundered and ridiculed by the rest of the nations around you.
>
> —EZEKIEL 36:4

Israel bore the shame of the nations.

Over the centuries the nations of the world shamefully stood by while the Jewish nation was nearly eliminated. I believe the following verse carries a clear word about God's view of the Holocaust:

> Therefore prophesy concerning the land of Israel and say to the mountains and hills, to the ravines and valleys: "This is what the Sovereign LORD says: I speak in my jealous wrath because you

have suffered the scorn of the nations. Therefore this is what the
Sovereign LORD says: I swear with uplifted hand that the nations
around you will also suffer scorn."

—EZEKIEL 36:6–7

Israel's treatment was the shame of the world. Hitler's terrors
in Germany alarmed the world, and at long last Israel was given her
homeland.

THE PROPHECY OF ISRAEL'S RETURN

God scattered the nation as a result of its sin.

I dispersed them among the nations, and they were scattered
through the countries; I judged them according to their conduct
and their actions.

—EZEKIEL 36:19

However, God promised that the nation would be regathered. God
has never canceled the covenant of the land.

For I will take you out of the nations; I will gather you from all the
countries and bring you back into your own land. I will sprinkle
clean water on you, and you will be clean; I will cleanse you from
all your impurities and from all your idols.

—EZEKIEL 36:24–25

British clergyman Thomas Newton, Bishop of Bristol (1704–1782),
saw God work to preserve the Jews throughout history:

The preservation of the Jews is really one of the most signal and
illustrious acts of divine Providence…And what but a supernatural power could have preserved them in such a manner as none
other nation upon earth hath been preserved. Nor is the providence of God less remarkable in the destruction of their enemies,
than in their preservation…We see that the great empires, which in
their turn subdued and oppressed the people of God, are all come
to ruin…And if such hath been the fatal end of the enemies and
oppressors of the Jews, let it serve as a warning to all those, who at
any time or upon any occasion are for raising a clamor and persecution against them.[3]

God promised the nation of Israel eventual abundant life and prosperity. Israel has yet to realize this fully. But God always will do what He promises!

> I will give you a new heart and put a new spirit in you; I will remove from you your heart of stone and give you a heart of flesh. And I will put my Spirit in you and move you to follow my decrees and be careful to keep my laws. Then you will live in the land I gave your ancestors; you will be my people, and I will be your God. I will save you from all your uncleanness. I will call for the grain and make it plentiful and will not bring famine upon you. I will increase the fruit of the trees and the crops of the field, so that you will no longer suffer disgrace among the nations because of famine. Then you will remember your evil ways and wicked deeds, and you will loathe yourselves for your sins and detestable practices. I want you to know that I am not doing this for your sake, declares the Sovereign LORD. Be ashamed and disgraced for your conduct, people of Israel!
>
> This is what the Sovereign LORD says: On the day I cleanse you from all your sins, I will resettle your towns, and the ruins will be rebuilt. The desolate land will be cultivated instead of lying desolate in the sight of all who pass through it. They will say, "This land that was laid waste has become like the garden of Eden; the cities that were lying in ruins, desolate and destroyed, are now fortified and inhabited."
>
> —EZEKIEL 36:26–35

THE PROPHECY OF ISRAEL'S REBIRTH

When we turn to Ezekiel 37, the story continues. The valley of dry bones pictures Israel scattered and dead among the nations. The inquiry, "Can these bones live?" (v. 3), raises the fundamental question of Israel's survival. Yet the nation lives today! What has helped this great nation survive?

Israel lives because of the Word of God.

God's Word brings the bones of the dead Israel together. When the Word goes forth, life comes!

> The hand of the LORD was on me, and he brought me out by the Spirit of the LORD and set me in the middle of a valley; it was full

of bones. He led me back and forth among them, and I saw a great
many bones on the floor of the valley, bones that were very dry. He
asked me, "Son of man, can these bones live?"

I said, "Sovereign LORD, you alone know."

Then he said to me, "Prophesy to these bones and say to them,
'Dry bones, hear the word of the LORD!'"

—EZEKIEL 37:1–4

Israel has survived because of the Spirit of God.

The creative breath of God brings life to God's chosen people. Here is
the wind of the Spirit! From the lips of God comes a life-giving breeze
that raises up a nation!

> Then he said to me, "Prophesy to the breath; prophesy, son of man,
> and say to it, 'This is what the Sovereign LORD says: Come, breath,
> from the four winds and breathe into these slain, that they may
> live.'" So I prophesied as he commanded me, and breath entered
> them; they came to life and stood up on their feet—a vast army.
>
> Then he said to me: "Son of man, these bones are the people of
> Israel. They say, 'Our bones are dried up and our hope is gone; we
> are cut off.' Therefore prophesy and say to them: 'This is what the
> Sovereign LORD says: My people, I am going to open your graves and
> bring you up from them; I will bring you back to the land of Israel.
> Then you, my people, will know that I am the LORD, when I open
> your graves and bring you up from them. I will put my Spirit in you
> and you will live, and I will settle you in your own land. Then you
> will know that I the LORD have spoken, and I have done it, declares
> the LORD.'"
>
> —EZEKIEL 37:9–14

Dr. Jack Van Impe, in his book *Israel's Final Holocaust*, gives a
description that I believe is very accurate concerning the interpretation
of Ezekiel's strange vision:

> The bones represent Israel. Their disconnectedness and dryness
> indicate the people of Israel's scattering and lack of hope. The
> graves are the nations in which they dwell. The imparting of sinew,
> flesh, and breath is a miracle timed for the last days. The Jews are
> to come out of their graves, i.e., the nations to which they have
> been scattered. They will return in unbelief and without spiritual

life, but finally after being settled in their land, there will come a time of conversion—new birth:

"Then you, my people, will know that I am the Lord, when I open your graves and bring you up from them. I will put my Spirit in you and you will live, and I will settle you in your own land. Then you will know that I the Lord have spoken, and I have done it, declares the Lord" (Ezek. 37:13–14, niv).[4]

The dead bones have come together in the ancient Jewish homeland. There is a body with flesh on it, but there is no spiritual life. Ezekiel 37 and Romans 11 anticipate the day when Israel will come to life as a nation after God Himself breathes on them that they may live!

THE PROMISE OF ISRAEL'S FUTURE

What persecution could not do in the natural, the church has almost done in the spiritual—eliminate the Jewish people from God's future plans.

The church has wrestled with many controversial subjects, but none more controversial than the question, "Is God finished with Israel?" As I previously discussed in chapter 2, there are at least three views when it comes to the question of Israel:

1. Two-Covenant Theology

2. Replacement Theology

3. "One New Man" Theology

For me the issue was settled when I determined in my own mind and heart that God was not finished with the Jewish people. I base my belief on what Paul wrote in Romans 9–11. If I believed that God was finished with the nation of Israel, I would have to cut those chapters out of my Bible!

More specifically the Apostle Paul devoted all of Romans 11 to the question of Israel and presented concrete evidence that God is not at all through with the Jewish people. It becomes obvious that Paul is talking about a literal future, about a literal people.

On more than one occasion the Apostle Paul had to defend his belief system. Whether before the religious zealots of his day, a Roman king, or among the churches he founded, Paul was not shy when it came to declaring the truth of the Word of God.

Imagine in your mind a courtroom. Paul is counsel for the defense. He has to prove that God has a future for the Jewish people.

In Romans 11 Paul makes the case for the defense. He calls five witnesses to prove his case.

Witness #1: He himself takes the stand (Rom. 11:1).

> I ask then: Did God reject his people? By no means! I am an Israelite myself, a descendant of Abraham, from the tribe of Benjamin.

If God has turned his back on His people, then how do you explain the conversion of the Apostle Paul? His conversion experience is presented three times in the Book of Acts (chapters 9, 22, and 26). I do not believe that these experiences were written just to brag on Paul, nor were they written just to highlight some flashy supernatural experience that most of us cannot identify with in our own conversion experience. I believe they were written as an illustration to show the coming conversion of the nation of Israel. It is God's plan to finish what He has started in regard to the Jews. His promises are yes and amen!

+ Paul was a "pattern" man: "However, for this reason I obtained mercy, that in me first Jesus Christ might show all longsuffering, as a *pattern* to those who are going to believe on Him for everlasting life" (1 Tim. 1:16, NKJV, emphasis added).

+ He called himself "one born out of due time": "Then last of all He was seen by me also, as by one born out of due time" (1 Cor. 15:8, NKJV).

Dr. Warren Wiersbe, in his book *Be Right* states:

> The accounts of Paul's conversion tell very little that parallels our salvation experience today. Certainly none of us has seen Christ in glory or actually heard Him speak from heaven. We were neither blinded by the light of heaven nor thrown to the ground. In what way, then, is Paul's conversion "a pattern"? It is a picture of how the nation of Israel will be saved when Jesus Christ returns to establish His kingdom on earth. The details of Israel's future restoration and salvation are given in Zechariah 12:10–13:1. The nation shall see Him…as their Messiah, repent, and receive Him. It will

be an experience similar to that of Saul of Tarsus when he was on his way to Damascus to persecute Christians (Acts 9).[5]

The importance of Paul's conversion is not the fact that he was saved but the *way* he was saved. I strongly believe that Paul was a pattern man and that is why he was first on the witness stand!

Witness #2: Let the prophet speak (Rom. 11:2–10).

> God has not cast away His people whom He foreknew. Or do you not know what the Scripture says of Elijah, how he pleads with God against Israel, saying, "LORD, they have killed Your prophets and torn down Your altars, and I alone am left, and they seek my life"?
>
> But what does the divine response say to him? "I have reserved for Myself seven thousand men who have not bowed the knee to Baal." Even so then, at this present time there is a remnant according to the election of grace. And if by grace, then it is no longer of works; otherwise grace is no longer grace. But if it is of works, it is no longer grace; otherwise work is no longer work.
>
> What then? Israel has not obtained what it seeks; but the elect have obtained it, and the rest were blinded. Just as it is written: "God has given them a spirit of stupor, eyes that they should not see and ears that they should not hear, to this very day."
>
> And David says:
>
> "Let their table become a snare and a trap, a stumbling block and a recompense to them. Let their eyes be darkened, so that they do not see, and bow down their back always."
>
> —NKJV

Paul draws from the life of Elijah to demonstrate the fact that God always has a remnant. Elijah thought he was all alone in his devotion to the Lord, but God reminded Elijah that there were more than seven thousand who had not bowed to Baal. Remember, Elijah's complaint against Israel was spoken in his darkest hour of personal crisis and right in the middle of national apostasy. The story is found in 1 Kings 18–19. Author and minister John Phillips writes:

> The mighty victory on Carmel, to which Paul refers, had dealt a devastating blow to Jezebel's power structure and to the Satanic cult of Baal on which it was based. But that victory had been

incomplete. The wily Jezebel had not sent all her prophets to the Carmel duel but had kept in reserve the four hundred prophets of the groves. Thus she was ready to counter Elijah's victory, which she did with energy and resolve, shaking even that fiery prophet's iron nerve. He fled! When he finally pulled himself up exhausted, it was to find himself far from the scene of conflict and beneath the historic crags of Horeb. Ashamed and disappointed, the prophet flung himself down. Then, tenderly the voice of God came to the man of God: "What are you doing here, Elijah?" (1 Kings 19:9).

In reply the prophet interceded, as Paul so pointedly puts it, against Israel. Then came the tempest, the earthquake and the fire, each suited to the prophet's mood... Why was not God in the tempest, the earthquake, or the fire? Why did God not send His servant back with a fresh commission against the prophets of the groves?...Unlike Moses who had interceded for Israel, Elijah interceded against them..."I only am left," complained the prophet. "I have reserved to myself seven thousand men, who have not bowed the knee to Baal," said God.[6]

Paul shows that now, just as in the past, God has His remnant. Those who are saved are not saved because of their birth or their nationality; they are saved because of pure grace. They are redeemed because they have been chosen by God in Christ Jesus.

Paul's point in these verses is that those who want to be saved can be saved, while those who refuse Christ are lost. For us, the message is that if we are saved, it is because of the grace of God! It is not our deeds, our birth, or our works. We are not saved because of who we are or what we have or can produce. Salvation is by grace alone (Eph. 2:8–9).

Paul is very clear on one thing—the hardening of Israel is not final nor is it in totality. It is clear proof that God has a future for the nation of Israel. This very hour finds a remnant of Jewish believers, as in Elijah's day, which is evidence that God is not finished with His chosen people.

Witness #3: The Gentiles are a witness to God's promise (Rom. 11:11–15).

I say then, have they stumbled that they should fall? Certainly not! But through their fall, to provoke them to jealousy, salvation has come to the Gentiles. Now if their fall is riches for the world, and their failure riches for the Gentiles, how much more their fullness!

> For I speak to you Gentiles; inasmuch as I am an apostle to the Gentiles, I magnify my ministry, if by any means I may provoke to jealousy those who are my flesh and save some of them. For if their being cast away is the reconciling of the world, what will their acceptance be but life from the dead?
>
> —NKJV

At the present time God is displaying His kindness to the Gentiles while He concentrates His severity upon the Jews. The underlying question of Romans 9–11 is, "Why?" Why are the vast majority of the Jews failing to experience God's promised blessings while many Gentiles are coming to faith in Israel's Messiah and abounding in His kindness? Because Israel rejected God. They refused the salvation offered by Jesus and His apostles. So God has temporarily hardened the Jews so that salvation may come to the Gentiles. But in God's good time Israel will be restored to a place of national prominence and blessing. That's the promise of Romans 11.

In the previous passage Paul said three tragedies occurred in Israel:

+ *They fell.* "I say then, have they stumbled that they should fall? Certainly not! But through their fall, to provoke them to jealousy, salvation has come to the Gentiles" (v. 11).

+ *They were diminished.* "Now if their fall is riches for the world, and their failure riches for the Gentiles, how much more their fullness!" (v. 12).

+ *They were cast away.* "For if their being cast away is the reconciling of the world, what will their acceptance be but life from the dead?" (v. 15).

Not a single statement suggests that God has placed a final judgment on Israel. He kept His promise to the Gentiles (Rom. 9:25–26), and He will also keep His promise to the Jews!

There are many who believe that because of Israel's failure, God has abandoned them altogether. To bolster their argument they point to the church—that is, to replacement theology (see chapter 2). Nothing could be further from the truth. Yes, God did introduce a new factor, the church, in which believing Jews and Gentiles are one in Christ (see Ephesians 2:11–22). Paul called this new factor a "mystery" (Eph. 3:3). This mystery is a sacred secret not revealed in the Old Testament. The question then is, "Has God abandoned His kingdom purposes for

Israel?" Absolutely not! The Bible makes it clear that Israel is merely set aside until the time comes for God's plan for Israel to be fulfilled.

The Gentiles have a vital role to play with regard to the Jewish nation. They are being used to provoke Israel to jealousy:

> But I say, did Israel not know? First Moses says: "I will provoke you to jealousy by those who are not a nation, I will move you to anger by a foolish nation."
>
> —ROMANS 10:19, NKJV

The Gentiles are enjoying spiritual blessings in Christ (Eph. 1:3). The Jews are spiritually bankrupt.

Witness #4: The lump of dough and the olive tree speak (Rom. 11:16–24).

Paul stopped for a moment and looked at Israel's past to show her hope for the future. We know from our own study of the Word of God that Israel was set apart and chosen by God as a special people.

Why? The Bible tells us that God's choice of Israel had nothing to do with merit. She didn't earn it. It wasn't because she was more numerous than other people in the world; as a matter of fact, she was the least (Deut. 7:7). It wasn't because Israel was more sensitive to God than other nations. Although God called her by name, Israel did not know Him (Isa. 45:4). It wasn't because Israel was more righteous than other nations. When God later confirmed His promise of land to the Jews, He reminded them that they were a rebellious, stiff-necked people (Deut. 9:6–7). If God chose to bless the nation of Israel not because she was more populous or spiritually responsive or righteous than other nations, just why did He choose the Jews?

The answer is, because of His grace! It was all grace. It was His sovereign purpose to do so. God cares what happens to His people and their land. God has chosen to love Israel!

Paul gave two illustrations from the Old Testament Scriptures to prove his case that God was not finished with the Jewish nation:

1. The lump of dough

> If the part of the dough offered as firstfruits is holy, then the whole batch is holy; if the root is holy, so are the branches.
>
> —ROMANS 11:16

Here Paul makes reference to Numbers 15:17–21. The first part of the dough was to be offered up to God as a symbol of the entire lump. In essence it was saying that the entire lump belonged to God. The basic idea was rather simple; if God accepts the part, He sanctifies the whole.

In using this illustration, it is easy to understand Paul's argument. God accepted Abraham as the founder (the lump of dough) of the Hebrew nation and in so doing set apart his descendants as well. No doubt Isaac and Jacob had their failings, but in spite of their sins God accepted the rest of the lump—the nation of Israel.

2. The olive tree

> If the part of the dough offered as firstfruits is holy, then the whole batch is holy; if the root is holy, so are the branches.
>
> If some of the branches have been broken off, and you, though a wild olive shoot, have been grafted in among the others and now share in the nourishing sap from the olive root, do not consider yourself to be superior to those other branches. If you do, consider this: You do not support the root, but the root supports you. You will say then, "Branches were broken off so that I could be grafted in." Granted. But they were broken off because of unbelief, and you stand by faith. Do not be arrogant, but tremble. For if God did not spare the natural branches, he will not spare you either.
>
> Consider therefore the kindness and sternness of God: sternness to those who fell, but kindness to you, provided that you continue in his kindness. Otherwise, you also will be cut off. And if they do not persist in unbelief, they will be grafted in, for God is able to graft them in again. After all, if you were cut out of an olive tree that is wild by nature, and contrary to nature were grafted into a cultivated olive tree, how much more readily will these, the natural branches, be grafted into their own olive tree!
>
> —ROMANS 11:16–24

The olive tree is a symbol of the nation of Israel (Jer. 11:16–17; Hosea 14:4–6). Some have mistakenly identified Paul's argument as a discussion concerning the relationship of individual believers to God, instead of a discussion about the place of Israel in His divine plan. It is clear to me that Paul was discussing Israel's future, not the individual believer's relationship to the Father.

Paul shows us that the olive tree represents the covenants with and promises to Israel, growing from its holy root—which is the Messiah, the Word of God—as well as the covenants made with the patriarchs. The natural branches are the people of Israel. Those who turned away from that relationship were broken off. Christians are simply the wild branches grafted in among the natural branches who "became a partaker [with them] of the root and fatness of the olive tree," which God established (v. 17, NKJV).

It is evident from Scripture, as well as from nature, that the root and trunk support the branches and not vice versa. In this position there is no room for pride or the notion that we Christians have replaced Israel, or that God rejected His own covenants and promises given to Abraham, Isaac, and Jacob. He cannot deny them or change them. God's promise and covenant with Abraham sustain Israel to this very day.

There is no room to boast or be arrogant, as the church has been prone to do, as both the natural branches and the engrafted wild branches remain only by faith (vv. 18–21). Paul reminded the Gentiles that they entered into God's plan because of faith, not because of anything good they had done. The church is an extension of a plan that preexisted it. There is only one tree, not two; we "wild branches" have been privileged to drink in new life from the cultivated, established tree.

To sum up Paul's argument at this point, the olive tree will flourish and bear fruit again. The roots are still good no matter how far Israel may stray from the truth of God's Word. God is still the God of Abraham, Isaac, and Jacob, and that will never change!

Witness #5: The Father takes the stand (Rom. 11:25–36).

> I do not want you to be ignorant of this mystery, brothers and sisters, so that you may not be conceited: Israel has experienced a hardening in part until the full number of the Gentiles has come in, and in this way all Israel will be saved. As it is written: "The deliverer will come from Zion; he will turn godlessness away from Jacob. And this is my covenant with them when I take away their sins."
>
> As far as the gospel is concerned, they are enemies for your sake; but as far as election is concerned, they are loved on account of the patriarchs, for God's gifts and his call are irrevocable. Just as you who were at one time disobedient to God have now received mercy as a result of their disobedience, so they too have now become disobedient in order that they too may now receive mercy as a result

of God's mercy to you. For God has bound everyone over to disobedience so that he may have mercy on them all.

Oh, the depth of the riches of the wisdom and knowledge of God! How unsearchable his judgments, and his paths beyond tracing out! "Who has known the mind of the Lord? Or who has been his counselor?" "Who has ever given to God, that God should repay them?" For from him and through him and for him are all things. To him be the glory forever! Amen.

Paul, like any good defense attorney, saved his best witness for last. God's very nature and character is at stake when it comes to the future of His chosen people, Israel.

Israel is a part of God's plan (Rom. 11:25).

The blinding of Israel as a nation is not final or complete; it is only partial and temporary. Paul declares that it will last "until the fullness of the Gentiles come in." We are living in an age primarily devoted to the time and seasons of the Gentiles. It is true that individual Jews are being saved, but until the "fullness of the Gentiles" is complete, the final restoration of the nation of Israel will not take place. Make no mistake about it: God can tell time, and He is never late for an appointment!

It is all because of an unchanging God (Rom. 11:27–32).

God is not capricious. He declares in Malachi 3:6: "I am the LORD, I change not" (KJV). We read in Numbers 23:19, "God is not a man, that he should lie; neither the son of man, that he should repent" (KJV). God will never break His promise to the nation of Israel, or He would not be true to His own perfect nature. His calling to His chosen people will not be changed.

It is extended because of God's grace (Rom. 11:30–32).

Just as you who were at one time disobedient to God have now received mercy as a result of their disobedience, so they too have now become disobedient in order that they too may now receive mercy as a result of God's mercy to you. For God has bound everyone over to disobedience so that he may have mercy on them all.

Paul constantly reminded the Gentiles that they were saved and had a spiritual obligation to Israel. In no uncertain terms he declared that Israel's hardness is only "in part" (v. 25), which means that individual

Jews can be saved today by the same grace and mercy that was extended to them and to us.

The evidence is overwhelming: Israel has a future! Next I want to turn my attention to her past. I plan to show the connections among the ancient civilization of Phoenicia, King Hiram of Tyre, Israel, and eventually you and me.

THE ANCIENT HIRAM CODE FOR END-TIMES PROSPERITY

CHAPTER 8

THE MYSTERY OF PHOENICIA

To remain ignorant of things that happened before
you were born is to remain a child.[1]
—CICERO

THE PHOENICIAN CIVILIZATION is a remarkable secret of history. The Phoenicians' connection with David found in Scripture has no explanation. We are simply told that Hiram built David's palace and helped Solomon because he loved David.

Remarkably the Phoenician civilization lasted about three hundred years longer than Judah. During that season they experienced remarkable wealth and status before finally falling to Alexander the Great around 322 BC.

Though there is no direct proof, it seems that Hiram and at least one generation after him embraced Yahweh, the God of Israel, and their great blessing flowed in connection with Israel's. It was Jezebel's generation and forward that lost the blessing, which led to the downfall of both Judah and, later, Phoenicia.

It is important to understand that the blessing came on Hiram and his people because they loved Israel and built David a house. Typically, it seems to me, those who love Israel today and love the church, which is David's Tabernacle (as you will see in this chapter), can unlock the Hiram Code and live in blessing and confidence in these last days. (Also, there is a strange and fascinating connection to the Cherokee Indians of North America.)

Anyone who knows me or has been a part of my ministry for any length of time knows two things about me: First, I love Israel unashamedly, without reservation. Genesis 12:3, "I will bless those who bless you, and I will curse those who curse you," has been the banner hung across my heart for nearly sixty years! The nation of Israel and the Jewish people have always been close to my heart. We have invested time, resources, and energy into bringing others to the knowledge that when we bless Israel, God blesses us!

Second, I am fascinated by archaeology and science. I love the way God reveals Himself and proves His Word through nature around us as well as through archaeology and study of the past. In my more than six decades of life, I've learned that if skeptics and critics will simply be honest and look at the facts, the Bible will come out as being exactly what it is: the historically accurate account of the love of God to man; the true, living, and infallible Word of God.

The more I have studied ancient secrets, the more fascinating and intriguing they have become. The revelations that scientists have made in recent years are shattering our understanding of our own history.

Did you know that

+ The ancient craftsmen of Phoenicia intermarried with the Jewish tribes of Dan, Napthali, and Zebulon;

+ Rebekah, Isaac's wife, was Syrophoenician (Gen. 25:20);

+ Rachel, Jacob's wife, was Syrophoenician (Gen. 31:20);

+ Naaman the leper was Syrophoenician (Luke 4:27);

+ Jesus healed a Syrophoenician (Mark 7:24–30); and

+ The Cherokee Indians share twenty-six genetic markers with the Phoenicians and five with the Jewish people?

And, as we will soon see, there is so much more!

You may be thinking the same thing I thought when I sat in a world history course in college: "Why is it important that I learn all of this stuff about ancient history? It has no bearing on my life today." I was wrong to think that then, and you would be wrong to think that today! It is important because it all connects together. It will help us understand where it all started and how it relates to us.

We will spend a great deal of time in this chapter and the next two examining the connections among King Hiram, David, Solomon, the nation of Israel, and the church. Before we do, it will be beneficial to look at a brief background and consider the importance of the ancient civilization of the Phoenicians.

WHO WERE THE PHOENICIANS?

The question of when, where, and how the Phoenicians and their society originated is an intriguing one due to their role as carriers of goods, discoveries, and practices that profoundly affected other well-known societies in antiquity. In fact, social interactions may have contributed to the rise of the Phoenician society.

It is more than likely the Phoenicians were the original inhabitants of the eastern Mediterranean region. According to DNA tests conducted in Lebanon, that area has been inhabited by the same people since the beginning of known history.

> It is not certain what the Phoenicians called themselves in their own language; it appears to have been Kena'ani (Akkadian: Kinahna), "Canaanites." In Hebrew the word kena'ani has the secondary meaning of "merchant," a term that well characterizes the Phoenicians.
>
> The Greeks gave the new appellation Phoenicians to those Canaanites who lived on the seacoast and traded with them. Phoenicia is the Greek work for "purple." The most probable reason for giving this name is the famous Tyrian purple cloth which the Phoenicians manufactured and sold to the rich of the ancient world.[2]
>
> Given the Phoenicians' go-between role, and their serious interactions with many societies in the Mediterranean region, their origin date takes on additional significance. It marks the beginning of the Phoenicians' impact—great or small—on each of those other societies, which included the Egyptians, Mycenaeans, Hittites, Hebrews, Assyrians, Babylonians, Persians, Greeks, Etruscans, Romans and other lesser-known societies.[3]

All of the eastern coast extending north and south, and the land extending farther east, was known as Canaan. This was the land Abraham settled as part of the covenant promise God made with him. Later God chose Moses to deliver the Israelites back to this Promised Land. By 1200 BC the Israelites had finally settled the land. Kerry W. Cranmer, MD, in his book, *Tyre: The Invincible*, states the following:

> Prior to the time of Moses, the area known as Phoenicia was a collection of autonomous city states. The first cities to emerge in prominence were Byblos and Sidon. Byblos rose as a great city very early.
>
> The one-time director general of antiquities of Lebanon, Emir

Maurice Chehab, stated that Byblos was settled by fishers and farmers 6,000 years ago. "From early times it called itself the oldest city in the world" (*National Geographic*: Aug. 74, p. 154). The merchants of Byblos became famous for their sale of papyrus from Egypt. Papyrus was paper made of pressed reeds. The merchants of Tyre traded goods with the Egyptians for the papyrus and then sold it to the merchants of Byblos, who in turn retailed it to the world. The ancient scribes of Israel purchased the papyrus from Egypt and then recorded the words of the prophets. This amazing paper from Byblos was so highly valued that even today those written pages are named after that city. Today we call them the Bible.[4]

Many historians believe that Phoenician cities existed prior to 1200 BC but the Phoenicians did not become differentiated from their neighbors until the arrival of the "sea peoples," as they were called. Mystery and controversy surround the origin of the sea people. They could be called the "pirates of the ancient world" because they attacked cities from the land of Canaan to the Egyptian Delta. After a stunning defeat at the hands of Ramses III at the Battle of Pelusium in 1149 BC, the sea people were pushed back to settle in the southern coastal areas of Phoenicia. They were absorbed in the culture and created the seagoing financial giant that was Phoenicia. It is interesting to note the sea peoples later became known as the Philistines. They paved the way for Hebrew, Greek, and Roman cultures, from which our Bible came!

A SMALL CITY WITH A BIG IMPACT!

Around 1200 BC the sea peoples made a lasting impact on the cities of Tyre and Sidon. For reasons many do not understand, only Tyre, Sidon, and the Hebrew civilization made peace with them. Tyre was not destroyed; in fact, the people of Tyre became specialists in seafaring and maritime activities. Tyre, though less than one square mile in size, was one of the world's greatest leaders of trade and commerce for centuries. Most historians agree that Tyre was the richest of all nations and controlled Phoenicia and the eastern Mediterranean coast.

A case in point

The exploration of the Tyrians was legendary. Their far-reaching expeditions turned the Mediterranean Sea into the Phoenician Lake:

The actual name for this body of water stems from their legendary maritime activities and remains the Medi-Tyrian Sea. As a matter of fact, the prefix "medi" implies middle. Perhaps Tyrian voyages included sailing the Atlantic and the Indian Oceans, with the Mediterranean in the middle. It could simply represent a body of water in the middle of the surrounding lands.[5]

Just how far did the seafarers of Tyre go in their explorations? In the fifth century BC, Hanno II from Carthage (a colony of Tyre) sailed past the Pillars of Hercules to the Gulf of Guinea. Around the same time Himilco sailed to what is now known as Great Britain.[6]

It was also reported that the mariners brought back gold from southeast Africa (Zimbabwe-Rhodesia). Diodorus of Sicily, in his first century BC writings, said:

> The Phoenicians discovered, "in the deep, off Libya (Africa) an island of considerable size...fruitful, much of it mountainous...Through it flows navigable river..." The first lands west of Africa with the specifications are South America and the islands of the Antilles. Many Greek and Roman writers maintain that there was land lying far to the west.[7]

There is some disagreement on how far west the explorations took them. Some have conjectured that perhaps the gold found in King Solomon's mines did not come from the Middle East or southern Africa:

> It's very possible that everyone has looked in the wrong continent for the gold mines of Ophir. The origin of the Amazon, a "deep navigable river," begins in Peru. The amazing Inca Indians were known for their advanced civilization and ample supplies of gold and silver.[8]

> In pre-Columbian South America, the Incan civilization had a mysterious forebear, the Olmecs. Hieroglyphic symbols were also discovered in addition to Incan symbols. Deciphering of the hieroglyphics is still an ongoing process. It is also true that hieroglyphics were not common in pre-Columbian South America. This method of writing and communication was best known between Egypt and Tyre during this same period.[9]

COMING TO THE AMERICAS?

In 1996 Mark McMenamin, professor of geology at Holyoke College, proposed a theory that Phoenician sailors discovered the New World around 350 BC. The Phoenician state of Carthage minted gold staters in 350 BC bearing a pattern, in the reverse exergue of the coins, which McMenamin interpreted as a map of the Mediterranean with the Americas shown to the west across the Atlantic.

If McMenamin is correct, neither Columbus nor the Vikings were the first non-natives to set foot on the Americas. McMenamin, who in 1995 led an expedition that discovered the oldest animal fossil found to date, may have made another discovery. Upon his examination McMenamin determined that coins' designs are actually maps of the ancient world, an area that includes the Mediterranean Sea and the Americas. In addition to this discovery, the impression of the maps on these coins indicate that Carthaginian explorers had sailed to the New World.

In fact, it was his interest in the Carthaginians as explorers that led McMenamin to study the coins. The Carthaginians were closely linked to the Phoenicians of the Middle East in culture, language, and naval enterprise. Both peoples are widely credited with significant sailing exploits through the Mediterranean, to the British Isles, and along the coast of Africa.

Often interpreted by scholars as letters in Phoenician script, the design on one of the coins is of a horse standing with symbols appearing on the bottom of the coin. Scholars were baffled when in 1960 their theory was discounted. Studying the images more carefully, McMenamin was able to see that the design was a representation of the Mediterranean in the midst of Europe and Africa with the British Isles to the upper left. Further left is an image of the Americas. Because of his interest in Carthage, McMenamin became a master of the Phoenician language and wrote two pamphlets on his discoveries concerning the Carthaginian coins. One pamphlet, written in Phoenician, is the first newly published piece written in that ancient language in fifteen hundred years.

McMenamin has submitted a paper on his theory to *The Numismatist*, a leading journal in the study of coins, and will seek to gain access to a number of coins currently held in European collections. At the very least he hopes his theory will focus new scholarly attention on ancient Carthaginian culture, and it may well reveal that it was Africans, not Europeans, who discovered the New World.[10]

Alan Campbell is the pastor of the Cregagh Covenant People's

Fellowship in Belfast, Northern Ireland; director of Open Bible Ministries; and a prominent scholar and lecturer. Pastor Campbell penned an article outlining his view on the influence of the Phoenician civilization with regard to the question, "Did the Phoenicians discover America?":

> The term Phoenician is a general one, which covers not only the sea-faring peoples based in the ancient cities of Tyre and Sidon (on the coast of modern Lebanon), but also the sea-roving Israelite tribes of Dan, Asher and Zebulon, whose tribal territories in Canaan were adjacent to these city states on the East Mediterranean coastline. These peoples planted trading posts and mercantile colonies along the shores of North Africa and Spain: and they engaged in a flourishing tin trade with the Southwest corner of the British Isles, their ships passing through the Straits of Gibraltar, then known as the "Pillars of Hercules."
>
> As long ago as 1913, author T. C. Johnston in his book *Did the Phoenicians Discover America?* claimed that the American continent was discovered and settled by Phoenicians and Hebrews who kept in contact with the Middle East for some three hundred years. He claimed that North America was the Biblical Ophir, visited by the fleets of King Solomon, and he outlined some twenty-six points of comparison between the civilization of the Eastern Mediterranean homelands of the Phoenicians, Hebrews, and the Mayan, Inca, and Aztec civilizations in the New World.
>
> More recent research by Professor Barry Fell points to Punic or Phoenician inscriptions found in New England, Ohio and West Virginia, and also the discovery of coinage and trade goods in the United States which had come from the Phoenician city of Carthage in North Africa.[11]

Other important discoveries have proven to be both enlightening and controversial when it comes to the question of the Phoenician/Hebrew influence on the Americas. These are a few examples.

The Bat Creek Stone and the Cherokee Nation (see the addendum at the end of this chapter).

The Bat Creek Stone was professionally excavated in 1889 from an undisturbed burial mound in eastern Tennessee by the Smithsonian's Mound Survey project. The director of the project, Cyrus Thomas, initially declared that the curious inscriptions on the stone were "beyond question letters of the Cherokee alphabet."[12]

Photo: Scott Wolter

In the 1960s, Henriette Mertz and Corey Ayoob both noticed that the inscription, when inverted from Thomas's orientation to that of the above photograph, instead appeared to be ancient Semitic. The late Semitic languages scholar Cyrus Gordon (1971a, 1971b, 1972) confirmed that it is Semitic, and specifically Paleo-Hebrew of approximately the first or second century AD. According to him, the five letters to the left of the comma-shaped word divider read, from right to left, LYHWD, or "for Judea." He noted that the broken letter on the far left is consistent with *mem*, in which case this word would instead read LYHWD[M], or "for the Judeans."[13]

The Los Lunas Decalogue Stone

You can find information about this on several Internet sites, including Wikipedia.

The greatest gift: invention of the alphabet

Probably the most visible and long-lasting impact the Phoenicians made on civilization was the creation of the Phoenician alphabet. Many believe that the Phoenician alphabet gave birth to the Greek alphabet. As Herodotus told us, and virtually all linguists have confirmed, the Greeks improved it considerably by adding vowels, thus creating their own alphabet. This not only allowed the recording of history throughout the ages, from Herodotus to Gibbons to the history books used in classrooms today, but also the recording of science, philosophy, literature, and other knowledge contributed by the world societies. Other alphabets have been based upon the Phoenician model, including the Roman, Persian, Hebraic, Arabic, Brahimi (Indian and Southeast Asian), and Cyrillic (Russian).

There is a great deal of similarity between the Phoenician alphabet and the Hebrew alphabet, including numerals, which are nearly identical.

It is important to note the Phoenicians were instrumental in disseminating their form of writing, which became our modern alphabet, and in opening up various civilizations and cultures of the Mediterranean basin to one another.

Without this contribution of an alphabet, world history would have still happened; however, it would have been quite different, and much less of it would have been passed down to us today.

CAN ANYTHING GOOD COME OUT OF PHOENICIA?

Time and space permitted me to outline only certain indisputable facts, theories, even controversy, when it came to the influence of the Phoenician civilization—more specifically the ancient city of Tyre. There is enough historical documentation to prove that their influence reached every corner of the ancient world.

Without a doubt this ancient civilization played such an important role in history that three thousand years later we are still amazed by it. The mere fact that Tyre and Sidon are mentioned in more than seven chapters of the Bible is proof enough that there was more to the connection to our lineage than first thought. It is a fact that both Jesus and the Apostle Paul traveled a great distance in order to minister there.

As we will soon see, King David and his son Solomon developed a strong relationship with Hiram, the King of Tyre. Other kings of Israel also felt the urgency to align themselves with what often has been described as the financial capital of the ancient world—the city of Tyre.

The sound of this generation is the voice of the prophetic crying out to "pay attention" to the divine connection between the actions and attitude of King Hiram toward God's chosen people.

King Hiram of Tyre will now step to center stage. I will show you an amazing connection with this ancient Gentile king whom God used to bless David and Solomon.

Fact or fiction, fairy tale or history, the question remains: *Can anything good come out of Phoenicia? I believe the answer is a resounding yes!*

HIRAM, THE PHOENICIANS, AND THE CHEROKEE CIVILIZATION

From the beginning of human history Satan has hated the promised seed and declared war on the lineage of Jesus the Messiah. This hatred for Semitic peoples manifested in ancient times under Pharaoh of Egypt; Sargon and Sennacherib of Assyria; and Nebuchadnezzar of Babylon. In the twentieth century Hitler's hatred led to the separation of Jews into ghettoes and later into concentration camps. Ultimately millions died in the Holocaust.

What does this have to do with the ancient and modern Cherokee nation?

DNA

It is critically important to understand that there is as much as 35 percent Phoenician-Hebrew markers in the DNA of the Oklahoma Cherokee. Phoenicians (Syrians) and Hebrews are both descendants of Shem, the son of Noah, and are therefore Semitic people and cousins. Phoenicians are not Arabs![1] According to Chief Attakullakulla, in 1750 they came across the ocean from the rising of the sun.[2]

Syrophoenicians descended from Shem through Arphaxad, his son. Arphaxad begat Sala, who begat Ebon, from whom the Hebrews came. He had another son, Kenni, from whom the Syrophoenicians came. Therefore, like the Jews, the ancient Syrophoenicians were descendants of Shem—Semitic people, not Arabs!

This explains the relationship between Solomon and Hiram, and Solomon's willingness to allow Huram-Abi to help cast the metal objects for the temple. Huram-Abi was half Jewish of the tribe of Dan and half Syrophoenician! (See 2 Chronicles 2:10–13; see also http://en.wikipedia.org/wiki/Phoenicia.)

Strange as it may seem, the *haplo* groups that are Semitic Phoenician-Hebrew are in the Cherokee DNA. Is it possible that the Phoenician-Hebrew ships of Hiram and Solomon made it to America? (See chapter 8, "The Mystery of Phoenicia.")

IS THERE ANY OTHER PROOF?

The DNA is without question a link to Semitic origins in Phoenicia and ancient Israel. The real proof rises in Tennessee, part of the ancient Cherokee empire. The Cherokee lived in houses, had lodges in the shape of synagogues, prayed under prayer shawls, and called on the name of Yohawah.[3] They also called God Eloh.[4] In the *Cherokee History of the World*, written in 1890 by Sakiyah Sanders, the author mentions the Creation in seven days, the Flood, and the Tower of Babel. He claims this is a translation of Cherokee ancient writings and oral tradition.[5]

TENNESSEE CONNECTIONS

Living in Chattanooga and one of the origins of the Trail of Tears by which the Cherokee were marched to Oklahoma reservations in cruel seizure of their ancient lands, I live with the echoes of Cherokees all around me.

Our community, called Brainerd, is named after David Brainerd, who came to our area from the Great Awakening in Massachusetts and gave his life as a witness to the Cherokee. Also, "Missionary Ridge," where the bloody Civil War battle by the same name was fought, was an ancient tribal headquarters. Why is this important?

Returning to the beginning of this chapter, it is important that you understand Satan's hatred of Shem and his Semitic descendants who would give us the Jewish race and ultimately our Messiah.

Revelation 12 describes the serpent posed to devour the promised seed of woman. Could it be that the treatment of the Eastern Cherokee was, at least from Satan's perspective, an anti-Semitic act? The Cherokee were relocated later. The German Jews under Hitler were relocated and placed in camps called concentration camps. In fact, according to the late author and minister John Phillips, Adolf Hitler patterned his treatment of Jews after American Indian reservations.[6]

There is much more evidence, but I wanted you to see the ancient war against God's people and His plan. I do not believe early Americans were Nazis, but I do believe that John Wesley Powell, an explorer and the first director of the Smithsonian Institute, and others believed Native Americans were savages and that it was the white man's destiny to take the land under the expansionist beliefs of Manifest Destiny. (For more on this doctrine, see wikipedia.org/wiki/Manifest_destiny.)

CONCLUSION

I recently traveled to the end of the Trail of Tears, where I met Jay Swallow, a spiritual leader among Native Americans. Dr. Swallow, who died shortly after my visit, shared with me the discovery of Phoenician gold coins dating back to AD 80 in the Cimarron River.

Could Phoenician and Hebrew vessels have made it to America? Were Hebrew roots already present in our nature? Could Hiram's and Solomon's ships have made it to America? Could America be the Ophir of Scripture? Only God knows.

CHAPTER 9

UNLOCKING THE HIRAM CODE

Now Hiram king of Tyre sent envoys to David, along with cedar logs and carpenters and stonemasons, and they built a palace for David.
—2 SAMUEL 5:11

No doubt one of the strangest characters in the Bible is King Hiram I. King Hiram ruled the ancient city of Tyre, a leading city-state of Phoenicia. Tyre is mentioned seventy times in the Bible. Although less than one square mile in size, Tyre was one of the greatest leaders of commerce and trade for thousands of years. It boasted famous shipbuilders and successful merchants, and was known as the financial capital of the ancient world. History has proved that Tyre's influence reached every corner of the world. Ancient colonies of Tyre were located in the Greek world on the Aegean Sea, North Africa, Carthage, Sicily, and Corsica.

IT'S GOOD TO BE THE KING!

Tyre had many kings, but no one was as famous as Hiram I. It was Hiram who was king when Israel formed a new nation under the rule of King David. During the golden age of Tyrian rule, they had developed a far-reaching empire. The development of many kinds of ships enabled them to explore, colonize, and develop trade relationships all over the known world.

- *Hiram* means "exalted one," or "bright white one." In Hebrew it means "high born." King Hiram I succeeded his father, Abibaal. King Hiram was born in 1000 BC and reigned from 982–947 BC.

- It was during his reign that Tyre grew from a satellite of Sidon into the most important of Phoenician cities.

- He worshipped Yahweh at a time when the worship of Baal was prevalent in his nation.

+ He ensured himself access to major trade routes to Egypt, Arabia, and Mesopotamia by aligning himself with King Solomon.

+ Because of his relationship with Israel, his rule was one of peace and not war.

+ He built the first freshwater cisterns in the known world.

+ He built two land bridges between Tyre and Lebanon that are still seen today.

+ He constructed the first arch of triumph, and its remains are still visible today.

+ His sarcophagus (tomb) is still visible today in Lebanon.

A TALE OF THREE KINGS: HIRAM, DAVID, AND SOLOMON

There was a strong spiritual connection between three great kings: David, Solomon, and Hiram. What started in the "natural" will become "spiritual" to us.

First the natural

King David captures Jerusalem.

In 2 Samuel 5 David is anointed king over all of Israel and establishes his capital city. He captured Jebus, which became Jerusalem, or the "City of David":

> All the tribes of Israel came to David at Hebron and said, "We are your own flesh and blood. In the past, while Saul was king over us, you were the one who led Israel on their military campaigns. And the LORD said to you, 'You will shepherd my people Israel, and you will become their ruler.'
>
> When all the elders of Israel had come to King David at Hebron, the king made a covenant with them at Hebron before the LORD, and they anointed David king over Israel.
>
> David was thirty years old when he became king, and he reigned forty years. In Hebron he reigned over Judah seven years and six months, and in Jerusalem he reigned over all Israel and Judah thirty-three years.
>
> The king and his men marched to Jerusalem to attack the

Jebusites, who lived there. The Jebusites said to David, "You will not get in here; even the blind and the lame can ward you off." They thought, "David cannot get in here." Nevertheless, David captured the fortress of Zion—which is the City of David.

On that day David had said, "Anyone who conquers the Jebusites will have to use the water shaft to reach those 'lame and blind' who are David's enemies." That is why they say, "The 'blind and lame' will not enter the palace."

David then took up residence in the fortress and called it the City of David. He built up the area around it, from the terraces inward. And he became more and more powerful, because the LORD God Almighty was with him.

—2 SAMUEL 5:1–10

Why did David lead all of Israel up against this city, a city that the Israelites had never been able to thoroughly defeat before? I believe there are several reasons. We will look at two.

First, Jerusalem was a city that God had promised to give to the Israelites, and a people that He had ordered the Israelites to destroy. Their presence among the Israelites was corrupting God's people (Judges 3:5–6). Saul was reluctant to deal decisively with attacks from Israel's enemies from without. He was even willing to live with the enemy dwelling within Israel. The Jebusites were left alone, so far as we can tell. Even the garrison of Philistines was not resisted until Jonathan could bear their presence no longer, virtually forcing both the Philistines and his father to act. (See 1 Samuel 13:3.)

David recognized that no kingdom could be viewed with fear (or even respect) if it were not able to expel its enemies from its midst. The Jebusites had to be dealt with, and David knew it. It was time for these enemies of God to be defeated. The defeat of the Jebusites and the taking of Jebus would be the first step in Israel's conquest of her enemies, a conquest that was partial in the times of Joshua and the judges. This victory would overshadow the victory of Saul and the Israelites over the Ammonites. (See 1 Samuel 11.) What a way to start a reign as king!

Second, David needed a new capital city. When David had been king of Judah alone, Hebron served well as his capital. But now David was anointed king of all Israel. He needed a capital that was farther north, one more centrally located that would unify the nation. Jebus was the perfect city. Israel's victory over the Jebusites would unite the nation. The possession of Jebus as David's new capital would do likewise. The city was virtually on the border of Judah and Benjamin. It was a city that neither the sons of Judah nor the sons of Benjamin had been able to capture; thus, taking this city as his capital would not seem to favor either of these two tribes. In addition to all this, its natural setting made it difficult to defeat (which is why the Israelites had not taken and held it before). It was in the hill country, on the top of more than one mountain, with valleys around it. With a little work, it was a virtual fortress (2 Sam. 5:9).

When the people of Jebus saw David and the Israelite soldiers coming against their city, it was not something new or frightening to them. In their history such attacks had occurred with some frequency, though never successfully. And so, safely behind the walls of the city, the Jebusites mocked David and his men. It was something like an arrogant bully threatening, "I can whip you, and your big brother, with one arm tied behind my back." Were they intimidated by David's army? Not at all! So they mocked them, bragging that they were so secure that they could turn their defense over to those who were blind and lame.

David's anger was aroused, much as it had been by Goliath's arrogant boasting. He took up the words of their boast in his orders to his men: "Let his men go and do battle with the 'lame and the blind,' and let them reach them by entering the city through the water tunnel." (See 2 Samuel 5:8.) The Jebusites thought they were secure but did not reckon on the fact that God was with David and nothing could prevent victory from coming into David's hand!

Is this attitude and action on David's part not a foreshadowing of how the ultimate King of Israel would come to Earth? Would the self-righteous not look the other way and walk on the other side of the street, lest they come into contact with a wounded man (Luke 10:25–37)? They wondered why Jesus would associate with sinners and be touched by the impure. The very people they shunned, Jesus sought. David was a prototype of the One who would come after him, who would seek out those who were infirmed and minister to them. (See Luke 4:16–21; 5:29–32; 7:18–23.)

Just as David represents the Messiah, the arrogant and boastful Jebusites represent the self-righteous, who scorn Jesus, and will eventually suffer defeat at His hand. David's enemies were defeated as he became greater and greater. David could not be stopped, for God was with him!

King Hiram builds David a house.

The first mention of Hiram in Scripture is in 2 Samuel 5:11: "Now Hiram king of Tyre sent envoys to David, along with cedar logs and carpenters and stonemasons, and they built a palace for David."

The rulers of Tyre cultivated a strong relationship with Israel. They wanted to make sure the financial success of Tyre was secure, and they did so by establishing and maintaining a purposeful connection with this newly formed nation under the leadership of Saul and David.

King Hiram entered David's life as David conquered Jerusalem, built fortifications, and established his capital city. It was during this moment in history that King Hiram came to David asking for nothing except to sow a seed into the young king's life. He gave David a house! You will see that this act released extreme favor on Hiram and his nation. David quickly accepted Hiram's offer and assistance, since some of the greatest artisans, workers of metal, and stone carving in the world were from Tyre. But that is not the end of the relationship.

King Hiram and Solomon's temple

It wasn't long before King Hiram discovered what was near and dear to Israel's heart. He helped build the temple in Jerusalem. After David died, Hiram continued the friendship with Solomon, providing materials and skilled workmen for the building of the temple:

> When Hiram king of Tyre heard that Solomon had been anointed king to succeed his father David, he sent his envoys to Solomon, because he had always been on friendly terms with David. Solomon sent back this message to Hiram:
>
> "You know that because of the wars waged against my father David from all sides, he could not build a temple for the Name of the LORD his God until the LORD put his enemies under his feet. But now the LORD my God has given me rest on every side, and there is no adversary or disaster. I intend, therefore, to build a temple for the Name of the LORD my God, as the LORD told my father David, when he said, 'Your son whom I will put on the throne in your place will build the temple for my Name.'
>
> "So give orders that cedars of Lebanon be cut for me. My men will work with yours, and I will pay you for your men whatever wages you set. You know that we have no one so skilled in felling timber as the Sidonians."
>
> When Hiram heard Solomon's message, he was greatly pleased

and said, "Praise be to the LORD today, for He has given David a wise son to rule over this great nation."

So Hiram sent word to Solomon: "I have received the message you sent me and will do all you want in providing the cedar and juniper logs."

—1 KINGS 5:1–8

So the friendship between Hiram and Solomon hereby increased more and more; and they swore to continue it forever. And the king appointed a tribute to be laid on all the people, of thirty thousand laborers, whose work he rendered easy to them by prudently dividing it among them; for he made ten thousand cut timber in Mount Lebanon for one month; and then to come home.... There were also of the strangers who were left by David, who were to carry the stones and other materials, seventy thousand; and of those that cut stones, eighty thousand. Of these three thousand and three hundred were rulers over the rest.[1]

Solomon reciprocated in the agreement. In return for King Hiram's help Solomon committed an annual supply of food:

And Solomon gave Hiram twenty thousand cors [about 3,600 tons or about 3,250 metric tons] of wheat as food for his household, in addition to twenty thousand baths [about 120,000 gallons or about 440,000 liters] of pressed olive oil. Solomon continued to do this for Hiram year after year. The LORD gave Solomon wisdom, just as he had promised him. There were peaceful relations between Hiram and Solomon, and the two of them made a treaty.

—1 KINGS 5:11–12

Now the spiritual

The connection between King Hiram and King David, and eventually King Solomon, was more than politically motivated. There is ample evidence in the historical records and Scripture to establish the fact that both sides benefited politically, financially, and militarily from having a strong relationship. But it is also important to know the spiritual effects of this relationship.

The connection between the Phoenician people, led by King Hiram, and Israel brought blessings. Because a Gentile king determined to have a relationship with Israel, the blessings of God flowed upon his people:

> King Solomon sent to Tyre and brought Huram, whose mother
> was a widow from the tribe of Naphtali and whose father was
> from Tyre and a skilled craftsman in bronze. Huram was filled
> with wisdom, with understanding and with knowledge to do all
> kinds of bronze work. He came to King Solomon and did all the
> work assigned to him.
>
> —1 KINGS 7:13–14

Jesse L. Cotton writes in the International Standard Bible
Encyclopedia:

> After David had taken the stronghold of Zion, Hiram sent mes-
> sengers and workmen and materials to build a palace for him at
> Jerusalem (2Sa 5:11; 1Ch 14:1). Solomon, on his accession to the
> throne, made a league with Hiram, in consequence of which Hiram
> furnished the new king of Israel with skilled workmen and with
> cedar trees and fir trees and algum trees from Lebanon for the
> building of the Temple. In return Solomon gave annually to Hiram
> large quantities of wheat and oil (1Ki 5:1 (Hebrews 15) ff; 2Ch 2:3
> (Heb 2:1–18) ff). "At the end of twenty years, wherein Solomon had
> built the two houses, the house of Yahweh and the king's house,"
> Solomon made a present to Hiram of twenty cities in the land of
> Galilee. Hiram was not at all pleased with these cities and contemp-
> tuously called them "Cabul." His displeasure, however, with this
> gift does not seem to have disturbed the amicable relations that had
> hitherto existed between the two kings, for subsequently Hiram
> sent to the king of Israel 120 talents of gold (1Ki 9:10–14). Hiram
> and Solomon maintained merchant vessels on the Mediterranean
> and shared mutually in a profitable trade with foreign ports (1Ki
> 10:22). Hiram's servants, "shipmen that had knowledge of the sea,"
> taught the sailors of Solomon the route from Ezion-geber and Eloth
> to Ophir, whence large stores of gold were brought to King Solomon
> (1Ki 9:26; 2Ch 8:17 f).[2]

> Now King Solomon sent and called Huram out of Tyre. He was
> the son of a widow from the tribe of Naphtali, and his father was a
> man of Tyre who worked in bronze, and he was filled with wisdom
> and understanding and skill to make all sorts of items in bronze.
> So he came to King Solomon and performed all his work.
>
> —1 KINGS 7:13–14, MEV

Hiram king of Tyre replied by letter to Solomon: "Because the LORD loves his people, he has made you their king."

And Hiram added: "Praise be to the LORD, the God of Israel, who made heaven and earth! He has given King David a wise son, endowed with intelligence and discernment, who will build a temple for the LORD and a palace for himself. I am sending you Huram-Abi, a man of great skill, whose mother was from Dan and whose father was from Tyre. He is trained to work in gold and silver, bronze and iron, stone and wood, and with purple and blue and crimson yarn and fine linen. He is experienced in all kinds of engraving and can execute any design given to him. He will work with your skilled workers and with those of my lord, David your father. Now let my lord send his servants the wheat and barley and the olive oil and wine he promised, and we will cut all the logs from Lebanon that you need and will float them as rafts by sea down to Joppa. You can then take them up to Jerusalem."

—2 CHRONICLES 2:11–16

Can you fathom that God sent a man who was half Jew and half Gentile to help build the temple? In light of the Jewish attitude of exclusivity as pertaining to the Gentiles in the first century, it is more unbelievable. The Jews of Jesus's day would have never accepted nor allowed a half-breed to have any part in things pertaining to their religion, traditions, or law. As hard as it is to believe, here was a man sent by King Hiram participating in the fashioning of the articles to be placed in the holy of holies! All of the design pieces of gold, silver, bronze, and iron were his handiwork. But, as pointed out in Scripture, Solomon maintained and cultivated a relationship with King Hiram, a Gentile king, and accepted his help!

King Hiram loved David and built him a palace. Why? Because he loved him! When Solomon was anointed king, Hiram continued to sow seed and bless the new king.

When Hiram heard Solomon's message, he was greatly pleased and said, "Praise be to the LORD today, for he has given David a wise son to rule over this great nation" (1 Kings 5:7).

There is so much more to the story than the fact that Hiram enjoyed a reign of peace and prosperity. In the next chapter we will see the divine connection between the Hiram anointing and the body of Christ today. How is it possible that something that happened thousands of years still has an effect today? Turn the page and find out!

CHAPTER 10

THE HIRAM CODE ACTIVATED TODAY

Now when He had taken the scroll, the four living creatures and the twenty-four elders fell down before the Lamb, each having a harp, and golden bowls full of incense, which are the prayers of the saints. And they sang a new song, saying: "You are worthy to take the scroll, and to open its seals; for You were slain, and have redeemed us to God by Your blood out of every tribe and tongue and people and nation, and have made us kings and priests to our God; and we shall reign on the earth."

—REVELATION 5:8–10, NKJV, EMPHASIS ADDED

I**T IS IMPORTANT** *to see this principle!* God used Gentiles (non-Jews) to erect, establish, and exalt His chosen people! How does that affect us today? First, consider two prophecies from Amos 9. Then I will show you how it is possible to walk in the Hiram anointing today.

PROPHECY #1: THE JEWS WILL BE RETURNED TO THEIR LAND

"I will bring back the captives of My people Israel; they shall build the waste cities and inhabit them; they shall plant vineyards and drink wine from them; they shall also make gardens and eat fruit from them. I will plant them in their land, and no longer shall they be pulled up from the land I have given them," says the LORD your God.

—AMOS 9:14–15, NKJV

Much has been written about the restoration of God's chosen people to their land. Even before May 1948 significant volumes of work were compiled for and against the notion that God's people would ever be restored to their land. I believe Scripture is clear that indeed the promises of God concerning Israel will not fail.

As England's most influential nonconformist preacher and popular theologian in the last half of the nineteenth century, Charles Haddon Spurgeon (1834–1892) added his considerable voice to the question of

Jewish restoration to the Promised Land. While the political, economic, and social issues involved in the restoration movement were varied and complex, Spurgeon "worked only through the power of the Word of God," and his views on this issue were driven by his interpretation of Scripture.

> Perhaps the clearest and most significant statement by Spurgeon as it relates to the restoration of the Jews to the land, was made in an address to the *British Society for the Propagation of the Gospel Amongst the Jews*. Delivered at the Metropolitan Tabernacle on June 16, 1864 [eighty-two years before the establishment of the state of Israel], Spurgeon preached on "The Restoration and Conversion of the Jews" and stated: "There will be a native government again; there will again be the form of a body politic; a state shall be incorporated, and a king shall reign. Israel has now become alienated from her own land. Her sons, though they can never forget the sacred dust of Palestine, yet die at a hopeless distance from her consecrated shores. But it shall not be so forever, for her sons shall again rejoice in her: her land shall be called Beulah, for as a young man marrieth a virgin so shall her sons marry her. 'I will place you in your own land,' is God's promise to them… They are to have a national prosperity which shall make them famous; nay, so glorious shall they be that Egypt, and Tyre, and Greece, and Rome, shall all forget their glory in the greater splendor of the throne of David.… If there be anything clear and plain, the literal sense and meaning of this passage [Ezekiel 37:1–10]—a meaning not to be spirited or spiritualized away—must be evident that both the two and the ten tribes of Israel are to be restored to their own land, and that a king is to rule over them."[1]

It was one thing for the Jews to be restored to the land; it was another thing for them to stay there! All the forces of hell arrayed against her. As soon as her independence was declared in 1948, Haj Amin al-Husseini, the grand mufti, declared: "The entire Jewish population in Palestine must be destroyed or driven into the sea. Allah has bestowed upon us the rare privilege of finishing what Hitler only began. Let the jihad begin. Murder the Jews. Murder them all!"[2]

Just a few hours after the declaration of Israel's statehood, some thirty-five thousand soldiers from six Arab nations arrayed themselves against a brand-new Israeli army. The majority of the Israeli soldiers had never seen a day of training, much less combat.

Since its establishment in 1948, the state of Israel has fought seven recognized wars, two Palestinian intifadas, and a series of armed conflicts in the broader Arab-Israeli conflict, including the following:

+ 1948 Arab-Israeli War (November 1947–July 1949)

+ Reprisal operations (1950s–1960s)

+ Suez Crisis (October 1956)

+ Six-Day War (June 1967)

+ War of Attrition (1967–1970)

+ Yom Kippur War (October 1973)

+ Palestinian Insurgency in South Lebanon (1971–1982)

+ 1982 Lebanon War (1982)

+ South Lebanon Conflict (1982–2000)

+ First Intifada (1987–1993): first large-scale Palestinian uprising against Israel in the West Bank and the Gaza Strip

+ Second Intifada (2000–2005): second Palestinian uprising; a period of intensified violence that began in late September 2000

+ 2006 Lebanon War (summer 2006)

+ Gaza War (December 2008–January 2009): three-week armed conflict between Israel and Hamas during the winter of 2008–2009

+ Operation Pillar of Defense (November 2012): military offensive on the Gaza Strip[3]

As we will see, there is a divine connection between the return of the Jews to their land and the fulfillment of a second prophecy in Amos 9.

PROPHECY #2: THE TABERNACLE OF DAVID WILL BE RESTORED

> "On that day [What day? When the Jews are restored!] I will raise
> up the tabernacle of David, which has fallen down, and repair its
> damages; I will raise up its ruins, and rebuild it as in the days
> of old; that they may possess the remnant of Edom, and all the
> Gentiles who are called by My name," says the LORD who does
> this thing.
>
> —AMOS 9:11–12, NKJV

Is there a New Testament connection to the tabernacle of David? Yes.
Listen to the Apostle James in Acts 15 as he becomes the arbiter at the
Jerusalem Council. Most if not all Bible students agree that this was
a pivotal moment in the spreading of the gospel of Jesus Christ to all
nations. The debate was simple at its core; on one side you had those who
said the gospel was restricted to the Jew. On the other side were those
who said the gospel was for all nations. It was left up to the Apostle
James to make a judgment.

> The whole assembly became silent as they listened to Barnabas and
> Paul telling about the signs and wonders God had done among
> the Gentiles through them. When they finished, James spoke up.
> "Brothers," he said, "listen to me. Simon has described to us how
> God first intervened to choose a people for his name from the
> Gentiles. The words of the prophets are in agreement with this, as
> it is written: 'After this I will return and rebuild David's fallen tent.
> Its ruins I will rebuild, and I will restore it, that the rest of man-
> kind may seek the Lord, even all the Gentiles who bear my name,
> says the Lord, who does these things.'"
>
> —ACTS 15:12–17

As James makes his argument to the Jerusalem Council, he quotes
from Amos 9 as well as from other prophets. He makes reference to
the Gentiles and the fact that the door of salvation was now open to
whoever would come. I believe that the restoration of David's tabernacle
is a sign that there will be a great harvest of souls among the nations.
King David's kingdom was greatly expanded under his anointing, so
King Jesus will bring in a great end-times revival that will expand His
kingdom. Although the expansion of God's kingdom is happening at this
very hour, you would never know it by listening to the modern media!

In his eloquent defense James reminds the council how even Peter, an Orthodox Jew, saw Gentiles receive the gospel when he presented it to them. The telling statement is found in Peter's declaration in verse 14: "Simon has described to us how God first intervened to choose a people for his name from the Gentiles."

James then elaborates: "The words of the prophets are in agreement with this, as it is written: 'After this I will return and rebuild David's fallen tent. Its ruins I will rebuild, and I will restore it, that the rest of mankind may seek the Lord, even all the Gentiles who bear my name, says the Lord, who does these things'" (vv. 15–17).

The tabernacle of David speaks of unity.

I believe the expansion of God's kingdom today is patterned after what happened in David's day. Why do I believe that? Go back and look at David's attitude toward the Gentiles and how he viewed them in relation to God's kingdom. In 1 Chronicles 16:1 when David delivered the ark to his tabernacle, "They brought the ark of God and set it inside the tent that David had pitched for it, and they presented burnt offerings and fellowship offerings before God." And then it says, "On that day David first delivered this psalm into the hand of Asaph and his brethren, to thank the LORD: Oh, give thanks to the LORD! Call upon His name; make known His deeds among the peoples!" (vv. 7–8, NKJV).

Who are the "peoples" to whom David is referring? Verses 23–24 tell you: "Sing to the LORD, all the earth; proclaim his salvation day after day. Declare his glory among the nations, his marvelous deeds among all peoples." The tabernacle of David is a symbol of the house of God—not just Israel's God, but also the God of the nations! In these last days multitudes can come from all nations to receive salvation and marvel at the glory of God.

Can you imagine it? Jews and Gentiles coming together as "one new man" under the protection of the canopy of God! Roman soldiers on the battlefield marched toward their enemy holding their shields. When arrows rained down on them, they would create a united covering by interlocking their shields, leaving no room for a single arrow to penetrate. That is a picture of the body of Christ in unity—impenetrable! When the body of Christ is united, nothing can penetrate or gain a foothold. The body stands as one, in one accord—a force to be reckoned with!

The tabernacle of David speaks of a revival of praise and worship.

I believe that rebuilding the tabernacle of David is related not only to the unity in the last days but also to a revival of the kind of worship that existed when David brought the ark back and placed it in the tent (tabernacle).

David was a man after God's own heart. He was a true worshipper. He didn't just go through the rituals. His worship was from the heart, and it was open and unreserved.

> One thing I ask from the LORD, this only do I seek: that I may dwell in the house of the LORD all the days of my life, to gaze on the beauty of the LORD and to seek him in his temple.
>
> —PSALM 27:4

In David's day there was no temple; there was only his tent. So when David talks about worship and prayer, he is not talking so much about formal rituals and ceremonies but something that came from deep within the heart. David speaks about prayer as a "seeking after." He speaks about worship in terms of "beholding the beauty of the Lord" (NKJV). For David it's all about a personal relationship with God.

Author and minister Maurice Sklar wrote the following about David's tabernacle:

> When David did *not* bring the ark of the covenant back to Israel in the proper way by the Levites carrying it, or *not* according to scriptural pattern, judgment came and Uzzah, who carried it improperly, died.
>
> David also was very specific about how and who were to be singing and playing music before the Lord in his tabernacle, and although we cannot know every detail, we can see that there was a very precise and definite pattern that was followed.
>
> God is a God of order and pattern in *all* He does.
>
> The musicians of David were highly skilled and trained. They were set according to ranks and under authority as to when and how they were to worship. There were precise instruments and vocal parts that were written out as well as times of spontaneous music and worship. There was great variety of dynamic range and also style in the music. And it was continuous—going on 24 hours a day for a number of years! This is the basic pattern that God gave to David in the old covenant.

Now we live in a better covenant, based on better promises, according to the book of Hebrews. We are to behold and experience the glory and live in the very presence of the open face of the Lord in a much greater way than Israel did, according to the book of 1 Corinthians.[4]

David was not shy about his love for the Lord, nor was he embarrassed about expressing his love for his heavenly Father before the congregation. I believe in the last days God desires for His people to worship according to the pattern of David, dancing before the Lord and rejoicing in His glory.

Davidic worship was practiced by the early church. The worship found in the Psalms is encouraged by Paul (Eph. 5:19; Col. 3:16) and James (James 5:13). The writer of Hebrews admonishes Christians to offer the sacrifice of praise (Heb. 13:15), a revelation received earlier by David (Ps. 51:15–16; 69:30–31). And Davidic worship has been a part of every great revival in church history!

Based on the pattern of worship in David's tabernacle, here are a few tangible ways we can express our worship today:

+ Singers and singing (1 Chron. 15:16–27)

+ Musical instruments (1 Chron. 23:5, 25:1–7)

+ Thanking the Lord (1 Chron. 16:4, 8, 41)

+ Clapping of hands (Ps. 47:1; 98:8; Isa. 55:12)

+ Shouting (1 Chron. 15:28; Ps. 47:1–5)

+ Dancing and lifting up hands (1 Chron. 15:29; 2 Sam. 6:14; Ps. 149:3; 150:4; 134; 141:2)

The reason there has been so much satanic opposition to a revival of Davidic praise and worship in the modern church is because the enemy knows the tabernacle of David is a model for church worship. The church landscape is littered with the bodies of those who have been involved in the "worship wars." Decades ago the battle lines were drawn between those who held on to "traditional" styles of worship and those who wanted to birth a reformation of praise and worship. What many have failed to understand is that the tabernacle of David is the major type of worship found in the Bible! The majority of the psalms were birthed in David's tabernacle.

HOW IS THE HIRAM ANOINTING RELEASED TODAY?

Five keys to unlock the Hiram anointing

1. The pattern of the Hiram anointing

Hiram loved David and Solomon so much that he helped build David a palace and Solomon a temple. As a result King Hiram experienced a reign of peace, prosperity, exploration, and profitable trade. Scholars have called this "the Golden Age of Phoenicia." The pattern is clear—when kings (Gentile leaders) support Israel, prosperity is released.

Ask Hiram.

Ask Cyrus.

Ask Xerxes.

Ask Ruth and Boaz.

Ask any modern-day Christian who loves and supports Israel!

2. The principle of the Hiram anointing

Hiram loved what David loved. The principle of the Hiram anointing is to love what God loves. How can we love God and not love all of His people, including the Jews? How can we say we love God and not be connected to the church of Jesus Christ? Failure to recognize this principle will disqualify you from receiving ongoing blessing and prosperity.

3. The practice of the Hiram anointing

The Phoenicians embraced the Atlantean Sea peoples. The sea peoples came and taught the Phoenicians seafaring, who then taught the Israelites the same skills. Three races came together! To put the Hiram code into practice is to recognize that there must not be division between the peoples. Division is a tool of Satan. We see it manifest on a relational level today between the races, political parties, and even geographical locations. There is power and anointing in unity of purpose (Ps. 133).

4. The promise of the Hiram anointing

God's plans and purposes are connected to times and seasons. David had a desire to build a temple and was denied. Solomon declared, "You know how my father David could not build a house for the name of the LORD his God because of the wars which were fought against him on every side, until the LORD put his foes under...his feet" (1 Kings 5:3, NKJV).

Solomon stepped out of his father's shadow to become the wisest man who ever lived, and he completed the temple of the Lord. With the help of Hiram and the blessing of the Lord, one of the greatest structures known to man was built. And it was all in God's timing!

As pastor of Abba's House (The House of David), I have wanted to complete many things, but at the time of this writing I have not yet done them all. I have to be content with the fact that some of these things may not be in God's timing. But I have a promise from God. He made it very clear that He wanted me to raise up a Solomon, a son in this house who will complete what I started. That is exactly what I am doing with my own son. But make no mistake, I still have plenty of "fight" in me yet!

The promise of the Hiram anointing is that as long as I lead this wonderful congregation to stay connected to Israel, and continue to be obedient to every word the Lord has given me, the work will continue for generations to come.

5. The power of the Hiram anointing

> Then the angel who talked with me returned and woke me up, like someone awakened from sleep. He asked me, "What do you see?" I answered, "I see a solid gold lampstand with a bowl at the top and seven lamps on it, with seven channels to the lamps. Also there are two olive trees by it, one on the right of the bowl and the other on its left." I asked the angel who talked with me, "What are these, my lord?" He answered, "Do you not know what these are?" "No, my lord," I replied. So he said to me, "This is the word of the LORD to Zerubbabel: 'Not by might nor by power, but by my Spirit,' says the LORD Almighty.
>
> —ZECHARIAH 4:1–6

I believe we are seeing a prophetic picture of the church in verses 2–4. Where do we see seven lampstands in the New Testament? In Revelation 2–3 we read the word of Jesus to the seven churches of Revelation. Zechariah also saw two olive trees by the lampstand (Zech. 4:4). The olive trees represent Jews and Gentiles (Rom. 9–11).

Here is an Old Testament prophetic picture of the Hiram anointing. It's the "one new man" coming together as one body (Eph. 3). When the body comes together—Jews and Gentiles—in divine connection, the anointing and power are released. When you face your "mountains of difficulty," remember it is "'not by might nor by power, but by my Spirit,' says the LORD Almighty" (Zech. 4:6).

Remember, it was Solomon who gave the anointing to Hiram in

symbol—Jew and Gentile connected in a clear covenant. As Hiram gave Solomon building materials, Solomon in return gave him

+ wheat, a picture of the word of God;

+ oil, a picture of the anointing; and

+ *shalom* (peace).

As a result, prosperity and blessings were released to the kingdom of Hiram for more than six hundred years!

> In this way Hiram kept Solomon supplied with all the cedar and juniper logs he wanted, and Solomon gave Hiram twenty thousand cors of wheat as food for his household, in addition to twenty thousand baths of pressed olive oil. Solomon continued to do this for Hiram year after year. The Lord gave Solomon wisdom, just as he had promised him. There were peaceful relations between Hiram and Solomon, and the two of them made a treaty.
>
> —1 Kings 5:10–12

Hello, Hiram! Who Are the Hirams Today?

> But you are a chosen people, a royal priesthood, a holy nation, God's special possession, that you may declare the praises of him who called you out of darkness into his wonderful light.
>
> —1 Peter 2:9

> And from Jesus Christ, who is the faithful witness, the firstborn from the dead, and the ruler of the kings of the earth. To him who loves us and has freed us from our sins by his blood, and has made us to be a kingdom and priests to serve his God and Father—to him be glory and power for ever and ever! Amen.
>
> —Revelation 1:5–6

When kings and priests build the church together, God's presence, provision, and peace are released. You can walk in the Hiram anointing, dethrone Satan, and receive favor for generations to come!

You may be thinking, "That's wonderful, but I still have to live in the real world." Is it possible to live with such an anointing as we just described? There is so much confusion and turmoil in the world, it's hard to take it all in. Jesus and the Apostle John had something to say about that very contradiction—*really living with what you see around you and what you know inside of you.* In the following chapters we will discover not only how to face the contradiction, but also to live in abundance and prosperity in the last days.

ISAAC'S SECRET FOR FAVOR IN TIMES OF FAMINE

CHAPTER 11

LIVING WITH CONTRADICTION

*When you encounter difficulties and contradictions, do not try
to break them, but bend them with gentleness and time.*[1]
—SAINT FRANCIS DE SALES

LIFE IS SUPPOSED to make sense. But sometimes life comes at you
so hard and fast that you wonder what just happened. If that has
ever happened to you, I can understand. No matter how long you have
been a believer, and no matter how long you have lived on this planet,
sometimes you feel like a walking, talking, breathing contradiction. One
day up, the next day down. One day I'm on top of the world, and the
next day I've got the world on my shoulders. It's called "living in the
contradiction."

All it takes is a quick view of the morning news to see that our world
is in a mess. We go to church on Sunday and hear one thing, and live the
rest of the week hearing and seeing something totally different.

Did you know that one of the greatest illusionists in the world, Harry
Houdini, did not die from an illusion that went wrong or due to an assis-
tant not doing his job properly? No, actually he died from a "sucker punch."
That's right, from a punch to the stomach that he was not ready for.

For you who feel as if you have been "sucker punched" by life—cheer
up. *We win*, even when it looks as if we lose!

By definition, the word *contradiction* means "the act of going against;
opposition; a declaration of the opposite or contrary; a statement that is
at variance with itself (often in the phrase *a contradiction in terms*); conflict or inconsistency, as between events, qualities, etc."[2]

What does it mean for Christians to "live in the contradiction"? It is
the difference between what we see around us and what we know inside
of us. Consider the following examples.

Isaac lived in the middle of a contradiction.

Isaac lived in a famine, without hope for the future. God told him
to stay where he was and sow into the barren soil. Even though in the

natural it didn't make sense (a contradiction), he obeyed God and reaped a hundredfold.

John the Baptist experienced the contradiction firsthand.

There came a point in the life of John when nothing made sense. No doubt he felt he was doing everything right, yet he found himself in a dark, depressing prison cell waiting to die. Things were not working out as he thought they would. John was going through something we all go through called the "process events" of life—when life doesn't match up with what we know. Up until his prison experience John had no doubts as to the identity of Jesus Christ.

> When John, who was in prison, heard about the deeds of the Messiah, he sent his disciples to ask him, "Are you the one who is to come, or should we expect someone else?"
>
> Jesus replied, "Go back and report to John what you hear and see: The blind receive sight, the lame walk, those who have leprosy are cleansed, the deaf hear, the dead are raised, and the good news is proclaimed to the poor. Blessed is anyone who does not stumble on account of me."
>
> —MATTHEW 11:2–6

David, a man after God's own heart, lived in the contradiction.

Reading the psalms is like reading the writings of a musical manic depressive—one minute he's up and the next he's down. "Why, my soul, are you downcast? Why so disturbed within me? Put your hope in God, for I will yet praise him, my Savior and my God" (Ps. 42:5).

David was living in the contradiction of trying to understand the gap between his anointing and the manifestation of the power of God in his life. His emotions were being integrated into his circumstances, into what he was seeing with his eyes and what he knew in his heart to be true. The process was actually working for him; he just didn't understand how something that looked bad could be good for him. Every right response to the process moved him to the next level of his assignment with a fresh and more powerful anointing.

Process is the term we use to describe something going on in our lives that we do not like. But when we understand that God has a purpose for our lives even in the middle of a contradiction, it takes the enemy out of the equation. The enemy will try to interfere with our God-given assignment, create confusion, and move us away from our destinies.

The kingdom of God is one of contradictions:

+ The way up is down.

+ If you want to be first, be last.

+ If you want to lead, learn to serve.

+ In order to live, you must die.

+ In order to get, you have to give.

+ If you want to rise to the top, start at the bottom.

WHERE IN THE WORLD ARE YOU?

In John 17 Jesus described what many have called the greatest contradiction of all—our relationship to the world. This chapter gives us Jesus's great high priestly prayer. In reality this is the Lord's Prayer. When Jesus taught His disciples to pray, "Our Father which art in heaven," that was not the Lord's Prayer but the model prayer, or the disciple's prayer.

I see four very clear contradictions concerning our relationship to the world. When you combine John 17 and 1 John 2 you will see a detailed view of what the world is and what it wants to do to each and every believer:

> I will remain in the world no longer, but they are still *in the world*, and I am coming to you. Holy Father, protect them by the power of your name, the name you gave me, so that they may be one as we are one.
>
> —JOHN 17:11, EMPHASIS ADDED

> Do not love the world or anything in the world. If anyone loves the *world*, love for the Father is not in them.
>
> —1 JOHN 2:15, EMPHASIS ADDED

What a contradiction! We are specifically told that we are "in the world," and then we are warned not to have an emotional tie to the very place in which we live—the apostle John makes it very clear that if we do, the love of the Father is not in us. He is saying, "You cannot love two exact opposites at the same time"—or as Jesus put it, "No one can serve two masters. Either you will hate the one and love the other, or you will be devoted to the one and despise the other. You cannot serve both God and money" (Matt. 6:24).

So, what does the word *world* really mean?

It does not mean the world of nature. When you look around and see all the beautiful flowers, trees, mountains, and oceans, you realize they are all part of God's wonderful creation. The Bible says in Acts 17:24, "The God who made the world and everything in it is the Lord of heaven and earth and does not live in temples built by human hands."

Neither is He talking about the world of men, or humanity. "For God so loved the world" (John 3:16). Jesus loved the world of humanity. As John 3:16 declared, God loved it so much that He sent His only Son to die on the cross for the sins of the world. We too must love people—not only our friends, but also even our enemies!

The word that both John (in 1 John) and Jesus (in John 17) use for *world* is *kosmos*, from which we get the words *cosmopolitan* and *cosmic*. Our word *cosmos* is taken from a verb that means "to order," "to arrange," or "to put in the proper condition." We get our English word *cosmetic* from the same Greek word *cosmos*. Every woman alive knows what cosmetics are: they represent the arrangement of things, or "putting things in order"!

Author Warren W. Wiersbe writes:

> This "world" named here as our enemy is an invisible spiritual system opposed to God and Christ. We use the word *world* in the sense of system in our daily conversation. The TV announcer says, "We bring you the news from the world of sports." "The world of sports" is not a separate planet or continent. It is an organized system made up of a set of ideas, people, activities, purposes, and so forth. And "the world of finance" and "the world of politics" are likewise systems of their own. Behind what we see in sports or finance is an invisible system that we cannot see, and it is the system that "keeps things going."[3]

The Bible has a lot to say about the world system.

The world has a ruler.

> The god of this age has blinded the minds of unbelievers, so that they cannot see the light of the gospel that displays the glory of Christ, who is the image of God.
> —2 Corinthians 4:4

> Now is the time for judgment on this world; now the prince of this
> world will be driven out.
>
> —JOHN 12:31

Jesus identified Satan as "the prince of this world." Satan has an organization of evil spirits (Eph. 6:11–12) working with him and influencing the affairs of this world.

The world has its children.

> The master commended the dishonest manager because he had
> acted shrewdly. For the people of this world are more shrewd in
> dealing with their own kind than are the people of the light.
>
> —LUKE 16:8

> As for you, you were dead in your transgressions and sins, in which
> you used to live when you followed the ways of this world and of
> the ruler of the kingdom of the air, the spirit who is now at work in
> those who are disobedient. All of us also lived among them at one
> time, gratifying the cravings of our flesh and following its desires
> and thoughts. Like the rest, we were by nature deserving of wrath.
>
> —EPHESIANS 2:1–3

Every student of the Bible knows that there are two families in existence—those who belong to the family of God, and those who belong to this world. The unsaved are the "children of this world." They did not know or understand Jesus when He ministered in a human body, and they do not understand you today. The children of this world are trapped in Satan's system and without the power of God are forever doomed.

People who do not have a relationship with Jesus Christ will either knowingly or unknowingly be used by Satan to fulfill his purposes, which are evil and destructive. They are energized by the "prince of the power of the air."

The world has its own brand of wisdom.

> We do, however, speak a message of wisdom among the mature,
> but not the wisdom of this age or of the rulers of this age, who are
> coming to nothing. No, we declare God's wisdom, a mystery that
> has been hidden and that God destined for our glory before time

began. None of the rulers of this age understood it, for if they had, they would not have crucified the Lord of glory.

—1 Corinthians 2:6–8

Who is wise and understanding among you? Let them show it by their good life, by deeds done in the humility that comes from wisdom. But if you harbor bitter envy and selfish ambition in your hearts, do not boast about it or deny the truth. Such "wisdom" does not come down from heaven but is earthly, unspiritual, demonic. For where you have envy and selfish ambition, there you find disorder and every evil practice. But the wisdom that comes from heaven is first of all pure; then peace-loving, considerate, submissive, full of mercy and good fruit, impartial and sincere.

—James 3:13–17

The wisdom of the world is upside down. For example, worldly wisdom says that it is illegal to open your Bible and read it in a classroom; yet when a young person gets in trouble and lands in jail, the first thing he or she receives is a copy of the Bible! Worldly wisdom is warped, perverted, and twisted. Worldly wisdom is the very opposite of what is godly, holy, and spiritual.

The world system is corrupt through its lust (2 Pet. 1:4). It is dirty, nasty, and totally opposed to everything the child of God stands for. Its purpose is to hinder God's people from being what they ought to be. The world is not a friend to the believer. It is the enemy to the Christian and will never "help" him get closer to God!

Living in the Contradiction

Let's examine Jesus's prayer in John 17 more closely and discuss four distinct contradictions concerning the child of God and his relationship to the world.

Contradiction #1: He is saved "out of the world."

I have revealed you to those whom you gave me *out of the world*. They were yours; you gave them to me and they have obeyed your word.

—John 17:6, emphasis added

If you are a child of God, you have been saved out of the world system. You have a new master, a new nature, a new purpose, and a new love.

And according to Philippians 3:20, you have a new citizenship in heaven. Because of that, heaven makes all of its resources available to the child of God for an abundant life: "So from now on we regard no one from a worldly point of view. Though we once regarded Christ in this way, we do so no longer. Therefore, if anyone is in Christ, the new creation has come: The old has gone, the new is here!" (2 Cor. 5:16–17).

Paul describes this experience as being "rescued." This literally means to be delivered, set free, and loosened from the grip of sin. The word *rescued* ought to be on the lips of every believer!

> Who gave himself for our sins to rescue us from the present evil age, according to the will of our God and Father.
> —GALATIANS 1:4

> For He has rescued us from the dominion of darkness and brought us into the kingdom of the Son he loves, in whom we have redemption, the forgiveness of sins.
> —COLOSSIANS 1:13–15

But Jesus is the One who comes to the rescue:

+ Bartimaeus was rescued from his blindness. Jesus not only gave back his sight in physical healing but also rescued him spiritually from his sin.

+ Zacchaeus was rescued from his greed. When no one else would have anything to do with him, Jesus went to dinner at his house and rescued him.

+ Lazarus was rescued from his tomb. For four days he lay in the darkness of the grave, but Jesus rescued him and brought him back to life.

+ The demoniac at Gerasenes was rescued from the unclean spirits. When Jesus saw the demoniac, He commanded the demons that possessed the man to tell Him their name. The demons answered, "Legion," because they were many. But Jesus rescued the demon-possessed man from the unclean spirits and gave him back his life.

+ Saul was rescued from the darkness of traditions and legalism on the road to Damascus. Jesus rescued Saul

and gave him the new name Paul, and a new life to go
along with it.

Pastor Michael P. Walther gave the following illustration in a sermon
titled "Blessed Is He Who Comes in the Name of the Lord":

> On August 30, 2005, Coast Guard Lieutenant Iain McConnell
> was ordered to fly his H46 helicopter to New Orleans and to keep
> that machine flying around the clock for what would turn out to
> be a heroic rescue effort. None of his crew were prepared for what
> they were about to see. They were ahead of every news crew in the
> nation. The entire city of New Orleans was under water. On their
> first three missions that day they saved 89 people, three dogs and
> two cats…On the fourth mission, despite twelve different flights
> to New Orleans, he and his crew were able to save no one. None!
> They all refused to board the helicopter. Instead they told the
> Coast Guard to bring them food and water. Yet they were warned
> that this [was] extremely dangerous. The waters were not going
> to go away soon. Sadly, many of those people perished because of
> their refusal to be rescued.[4]

Contradiction #2: He is living "in the world."

> I will remain in the world no longer, but they are still *in the world*,
> and I am coming to you. Holy Father, protect them by the power
> of your name, the name you gave me, so that they may be one as
> we are one.
>
> —JOHN 17:11, EMPHASIS ADDED

What a contradiction! First He saved us out of the world, and now
we're told we are still in the world. The truth is, being a Christian does
not take you physically out of this world. You still trade in the world's
economy, live in the world's houses, and—most of us—work a secular job.

Christians have a tendency to go to extremes. Some feel that since
we have to live in the world we should not have anything to do with the
world. There are some who even go to the extreme of isolation. They
solve the issue by moving to a mountaintop—or worse yet, joining a
cult and living totally isolated from society, including from their own
extended families.

We don't need to be isolated, but we need to be insulated. What does
that mean? The believer is somewhat like an astronaut. Astronauts must

wear pressurized spacesuits in order to survive in outer space. When an astronaut moves outside the safe environment of the space station to conduct routine inspections and repairs, the most essential equipment he must have is a pressurized suit. It is the spacesuit that allows him to breathe and to function normally. Zero gravity and zero oxygen is not man's natural habitat!

The Holy Spirit living within us gives us the resources necessary to live in the zero-gravity atmosphere of a polluted world system that is totally opposed to the things of God. Much has been written about the pollution of Earth's atmosphere in the last thirty years. But the "atmosphere" of the world's system is also so polluted spiritually that believers cannot breathe normally without the power of the indwelling Holy Spirit!

Is it possible to live in a world full of sin and still remain not sinless, but pure in your testimony? The answer is yes—but only by the power of the Holy Spirit!

Contradiction #3: He is not "of the world."

> I have given them your word and the world has hated them, for they are not *of the world* any more than I am of the world.
> —JOHN 17:14, EMPHASIS ADDED

Do you see what Jesus is saying? We are saved out of the world, yet we are still in the world. Now He says, "You are not of the world." You and I are *in* it, but we are not *of* it. We are still here, yet everything inside of us says we do not belong here.

Just as God has a purpose for every person, so does a corrupt world system. What the world wants to do is displace the love of God in your heart and replace it with the love of this world.

The world makes a very subtle approach to the believer. It does not come rushing headlong. No, it's much more deceptive than that.

Let's look at the downward spiral.

Can we just have companionship?

The approach is very subtle and easygoing. It may sound something such as this: "Well, why do you have to be so stuck up about your Christianity? Why don't you just go along to get along? You know, after all, you don't want to be different from the rest of us."

Before we get too far along with this idea that it's all right to be "friends" with the world and share a close companionship, we need to find out what God says about it in His Word:

> You adulterous people, don't you know that friendship with the
> world means enmity against God? Therefore, anyone who chooses
> to be a friend of the world becomes an enemy of God. Or do you
> think Scripture says without reason that he jealously longs for the
> spirit he has caused to dwell in us? But he gives us more grace.
> That is why Scripture says: "God opposes the proud but shows
> favor to the humble."
>
> —James 4:4–6

Sounds ominous doesn't it? Friendship and companionship with the
world is spiritual adultery! This scripture is a warning to all believers
that friendship with the world is equal to a married man flirting with
another woman. There are some who would argue that flirting is harm-
less, yet more than one marriage has been destroyed by the unfaithful-
ness of a spouse who started with so-called innocent flirting. Jesus said
that if you are a friend of this world, you are not a friend of God!

> If I had a dear brother who had been murdered, what would you
> think of me if I…daily consorted with the assassin, who drove the
> dagger into my brother's heart? Surely I, too, must be an accom-
> plice in the crime! Sin murdered Christ; will you be a friend to it?
> Sin pierced the heart of the Incarnate God; can you love it?[5]
>
> —C. H. Spurgeon

Companionship leads to contamination.

> Religion that God our Father accepts as pure and faultless is this:
> to look after orphans and widows in their distress and to keep one-
> self from being polluted by the world.
>
> —James 1:27

We are living in a dirty, rotten, filthy, grimy world. If you and I get
too close to it, some of the dirt is bound to rub off on us. You don't have
to be very old to remember a time when the things you see and hear
on the television or in the movies would have never been allowed. It is
almost impossible to work in the offices, factories, or even go to the mall
without hearing filthy language and dirty talk. Sometimes you just want
to go home and take a bath—not only physically, but also spiritually.
Why? It is a dirty, rotten world we live in!

Contamination leads to conformity.

> Therefore, I urge you, brothers and sisters, in view of God's mercy, to offer your bodies as a living sacrifice, holy and pleasing to God—this is your true and proper worship. Do not conform to the pattern of this world, but be transformed by the renewing of your mind. Then you will be able to test and approve what God's will is—his good, pleasing and perfect will.
>
> —ROMANS 12:1–2

When you get contaminated by the world, the Bible warns that you are in danger of being pressured into the world's mold. I like J. B. Phillips's translation of Romans 12:2: "Don't let the world around you squeeze you into its own mould, but let God re-mold your minds from within, so that you may prove in practice that the plan of God for you is good, meets all His demands and moves towards the goal of true maturity" (PHILLIPS).

The world system has a plan, and it is very simple: mold and pressure every person, including every believer, to its standard operating procedures. The world wants you to act as it does, go where it says to go, speak as it tells you to speak, and look like it tells you to look. The ultimate goal is that everyone will be the same—believers and nonbelievers alike.

> Addressing a national seminar of Southern Baptist leaders, George Gallup said, "We find there is very little difference in ethical behavior between churchgoers and those who are not active religiously. The levels of lying, cheating, and stealing are remarkably similar in both groups."
>
> Eight out of ten Americans consider themselves Christians, Gallup said, yet only about half of them could identify the person who gave the Sermon on the Mount, and fewer still could recall five of the Ten Commandments. Only two of ten said they would be willing to suffer for their faith.[6]

Conformity leads to condemnation.

> Nevertheless, when we are judged in this way by the Lord, we are being disciplined so that we will not be finally condemned with the world.
>
> —1 CORINTHIANS 11:32

I do not believe Paul is talking about losing your salvation. The downward spiral that begins with companionship will eventually lead to contamination. To be contaminated with the world system will bring about conformity. Left unchecked, conformity will ultimately lead to condemnation. I do not believe you can "sleep with the enemy" and still be vibrant and useful for Christ. A solid testimony for Christ is to be treasured, and, when lost, one of the most difficult things to reclaim.

Lot is a perfect example of someone who lived so close to the world's system that it eventually cost him everything. An article in *Our Daily Bread* best sums it up:

> Although Lot is referred to by Peter as "righteous Lot," he chose to live among the wicked in Sodom because he loved money and prominence. He was a double-minded man who wanted to serve God but who also wanted to enjoy the pleasures of this world. I believe this is evident from the fact that Lot chose to live in the plain bordering the wicked cities of Sodom and Gomorrah (Gen. 13:1–13). Once there, he moved into the city itself and became a part of its culture (19:1). It's true that he didn't give up his belief in the high moral standards he had learned from his uncle Abraham, and he didn't approve of the wicked things he saw and heard. But as an official at the city gate, he apparently had little impact on the wicked society of which he was a part. Lot's double-mindedness brought him much inner torment and rendered him spiritually powerless. He couldn't even convince his sons-in-law (and their wives) to leave Sodom before God's judgment fell. Only he, his wife, and the two daughters still living at home escaped. And his wife died instantly when she looked back, disobeying God's command. In the end, Lot lost the very things he wanted—possessions and position.[7]

Lot is an Old Testament example of a modern-day reality. He had become so attached to the world that it took an angel of God to get him out! There are many Christians today who would give everything they own to have the joy and passion for Jesus they used to have. At some point, living in the contradiction became too much. Instead of standing strong, they allowed the world's system to overwhelm them and slowly but surely rob them of their testimony for Christ.

Contradiction #4: He is sent "into the world."

> As you sent me into the world, I have sent them *into the world*.
>
> —JOHN 17:18, EMPHASIS ADDED

The contradiction is plain to see. We are in the world but not of it, yet He has sent us into the world. I believe the truth that Jesus wants us to see is that we are not sent into the world to condemn it, nor condone it, but to confront it with the gospel of Jesus Christ. To understand this truth is to keep your sanity in an otherwise insane world!

Many times we get discouraged when we think about the fact that as born-again, Spirit-filled Christians, we are quickly becoming a non-factor in a world gone mad. Before you throw up your hands and quit, remember two important truths:

1. *The world is not permanent.*

> The world and its desires pass away, but whoever does the will of God lives forever.
>
> —1 JOHN 2:17

Have you ever heard someone say, "Well, you know, that is just as sure as the world"? I know I have. The truth is, the world is fading away; it is a goner! First Corinthians 7:31 says, "The fashion of this world [passes] away" (KJV). One of these days the whole thing is going to come crumbling to the ground. Second Peter 3:10 says that one day "the elements shall melt with fervent heat" (KJV), and the world that you see around you will go out of existence. Remember, the only sure thing about this world system is that it will not be here forever.

It's time for believers to wake up and realize that a world system opposed to the things of God cannot and will not permanently satisfy you, because it is not lasting. Trying to get satisfaction from the world is like eating cotton candy. It may taste good for a moment, and satisfy your sweet tooth, but in the end it melts quickly and leaves nothing behind but a craving for more.

I once heard a preacher friend of mine say, "If you anchor your life in this world, you have anchored it to a floating island and you will pass away. Do not put your roots down in this world, do not put your hopes in this world, and do not fall in love with this world. It is not worth it."

2. Only the Word and will of God are permanent.

But whoever does the will of God lives forever.

—1 John 2:17

Inevitably, and sooner than most of us think, the world is going to pass away; but the person who does God's will, will abide forever. What that means to me is that Christians who devote themselves to doing the will of God will remain (abide) forever.

It will be impossible to put this world's system under your feet until you have seen a better view from heaven's perspective. The contradiction of what you see around you and what you know on the inside will be so confusing it might just overwhelm you unless you see a better world above.

Hebrews 11 describes how the Old Testament saints viewed the world's system. They were willing to live in tents in this world because they were looking for a city whose builder and maker is God (v. 10). They had discovered the secret: there is something better than the material things of this world. They had fallen out of love with the system and in love with the will of God!

D. L. Moody was instrumental in shaking two continents for the gospel of Jesus Christ. His influence is still being felt today through the Moody Bible College and other Christian enterprises that bear his name. The following appears in his biography:

> "Someday," D. L. Moody used to say, "you will read in the papers that D. L. Moody of East Northfield is dead. Don't believe a word of it! At that moment I shall be more alive than I am now!"
>
> He preached his last sermon in Kansas City on Nov. 23, 1899, from the text Luke 14:18: "And they all with one consent began to make excuse." When he gave the invitation, fifty stood to their feet and went across the street into the inquiry room. He was too ill to continue the Kansas City campaign, so he took the train back to Northfield. On Friday, Dec. 22, he went "home."
>
> Five years before his homegoing Moody had said, "If it can be said, faithfully said, over my grave, 'Moody has done what he could,' that will be the most glorious epitaph." Instead, 1 John 2:17 was chosen: "He that doeth the will of God abideth forever."[8]

CHAPTER 12

THE ISAAC EFFECT

Isaac planted crops in that land and the same year reaped a hundred-fold, because the LORD blessed him. The man became rich, and his wealth continued to grow until he became very wealthy. He had so many flocks and herds and servants that the Philistines envied him.
—GENESIS 26:12–14

GENESIS 26 TELLS the story of one of the greatest men of the Old Testament. His name is Isaac. Isaac went from living in the horror of drought, famine, and economic ruin, to living in such abundance that he was not only able to provide for his own family but also had enough left over to bless an entire city.

Pastor George Pearsons of Eagle Mountain International Church writes:

> Even though we have heard bad news about the economy, we are not subject to that news. Isaac reaped a hundredfold in a time of famine—he still reaped a bumper crop! That is a supernatural harvest. You, too, are walking in *the blessing* of kingdom prosperity. You are a symbol and source of prosperity, enlarging, expanding and being overtaken by *the blessing*! No matter where you are or where you go, you are *blessed*! Why is that? Because the kingdom of God is within you. It is vital for us during these times to develop a "kingdom-inside" mind-set. When we realize the kingdom of God is inside us, we will begin to understand that *the blessing* of kingdom prosperity is with us wherever we go.[1]

Isaac learned how to walk in God's provision and abundance in spite of his difficult surroundings. It would be safe to say that believers today are living in what Paul referred to in 2 Timothy 3:1 as "perilous times" (MEV). While we may not be facing a physical famine, we are certainly living in an age when *everything that can be shaken is being shaken*. Our economy is being shaken, unemployment is nearing record levels, and the value of the dollar is lower than it has been in fifteen years. The stock market is up and down. People in the world are hurting, and many are fearful. But as God's people, we don't have to be afraid.

Our world is turned upside down with divorce, suicide, drug dependency, alcohol abuse, criminal behavior, prostitution, sexual impurity, depression, pornography, eating disorders, and emotional and psychological disorders. Believers are constantly faced with a choice—live in fear or live by faith.

It is obvious that Isaac chose to live by faith and not by fear. He may have stumbled along the way, but at the end of the day he determined to go by what God said, not by what he saw with his natural eye. We have the same choice today! You are yoked to your beliefs. *The yoke you wear determines the burden you bear.* If you believe you "cannot," you will wear the burden of failure. If you believe you "can," you will wear the burden of success.

FAITH AND FEAR HAVE THE SAME DEFINITION

+ Faith is believing that what you cannot see will come to pass; fear is believing that what you cannot see will come to pass.

+ Faith attracts the positive; fear attracts the negative.

+ Faith attracts light; fear attracts attack.

The sum total of our lives is based on whether we operate in fear or faith. People with faith work with the little they have rather than waiting for the abundance they need.

To live in fear causes us to doubt our beliefs and believe our doubts. The good news is that Jesus came not only to save us but also to give us abundant life. This is much like a second blessing: eternal life plus "life to the fullest"! I'm convinced the reason so many Christians are not living life to the fullest is because they don't know what it is! Many Christians don't really think that such a life is available to them. How sad!

We live in and out of abundance. It's an up-and-down life for so many. That is a spiritual fact. Curiously, some of us find it hard to catch that vision. "Do we," writes Parker J. Palmer, "inhabit a universe where the basic things that people need—from food and shelter to a sense of competence and of being loved—are ample in nature? Or is this a universe where such goods are in short supply, available only to those who have the power to beat everyone else to the store?"[2]

Sad to say, many believers live by the "pie concept," which produces an attitude of fear and not faith. The pie concept is simply the belief that there is one pie with so many slices. Once you take your slice, that's all you're ever going to get, so don't ask for anything more! You may think this is a ridiculous philosophy to live by; however, this attitude is promoted in almost every segment of our society, including the church.

The pie concept says we are running out of resources, including oil, natural gas, forest, money, clean water, clean air, land, etc. If you buy into the lie that the pie concept is real, then you live life with a negative view, never expecting anything more, and certainly never receiving anything more.

For us, scarcity or abundance is mainly a matter of perspective on life. Charles Rush shares author David Steindl-Rast's point of view:

> "Abundance," he says, "is not measured by what flows in, but by what flows over. The smaller we make the vessel of our need…the sooner we get the overflow we need for delight." Almost all of us, at some point in our lives, get caught on the same treadmill of consumption that wearies our American souls. As soon as "our cup runneth over," what do most of us do? Why, we go out and buy a bigger cup! That means we are always living with the illusion of scarcity, always bemoaning the gap between what's in our cup and the rim—when in reality we, of all the people on the planet practically, are the most blessed financially.[3]

I have pastored churches for more than forty years—from the small country churches to large city churches. I have encountered many people with the attitude of "lack." Many of these people have big dreams that never become reality, mainly because they don't believe God wants them to live in abundance. They live from measure to measure, never experiencing the fullness God wants to provide. They may hear the truth with their heads, but it never seems to translate to their hearts. God desires that we live not only in abundance, but also exceedingly beyond anything we could think or ask! (See Philippians 4:19; Ephesians 3:20.)

So, can you prosper in a famine? Is it possible to live by another set of economic principles than those promoted in our culture today? Why don't we allow Isaac to show us how to live in abundance and prosperity? It worked for him and it will work for us.

CONSIDER THE MAN

Some have suggested that Isaac is an Old Testament type and shadow of how a believer should operate during severe shortage and lack. While everything around him was collapsing and falling apart, Isaac learned the secret of supernatural abundance.

It's only natural to focus attention on Isaac's supernatural harvest of a hundredfold. But before we look at the "method" he used, we need to take a closer look at the man himself. Why? I find that in every case God is more interested in who the person is than what the person can produce.

1. Isaac was an only child.

Isaac was the only son of Abraham and Sarah. He was a result of God's promise to Abraham that his descendants would be a great nation:

> For it is written that Abraham had two sons, one by the slave woman and the other by the free woman. His son by the slave woman was born according to the flesh, but his son by the free woman was born as the result of a divine promise.
>
> —GALATIANS 4:22–23

This "child of promise" took a long time—twenty-five years passed between when the promise was spoken in Genesis 12 and when it was delivered in Genesis 21. I'm sure there were times that Abraham wondered if the promise was ever going to be fulfilled. He even went so far as to try to help God by producing another child by the slave woman Hagar. Abraham discovered—like most of us do—that God does not need any help in fulfilling His promises! The promise of God can never be fulfilled by the works of the flesh (Ishmael) but only by obedience to His Word, no matter how long it takes.

2. Isaac was a miracle child.

In the natural Abraham and Sarah should never have had a baby. Abraham was one hundred years old and Sarah was ninety when Isaac was born (Gen. 17:17; 21:5). They were long past childbearing years; it's no wonder they laughed when they heard the news. In fact, the name Isaac means "to laugh" (Gen. 17:19). Isaac brought joy and laughter to his parents, his house, and his friends.

3. Isaac was a "pattern" child.

According to Acts 7:8, Isaac was the first baby to receive circumcision on the eighth day. The fact that he was the first to receive God's blessing and favor by birthright (Rom. 9:7) brought conflict with Ishmael, Abraham's son by the handmaid Hagar. Genesis 21 records the day Isaac was weaned, which was a cause of great celebration for the family but a source of consternation for Ishmael. The family relationship was so strained that Sarah sent Hagar and Ishmael away. Abraham was comforted by the fact that God told him Ishmael would also become the father of a great nation (Gen. 21:8–21).

4. Isaac was a "covenant" child.

Isaac inherited far more from Abraham then material possessions. From early childhood God's favor was evident every step of the way. Isaac's circumcision was a sign of the covenant with God. The evidence of God's favor and covenant with him was seen in the sending away of not only Ishmael, but also later the sons of Abraham's concubines (Gen. 25:6). Isaac inherited all that Abraham had, including the abundance and provision that God's blessings afford.

5. Isaac became a godly man.

To take on this Abrahamic covenant was not a simple task. Isaac had to be placed on the altar before he could carry on the covenant. When Isaac was a young man, God tested Abraham's faith by commanding him to sacrifice Isaac as an offering. When Abraham placed Isaac upon the altar, an angel appeared, stopping Abraham from sacrificing his son. God provided a ram in place of Isaac. This event showed clearly that Isaac was God's choice to carry on the covenant (Gen. 22).

Isaac married Rebekah when he was forty years old, after God directed one of Abraham's servants to her. Isaac loved Rebekah. Rebekah was a comfort to him after his mother's death (Gen. 24:67).

Like Sarah, her mother-in-law, and Rachel, her future daughter-in-law, Rebekah was barren. Isaac pleaded with the Lord, and He heard his plea (Gen. 25:20–21). In all three generations—from Abraham to Isaac to Jacob—the children of promise were born as a result of divine answers to prayers. Their wives were barren but became fruitful with just a touch of the master's hand.

When Isaac was sixty years old, after having been married for twenty years, God gave him his twin sons, Jacob and Esau (Gen. 25:24–26).

Since Abraham died at the good old age of 175 (Gen. 25:7–8), he lived to see his grandsons grow to the age of fifteen.

Isaac was seventy-five years old when Abraham died. He then became the patriarch of the community. Interestingly enough, Abraham also became a patriarch at the age of seventy-five, when he left Haran and went to the land of Canaan (Gen. 12:4–5). But that was a hundred years earlier.[4]

FAST-FORWARD TO GENESIS 26

There is a world of difference between a rerun and an instant replay. A rerun is simply seeing the same thing over again. An instant replay is seeing something over, but not all of it. It is looking at certain events again, usually much more carefully. The critics have tended to view Genesis 26 as a rerun, and not a very good one at that. They, of course, are right in recognizing the similarities between Isaac's experiences in this chapter and those in the life of Abraham in the previous chapters. However, they misinterpret the similarities in such a way as to suggest that they do little, if anything, to benefit us. Indeed, they even question the historicity of these events in the life of Isaac.[5]

I would like to focus our attention on Genesis 26 as if it were an instant replay. This is the only chapter in the Book of Genesis devoted exclusively to Isaac. While he is mentioned in other chapters, he is not the focus of attention. Here Isaac's life is summed up in the events described, each of which has a striking parallel in the life of his father, Abraham. These similarities are, I believe, the key to rightly understanding and applying this passage to our own lives.

Isaac learned a very valuable lesson. When you obey God's instructions, blessing and prosperity follow. Of course, the opposite is also true. We learn from Scripture that disobedience opens the door to curses. In Genesis 26 Isaac is presented with the choice—obey and be blessed, or disobey and be cursed. He chose the former rather than the latter.

WE NEED TO LEARN THE SAME LESSON

Whoever disregards discipline comes to poverty and shame, but whoever heeds correction is honored.

—PROVERBS 13:18

God has given certain instructions to help people break the chains of poverty and barrenness. Right now there are people living in a barren land, a land of famine. God has given certain instructions to help us break free from "lack." To my amazement, people refuse the instructions and continue to live in a desert.

God's people act like the proverbial father who buys toys for his children on Christmas and tries to put the toys together without reading the instructions. Not that I've ever done that (with my tongue firmly planted in my cheek). But the truth of the matter is, it's always easier to read the instruction manual if you want to do the job right:

> Moreover all these curses shall come upon you and pursue and overtake you, until you are destroyed, because you did not obey the voice of the LORD your God, to keep His commandments and His statutes which He commanded you. And they shall be upon you for a sign and a wonder, and on your descendants forever. Because you did not serve the LORD your God with joy and gladness of heart, for the abundance of everything, therefore you shall serve your enemies, whom the LORD will send against you, in hunger, in thirst, in nakedness, and in need of everything; and He will put a yoke of iron on your neck until He has destroyed you.
> —DEUTERONOMY 28:45–48, NKJV

Many people make the mistake of judging themselves by their *intentions* and other people by their *actions*. In doing this, they forget that the roads to poverty, divorce, and death are paved with good intentions. A good intention is actually the voice of the Holy Spirit communicating to your spirit the will of God in a certain situation. Then your spirit communicates with your intellect, and your intellect agrees that the instruction it has received from the Spirit is the right way to act in order to illuminate God's character to a world that is seeking workable truth.

James 1:22 declares that when we fail to follow through with corresponding actions to God's instructions, we deceive ourselves; we do not, however, deceive those whom we are trying to convince that the way of God is better than anything the world can offer.

Instruction or knowledge can only benefit us when we are willing to act upon it. I have met many so-called wise men who are poor and wretched. In their own minds they truly believe that they are legendary, yet they have very little or no fruit within their lives to back up their so-called wisdom. Isaac acted upon the Word of God. He did not sit back and say, "I deserve to be blessed; I don't have to do anything in response to God's instruction."

Unless the believer acts in faith on the Word of God, he cannot justly hold back the thieves of abundance. *Curses don't come to teach you a lesson.* Curses come because people refuse to listen to the Word of God and obey the instructions of the Book! The law of traffic control says there is a way to drive that is very safe. Stop at the red light and drive on through the green light. If you choose to do it another way, it is not the city's fault if you get a ticket for breaking the law.

Curses are very real and can affect our lives. Curses come for a reason, as stated in Proverbs 26:2: "Like a flitting sparrow, like a flying swallow, so a curse without cause shall not alight" (NKJV).

Just as a bird alights on its appointed place because it has a right to be there, so a curse alights upon us for a cause: "But it shall come to pass, if you do not obey the voice of the LORD your God, to observe carefully all His commandments and His statutes which I command you today, that all these curses will come upon you and overtake you" (Deut. 28:15, NKJV).

Be careful not to place your faith in the world system and doubt the Word of God—you will end up doubting your beliefs and believing your doubts. Lack of knowledge causes failure: "My people are destroyed from lack of knowledge" (Hosea 4:6).

There are a total of fifty-three verses of Scripture that discuss curses. Some of the types of curses mentioned are mental, emotional, physical, and relational curses, oppression, failure, lack, defeat.

But God states His will this way:

> Now it shall come to pass, if you diligently obey the voice of the LORD your God, to observe carefully all His commandments which I command you today, that the LORD your God will set you high above all nations of the earth. And all these blessings shall come upon you and overtake you, because you obey the voice of the LORD your God.
> —DEUTERONOMY 28:1–2, NKJV

Take time to read Deuteronomy 28. Meditate and rejoice over the many blessings that God outlines for those who are obedient to His Word, such as exaltation, health, fruitfulness, victory, God's favor.

Who would not want to receive those blessings of God's abundant provision? They are listed in the Word of God not only for the nation of Israel but also for us today. In the next chapter we will see how Isaac walked in the hundredfold blessing.

CHAPTER 13

LAST DAYS GENEROSITY

OPERATING THE ISAAC EFFECT

Living in a man-run society and business community, it is easy to get the idea that man is your source and supply. This is where you miss the truth of God's Holy Word. God often uses man as the means, but God Himself is the source. All other sources are instruments only.[1]

—ORAL ROBERTS

I SAAC DID NOT walk into the hundredfold blessing overnight. Nor will you! Because we live in a microwave society, we want everything "right now." It doesn't always work that way with God. It is true that some miracles are instantaneous, but I find more proof in the Scriptures, and in life, that miracles are a process. It seems that every time we ask God for a miracle, He gives us an instruction to obey.

CONSIDER HIS METHODS

Famine was occurring in Canaan during Isaac's day just as it had in his father Abraham's. In the natural everything was against him.

> Now there was a famine in the land—besides the previous famine in Abraham's time—and Isaac went to Abimelek king of the Philistines in Gerar.
>
> —GENESIS 26:1

> [God] seems to do nothing of Himself which He can possibly delegate to His creatures. He commands us to do slowly and blunderingly what He could do perfectly and in the twinkling of an eye.[2]
>
> —C. S. LEWIS

Isaac's three-step process to hundredfold increase

1. He obeyed ("So Isaac stayed").

> The LORD appeared to Isaac and said, "Do not go down to Egypt; live in the land where I tell you to live. Stay in this land for a while,

and I will be with you and will bless you. For to you and your
descendants I will give all these lands and will confirm the oath
I swore to your father Abraham. I will make your descendants as
numerous as the stars in the sky and will give them all these lands,
and through your offspring all nations on earth will be blessed,
because Abraham obeyed Me and did everything I required of him,
keeping my commands, my decrees and my instructions." So Isaac
stayed in Gerar.

—GENESIS 26:2–6

When the Lord appeared to Isaac in the city of Gerar, Isaac was
simply following in his father's footsteps. He might have been thinking,
"My father went to Egypt during the famine, and God blessed them
there. If I leave and go to Egypt, God will bless me the same way."

Isaac was living in the city of Gerar. If you study a map of the land,
you will see that Gerar is the last inhabited city in Canaan before
entering the Wilderness of Shur along the well-traveled caravan route
between the nation of the Philistines and Egypt. While Isaac was in
Gerar, the Lord appeared to assure him of His presence, to reaffirm the
Abrahamic covenant, and to warn him not to go down to Egypt. These
are valuable lessons for all of God's people to remember when they go
through times of testing. His presence and promises are as sure as His
Word, though at times it may seem to the contrary, especially when the
way is hard. But God's promise remains—"I will never leave you or for-
sake you"—and it is foundational to our faith.

Equally important is the charge to not "sell out" to the world during
our trials. "Woe to those who go down Egypt for help," the prophet
Isaiah warned the nation of Israel many years later (Isa. 31:1). The world,
typified by Egypt, is at enmity with God, and as such, attempts to lead
us away from dependence upon Him. Its promises of help during personal trial are alluring, yet the hardships from which we so desperately
want to be excused are often compounded as we abandon the pathway of
faith and exclude the Lord from our decisions.

If we want the Word of God to have authority in our life, there is
only one way—obey it. If we want the Holy Spirit to have authority
in our life, there is only one way—obey Him. If we always obey
impulses of fear or doubt or resentment, what will have authority
over our minds? Fear, and doubt and resentment.[3]

—TOM MARSHALL

It made no sense to Isaac's natural mind to stay in an area where a famine was raging. Miracles never make sense to the natural mind, nor are they explained by natural methods. The Lord promised to bless him in adverse conditions because he was doing a different thing in Isaac's day than in Abraham's, and it was vital for Isaac to obey God's command.

The same is true in our generation. We must be willing to "go with the flow" and not be tempted to fall back into old patterns and old ways of doing things. We can certainly learn from what God did in the past, but we must always be open when God is ready to do a new thing.

> Forget the former things; do not dwell on the past. See, I am doing a new thing! Now it springs up; do you not perceive it? I am making a way in the wilderness and streams in the wasteland. The wild animals honor me, the jackals and the owls, because I provide water in the wilderness and streams in the wasteland, to give drink to my people, my chosen, the people I formed for myself that they may proclaim my praise.
>
> —ISAIAH 43:18–21

If you want to see God's hand move in your situation, refuse to be famine driven. During tough times the temptation is to pack up and move on to other things instead of asking God for His instructions. A famine can have royal purposes if allowed to drive you closer to God. Being famine driven will cause you to end up in Egypt, forsaking God-given dreams and purposes. It is possible to be fruitful even in the midst of a famine, as we see in the life of Isaac. Life happens and challenges are real, but that doesn't mean you should quit and allow circumstances to overwhelm you.

If Isaac would have disobeyed God and done what was popular and left for Egypt, he never would have been blessed to the degree that God blessed him. There is a great blessing in obedience! As Isaiah 1:19 says, "If you are willing and obedient, you will eat the good things of the land."

2. He sowed ("Isaac planted crops").

> Isaac planted crops in that land and the same year reaped a hundredfold, because the LORD blessed him.
>
> —GENESIS 26:12

Isaac tapped into God's plan of economy and saw a miracle harvest. There are certain principles in God's created universe that are irrefutable.

For example, you may stand up and declare that the law of gravity is not real, and it is your right to do so. You can hold that view as long as you like; that is, until you step off the edge of a tall building and discover that what you believed was a lie! One of God's universal, irrefutable principles is called "seedtime and harvest." Genesis 8:22 declares, "As long as the earth endures, seedtime and harvest, cold and heat, summer and winter, day and night will never cease."

God has put in place not only natural laws that are immutable but also spiritual laws that are inviolable. Isaac planted crops (he sowed) and reaped a hundredfold harvest, and he found out that God's principles work even in a famine!

> Remember this: Whoever sows sparingly will also reap sparingly, and whoever sows generously will also reap generously. Each of you should give what you have decided in your heart to give, not reluctantly or under compulsion, for God loves a cheerful giver. And God is able to bless you abundantly, so that in all things at all times, having all that you need, you will abound in every good work. As it is written: "They have freely scattered their gifts to the poor; their righteousness endures forever." Now he who supplies seed to the sower and bread for food will also supply and increase your store of seed and will enlarge the harvest of your righteousness. You will be enriched in every way so that you can be generous on every occasion, and through us your generosity will result in thanksgiving to God.
>
> —2 Corinthians 9:6–11

Author and conference speaker Mark Gorman wrote in his book *God's Plan for Prosperity*:

> As we talk about the law of the harvest there is one thing that we must remember; God does not owe you a harvest just because you are saved. We have to not only break the spirit of poverty, but also a welfare mentality which causes people to think that God owes them a financial blessing just because they have a need. Second Corinthians 9:10 says, "God gives seed to the sower." It doesn't say that He gives seed to the needy, the poor, the widow, the orphan, or even the righteous. He only gives seed to the sower! Why? Because, He doesn't want the seed to be wasted. He knows that only a sower would use the seed properly. If you want God to put seed into your

hand, you must first develop the heart of a sower. God is looking for people with a heart of a sower so he can put seed into their hands that will produce an abundant harvest.[4]

Seven principles of seedtime and harvest

1. Seed must be planted.

This first principle may seem so obvious that we overlook it. Although there are many things you can do with a seed, there is only one thing you can do that will produce a harvest, and that is to plant the seed. When good seed is sown in good soil, in due time an abundant harvest will be produced. It's just that simple.

Seed must go into the ground. As long as it's in your possession, it can only do what you can do. But when you release the seed from your hand, God will release the harvest from His hand.

When you plant an apple seed, it will produce a tree, which will then yield a harvest of fruit. Many apples will result from one seed. This harvest not only gives a generous supply of seeds to continue the process, but it also produces an abundant return of "bread for food." God has created a system that blesses the person who is willing to sow with a generous spirit, not out of obligation. God has always intended to bless us with increase, which will happen when we live by and respect the laws that He has established.

There are many people who believe that God's blessings are restricted to spiritual experiences and emotional well-being. Any farmer will tell you that if he plants wheat, he will receive wheat in return. The seed being planted may be described as whatever you need, whether acceptance, friendship, or finances.

2. You will reap only what you sow.

> Then God said, "Let the land produce vegetation: seed-bearing plants and trees on the land that bear fruit with seed in it, according to their various kinds." And it was so. The land produced vegetation: plants bearing seed according to their kinds and trees bearing fruit with seed in it according to their kinds. And God saw that it was good.
>
> —GENESIS 1:11–12

There is a consistent theme in the Creation account. Every seed has within its own makeup a unique DNA that will allow it to reproduce only itself. If you plant corn, you reap corn, not wheat. The same is true with grapes or any other vegetable or fruit. The law of sowing and reaping also has a negative side. If you sow bitterness and hate, that is what you will reap. You cannot expect to reap joy and happiness when you sow seeds of discord. Remember, you always reap what you sow! As Galatians 6:7–11 says:

> Do not be deceived: God cannot be mocked. A man reaps what he sows. Whoever sows to please their flesh, from the flesh will reap destruction; whoever sows to please the Spirit, from the Spirit will reap eternal life. Let us not become weary in doing good, for at the proper time we will reap a harvest if we do not give up. Therefore, as we have opportunity, let us do good to all people, especially to those who belong to the family of believers.

3. *You do not reap a harvest at the same time that you sow your seed.*

> We do not want you to become lazy, but to imitate those who through faith and patience inherit what has been promised.
> —Hebrews 6:12

A wise farmer knows there will be a long period of growth after his seed is sown. This knowledge keeps him from growing discouraged as he waits for his return. Believe it or not, there is no such thing as instant success when it comes to reaping a harvest, either in the natural or in the spiritual. A wise farmer also knows that some crops take longer than others to produce a harvest. Our culture demands instant gratification, which is nothing more than a form of insanity.

Impatience will cause crop failure faster than anything I know. Godly patience will keep you from quitting when you don't see an immediate harvest. The successful farmer knows it takes time, lots of energy, and patience to reap the kind of harvest that he wants.

> Be patient, then, brothers and sisters, until the Lord's coming. See how the farmer waits for the land to yield its valuable crop, patiently waiting for the autumn and spring rains.
> —James 5:7

4. *You will always reap more than you sow.*
The amount of your harvest is determined on the day you plant your

seed, not on the day you go into the field to bring in the crop. A farmer knows that if he wants a generous harvest, he must sow generous seed.

> Remember this: Whoever sows sparingly will also reap sparingly, and whoever sows generously will also reap generously.
>
> —2 CORINTHIANS 9:6

Many people do not realize an abundant harvest because they spend more time complaining about what they don't have than rejoicing in what they do have. Always remember that to reap an abundant harvest, start with what is in your hand. Remember Moses? When God called him to lead His people out of bondage, all he had was a stick and a stammer—and God used him mightily!

5. If you want a harvest, perseverance is a necessity.

You do not build character or maturity by going to church every time the doors are open. If we are willing to take time to sow generously and wait patiently, while at the same time enduring the pressure and trials of life, we will see God work miracles.

> Let us not become weary in doing good, for at the proper time we will reap a harvest if we do not give up.
>
> —GALATIANS 6:9

Many years ago I heard an old preacher say, "We reap the full harvest of the good only if we persevere; the evil comes to harvest on its own." I say *Amen* to that!

Lack of perseverance will kill a harvest. Impatience will lead to indifference. Whether you are dealing with family relationships, friendships, business associates, or spiritual matters, all require patience and careful attention. Paul said: "For I am already being poured out like a drink offering, and the time for my departure is near. I have fought the good fight, I have finished the race, I have kept the faith. Now there is in store for me the crown of righteousness, which the Lord, the righteous Judge, will award to me on that day—and not only to me, but also to all who have longed for his appearing" (2 Tim. 4:6–8).

Paul had the heart of a finisher. He endured hardships, disappointments, and many trials, and he knew that in order to finish the race, perseverance was required. He admonished his young protégé Timothy to keep on no matter the circumstances.

In order to realize an abundant harvest, we must persevere and keep three important essentials in mind:

+ Plant correctly

+ Cultivate consistency

+ Give constant attention

6. *Do not let past crop failures rob your future harvest.*

I don't think anyone would disagree with the fact that life can be cruel. I don't know of anyone without a story that includes roadblocks and detours. I have met many people whose lives are filled with mistakes and blunders they've made, but I always encourage them: "Remember, you have a choice for your future. It's really not about what happened to you yesterday that counts. The question is, what are you going to do about your tomorrow? You can grin and bear it, or you can put your head down, dig in your heels, and change it!"

There is not a farmer alive that does not know what it's like to experience crop failure. It's never a question of "Will it happen?" but "How will I handle it when it happens?" The first thing many people do is blame circumstances or other people for a bad harvest. You can play the blame game, or you can accept responsibility for what went wrong, fix the mistakes, and move forward.

The Israelites are a prime example of giving up. They spent the majority of their time wandering in the wilderness, constantly complaining and wanting to go back to Egypt. They demonstrated what many people already know: sometimes it's easier to go back to the old way of life and not persevere to new levels with God. They blamed God, Moses, and anything or anyone they could think of to deflect attention from their own disobedience.

7. *Your current harvest must be properly handled to ensure a future harvest.*

A wise farmer will never eat all of his seed. He knows the importance of replanting his best seed to ensure a future harvest.

Here are four steps to ensure the proper handling of your harvest:

1. Give a portion of your harvest to God.

2. Enjoy a portion of your harvest.

3. Reserve a portion of your harvest for future planting.

4. Do not be satisfied with just one harvest; rather, continually sow to the future.

The essence of God's plan of economy is that He desires abundance in your life so that after meeting your own needs you can joyfully give to others. The law of seedtime and harvest was true in Isaac's day, and it's still true today!

3. He reaped (*"And the same year [he] reaped a hundredfold, because the Lord blessed him"*).

Isaac sowed in a land where nobody was sowing due to the famine. I'm sure people laughed at him as they watched him sow in a land that in the natural could not produce a harvest. There is no doubt in my mind that he was mocked for such a foolish venture. As Jesus would share centuries later, it takes "good seed" in "good soil" to produce a thirtyfold, sixtyfold, or hundredfold harvest (Mark 4:1–9). Obviously Isaac had good seed, but he was sowing in an area that was dry, dusty, and for all intents and purposes, dead. It would take a miracle from God for anything to be produced in such conditions.

Not only did he receive a hundredfold return, but he also received it in the same year that he sowed. In other words, he didn't have to wait until the famine was over or until things got better. He received it during the famine while everyone else was suffering! Why would Isaac sow seed in dead soil where no one else was sowing? He did it because God had promised to bless him regardless of the conditions.

CONSIDER THE MESSAGE OF THE MIRACLE

Here are three important thoughts to keep in mind:

1. When you face lack, don't eat your seed.

We are tempted to eat our seed instead of sowing it. But without sowing, there will be no harvest. Continue to sow in times of lack so that the future will have a harvest instead of continuing famine and dry season.

+ When others were living in fear—Isaac sowed!

+ When others were believing for disaster—Isaac sowed!

+ When others were planning for failure—Isaac sowed!

- When others were storing up what they had—Isaac sowed!

- When others were holding back—Isaac sowed!

Isaac was not ruled by fear of the famine; he planted in faith. It takes faith to plant seed in a famine! God rewarded his faith by making him very prosperous. Isaac sowed into God's gift, the land that God would give to him and his descendants. What did Isaac sow into? His inheritance!

2. Always recognize the source of your miracle.

Isaac sowed not only physically but also spiritually. According to Genesis 26:25, "Isaac built an altar there and called on the name of the LORD. There he pitched his tent, and there his servants dug a well." Isaac recognized where the power to prosper in a time of famine came from.

> But remember the LORD your God, for it is he who gives you the ability to produce wealth, and so confirms his covenant, which he swore to your ancestors, as it is today.
>
> —DEUTERONOMY 8:18

Not only did Isaac sow into his inheritance, but he also sowed into God's kingdom by bringing his offering to the Lord. As a result, he redug the wells that the enemy had stopped up and the wells the famine had dried up.

> The blessing of the LORD brings wealth, without painful toil for it.
>
> —PROVERBS 10:22

Isaac became great. He gained more and more until he became very wealthy and distinguished. He owned flocks, herds, and a great supply of servants—so much that the Philistines envied him. Because Isaac trusted in God and not in himself or in the elements, he prospered while others were struggling. If you obey God, He can multiply you in the midst of the worst circumstances of life and grant you favor. Even in the middle of famine—when everyone else is decreasing, losing, and going under—you can be prospering, increasing, and multiplying!

Notice that it was not until Isaac separated himself so completely from the Philistines that they began to seek him out—not, by the way, because they had changed their minds about Isaac. Look at Genesis 26:28. They were drawn to Isaac because, as they say, "We saw plainly that the LORD was with you" (MEV). Even people who do not know God can see the evidence of God's presence. This knowledge led the Philistines to want a peace treaty with Isaac.

When the world came knocking, Isaac's response was to accept them. We would be wise to do the same. The working of God in his life made his presence unbearable to his godless neighbors, so they rejected him. But God continued to bless him and, in fact, continued driving a wedge between Isaac and the Philistines. Why? I'm convinced it's because God doesn't want the world influencing us; He wants us to influence the world. Through a series of events God brought exactly that about. He made His work in one man's life obvious so that the world would eventually seek Him out.

3. Don't go by what you see, but by what God says.

God's instructions never make sense to the natural mind. Consider these examples:

- *To Joshua:* March around in circles thirteen times. (What a battle plan!)

- *To Naaman:* Dip seven times in the Jordan, and you will be healed.

- *To the servants in John 2:* Fill your water pots with water and draw out wine.

- *To the blind man in John 9:* Walk two miles and wash in the pool of Siloam (after having clay formed with spit put on his eyes!).

- *To the dead man in John 11:* "Come forth!"

- *To His disciples in John 6:* Take that small lunch and feed more than five thousand people.

A specific action is always required to unlock God's supernatural involvement. God never requires you to do something that is impossible. The only instructions God ever gives are actions that anyone and everyone in the world could do.

FINALLY

Do we have a New Testament example of how to respond in hard times? *Yes*. God recognized a famine in the land, a famine of righteousness. He used the same principle by sowing in the time of famine.

> For God so loved the world that he gave his one and only Son, that whoever believes in him shall not perish but have eternal life.
> —JOHN 3:16

God sowed His Son, both physically and spiritually, in the time of famine, and He expects a return. God, in His grace, blesses His people despite the situation, despite their sins, and despite opposition.

> The world is full of abundance and opportunity, but far too many people come to the fountain of life with a sieve instead of a tank car…a teaspoon instead of a steam shovel. They expect little and as a result they get little.[5]

So cheer up, child of God! Refuse to live with a poverty mentality, and choose to live according to God's plan of economy. You will be amazed at what the *Isaac effect* will do!

CHAPTER 14

PROSPERING IN THE LAST DAYS

*When a man becomes a Christian, he becomes industrious, trust-
worthy, and prosperous. Now, if that man, when he gets all
he can and saves all he can, does not give all he can, I have
more hope for Judas Iscariot than for that man!*[1]

—JOHN WESLEY

N O SERIOUS STUDENT of the Bible would deny we are living in
the last days. In these days of war and rumors of war, hysteria
seems to grow concerning a possible end to everything as we know it.
In the last decade popular movies have adapted the theme of disaster
and world-ending scenarios. In one a giant meteor is on a crash course
with the earth; in another nations turn their nuclear weapons upon one
another in a massive holocaust. It seems the more dramatic the fear, the
better the box office turnout!

I believe the movie industry simply echoes the fears of our day.
Besides the insanity in the Middle East, with crazed and demonic
leaders trying to acquire biological and nuclear weapons, we also face
a rash of new fears concerning natural disasters. Global warming, solar
flares, changing weather patterns—all these prompt anxious debate.

There are so many hotspots around the world that it would be nearly
impossible to list all of them here. But one area that concerns many
believers is the current economic crisis being felt from New York to
London, from Beijing to Bangkok, from Frankfurt to Moscow. The
financial capitals of the world are linked together and face daily challenges to keep a global recession in check. Decades ago the average
believer felt these things did not apply to the church; they were applicable only to the "other guy." In this day of technological wonders and
social media, we are discovering that almost no one is ignorant of the
somber and depressing state of affairs.

Is it possible to live in blessing and walk in prosperity in such a bleak
economic environment? Can we, like Isaac, learn to be blessed in a
barren land? The answer is an unequivocal, *yes we can!*

Al Mohler states:

> This current crisis should also remind Christians that we are not
> called to be mere economic actors, but stewards. Everything we are,
> everything we do, and everything we own truly belongs to God and
> is to be at the disposal of Kingdom purposes. This world is not our
> home and our treasure is not found here. We are to do all, invest
> all, own all, purchase all to the glory of God.[2]

Living in God's plan of economy begins with choices. First, we must
choose this day whom we will serve—God or man.

> But if serving the LORD seems undesirable to you, then choose for
> yourselves this day whom you will serve, whether the gods your
> ancestors served beyond the Euphrates, or the gods of the Amorites,
> in whose land you are living. But as for me and my household, we
> will serve the LORD."
> —JOSHUA 24:15

Making the right choices is the foundation for living in kingdom
economics. Personal choices determine our personal economic situation. The combined choices of all citizens shape the economy as a whole.
In addition, choices of those in authority greatly impact the national
economy, for government is the house in which the economy lives.

C. H. MacIntosh, writing in 1882, compared the way nonbelievers
and believers approach kingdom knowledge:

> He [the nonbeliever] measures everything by his own standard,
> and rejects whatever he cannot reconcile with his own notions. He
> lays down, with marvelous coolness, his own premises, and then
> proceeds to draw his own conclusions; but if the premises are false,
> the conclusions must be false likewise. And there is this invariable
> feature attaching to the premises of all skeptics, rationalists, and
> infidels—they always leave out God; and hence all their conclu-
> sions must be fatally false. On the other hand, the humble believer
> starts with this great first principle, that God is; and not only that
> He is, but that He has to do with His creatures; that He interests
> Himself in, and occupies Himself about, the affairs of men.[3]

Our worldview determines the state in which we live. We must start
with the premise that there is a God who created all things, including

man, and that God is concerned about the economy, our nation, and how we manage our households. Viewing man from God's perspective has great implications for economics. The Christian view of man includes the following:

- Man is created in the image of God and hence has great value.

- Man has many characteristics of his Creator, including the ability to choose.

- Man makes his choices based on his worldview.

God is, and He has revealed Himself in His Word. He has also revealed principles for all of life (including the economy). So men who claim to be Christian must reason from those principles to be truly Christian and to obtain the fruit of obedience. To make the right choices concerning our stewardship, we must understand that there are two divergent "kingdoms" in conflict. What are these two opposing kingdoms, and what does all this have to do with economics?

Jesus went about preaching the gospel of the kingdom. In Matthew 6 He told us to seek the kingdom first. The topic of "the kingdom" is expressed throughout His parables. Yet it is also clear that Jesus recognized another kingdom. These two kingdoms have different worldviews, and as such, they are in constant conflict with each other.

When tempted by Satan in the wilderness, Jesus pointed to the fact that another kingdom was in operation:

> Again, the devil took him to a very high mountain and showed him all the kingdoms of the world and their splendor. "All this I will give you," he said, "if you will bow down and worship me."
> —MATTHEW 4:8–9

Was it possible for Satan to give these kingdoms to Jesus? Did he have the authority to do so? Jesus referred to Satan as the "ruler of this world" in John 12:31 (MEV). Paul referred to Satan as "the god of this world" in 2 Corinthians 4:4 (KJV). Obviously the answer is yes, he did have control of another kingdom.

First, it is important to realize that these two kingdoms—the kingdom of God that Jesus spoke about and the kingdom of this world—are essentially two completely different realities. Each reality is expressed by our worldview. Our worldview determines our behavior, not only in the marketplace, but also in our approach to life itself. Just as these kingdoms are in conflict with each other, so these worldviews are also in conflict.

For example, one worldview may be represented in the secular business environment as a drive for success at any cost. It is played out through a variety of expressions:

+ Manipulation of clients

+ Greed

+ Selfish ambitions

+ Self-promotion

+ Self-interest

These and other expressions become the top priority in dealings with others.

On the other hand, we may experience the worldview of the kingdom through integrity in business dealings. Here are a few of these expressions:

+ Generosity and loyalty

+ Faithfulness; honoring our commitments even when it costs us

+ Loving and blessing those who use us and seek to destroy us

Our behavior always exposes the worldview of the kingdom in which we are operating. These two kingdoms are direct opposites by their very nature.

What does all this have to do with economics? It is impossible to be a participant in either of these kingdoms, with their respective worldviews, without living by the system of economics required by those kingdoms. Just as the kingdom of God and the kingdom of this world are polar opposites, so these economic systems are also polar opposites in their objectives, methods of operation, and their impact on the lives of individual participants. Each economic system produces fruit in our lives that reflects the nature of the author of the system.

Dr. Francis A. Schaeffer, author and Christian apologist, states:

> People have presuppositions...By "presuppositions" we mean the
> basic way that an individual looks at life—his worldview. The grid
> through which he sees the world. Presuppositions rest upon that
> which a person considers to be the truth of what exists. A person's
> presuppositions provide the basis for their values—and therefore
> the basis for their decisions.[4]

We must realize that when we were born, we were dropped into
a battle zone. Just as in any "real-time war," every single one of us is
involved—and we are not allowed to remain neutral. Although this war
is global in nature, it becomes personal to every one of us. The battle
lines are drawn between God and Satan, and the ultimate confrontation between the forces of hell and the forces of God will soon erupt. It
is a sad state of affairs that most Christians who occupy our pews on
Sunday mornings are unaware of the immediacy of the conflict.

It may appear that things are normal; nevertheless the armies are
amassing through clear-cut battle lines. The "kings of the earth" (the
world's system) will take their stand against the Lord and His anointed
(the church). Spirit-filled believers are the only hope for a world sinking
slowly into the pit of despair, fear, and bondage.

When faith and kingdom economics operate in unison, we give first,
without any thought of return. When the world system is in operation,
instead of giving, we take. The worldview of the kingdom will always
view others first. The polar opposite is a worldview that is based on putting oneself first. This "me first" mentality has invaded the church. In the
American church it's called the "bless me first" theology. All the attention is based on the individual and what he or she can receive, never on
the corporate level. There is coming a day when the church will wake
up and realize that it's going to take a corporate anointing on a united
church, with a united front, to storm the gates of hell!

To live in supernatural abundance, we must operate according to
God's plan of economy. That act of giving first, before you receive, is
faith. The essence of Luke 6:38 is "give first, receive later." When you
take the first step to open your hand to give, it will be given back to you
far more abundantly than you gave. The measure in which you gave will
determine the measure in which you will receive.

I believe that Jesus was giving insight into kingdom economics when
he stated in Luke 6:38, "Give, and it will be given to you. A good measure, pressed down, shaken together and running over, will be poured
into your lap. For with the measure you use, it will be measured to you."

"Give" is a command. The last part of that verse will not be fulfilled until the first part is obeyed. This command is personal. *You* means everyone can get in on it. *It* is a big word; *it* represents whatever is given. Sow love and get love. Sow friendship, and you will get friendship. I believe Jesus left it open ended so that we could fill in the blank.

Notice three descriptions here: "good measure," "pressed down," "shaken together and running over." These words describe how God wants to give back to us. When I open my hand to God, He unlocks the windows of heaven to pour out abundance so great that I will be amazed and astounded at His awesomeness. The Apostle Paul put it this way in Ephesians 3:20: "Now to him who is able to do immeasurably more than all we ask or imagine, according to his power that is at work within us."

Why is giving the key to everything? It is because we are never more like our heavenly Father than when we are living with a giving spirit. How we give impacts how we live! The key is not in formulas to make money and accumulate more things, but it is about a lifestyle that freely receives God's grace, and freely releases it every day and in every way to everyone. God is not a glorified slot machine in the sky, where if you dispense enough prayer coins you might hit the jackpot of prosperity and abundance!

> Where your pleasure is, there is your treasure; where your treasure
> is, there is your heart; where your heart is, there is your happiness.[5]
>
> —AUGUSTINE

WHAT DO *PROSPERITY* AND *ABUNDANCE* REALLY MEAN?

From my point of view, it seems that those two words do not necessarily refer to a person who has lots of money in the bank or owns great material possessions. The promise from God is that all of our needs will be met and there will be enough left over to share.

In short, when I think in terms of God's provision, I do not necessarily think of wealthy or rich people. I personally believe that having God's provision means that we succeed in whatever He has called and commissioned us to do.

The apostle John says, "Beloved, I pray that you may prosper in all things and be in health, just as your soul prospers" (3 John 2, NKJV).

If you study John's third epistle, you will discover that he wrote under the inspiration of the Holy Spirit telling us that God wants us to "prosper" in all things and be in "health" just as our "soul prospers." This covers every area of life, including the material.

By using the word *prosper*, John is saying, "to have a prosperous or successful journey or accomplish what you intend to with success." It's the same word that Paul used in Romans 1:10 (KJV) when he prayed that he may have "a prosperous journey by the will of God" to visit and minister to the Christians in Rome. If you think that having a prosperous journey would include first-class accommodations and a big welcome on the other end, you would be wrong.

In order to get to Rome, his destination, Paul endured hardship, suffering, and fear. After the trauma of shipwreck (remember, God told him no one would suffer loss), being thrown onto an island as a castaway, and being bitten by a viper, Paul was witness to a supernatural power from God. That which appeared to be disaster God used for His glory when a revival exploded and many were saved and healed.

Paul made it to Rome and had a prosperous journey, but I can guarantee it was not comfortable or luxurious—it was prosperous because he accomplished the purpose of God!

From studying Scripture, I believe *abundance* means having all that's needed, plus something to spare or something left over to share with others. Walking in abundance lifts you out of your own needs and puts you in the cycle where you receive from the Father and generously turn and meet someone else's need.

Jesus went about preaching the gospel of the kingdom everywhere He went. Jesus made more than 150 references to the "kingdom" in the New Testament. When He taught us how to pray, He included the phrase, "Thy kingdom come." In Matthew, Mark, and Luke one out of every six verses deals with money. Of the twenty-nine parables Christ told, sixteen deal with a person and his money. So it would appear that with all of His teaching about the kingdom, He places a great deal of emphasis on our stewardship of material things. It is possible to live in prosperity and abundance in the last days if we choose to live according to divine kingdom principles. I suggest that those principles include a clear understanding about giving.

The Bible teaches four levels of giving that reflect kingdom economics.

1. The tithe

> A tithe of everything from the land, whether grain from the soil or
> fruit from the trees, belongs to the LORD; it is holy to the Lord.
>   —LEVITICUS 27:30

The word *tithe* means "tenth." God's Word teaches us that the first 10
percent of everything that comes into our hands is already God's property, even before we receive it. Every time your boss pays you, he gives
you the money you earned and the money that belongs to God. By the
way, the government's portion has already been removed.

Tithing is not a suggestion or an option. It is not something that is
driven by emotion or greed. It is a commandment given by God.

> "Will a mere mortal rob God? Yet you rob me. But you ask, 'How are
> we robbing you?' In tithes and offerings. You are under a curse—your
> whole nation—because you are robbing me. Bring the whole tithe
> into the storehouse, that there may be food in my house. Test me in
> this," says the LORD Almighty, "and see if I will not throw open the
> floodgates of heaven and pour out so much blessing that there will
> not be room enough to store it. I will prevent pests from devouring
> your crops, and the vines in your fields will not drop their fruit before
> it is ripe," says the LORD Almighty. "Then all the nations will call you
> blessed, for yours will be a delightful land," says the LORD Almighty.
>   —MALACHI 3:8–12

It is also interesting to note that God offers to reward us for giving
Him His own property. He could just say, "Give Me My money, or
there's going to be trouble!" Instead, He blesses us for obeying Him. I'm
sure that you would agree that it's better to be 90 percent blessed than
100 percent cursed.

I have met many people in my ministry who have made a huge mistake by assuming that tithing is an option. By making this false assump-
tion, they place themselves in the position of being thieves who have
stolen from almighty God. The God who created the earth and all that
is in it, who has all power and all knowledge, is the last person you
would want to steal from.

Without a doubt there are many opinions concerning the tithe. Some
would argue that tithing is not taught in the New Testament at all. The
answer is obvious: all you have to do is remove Matthew, Luke, and the

Book of Hebrews—then it's not mentioned at all. Just tear out those three books of the Bible, and you will be fine! As ridiculous as it sounds to remove three books of the New Testament, it is no more ridiculous than to suggest that something is not taught in the New Testament when it is clearly found in three different books.

Mark it down: when someone wants to argue whether tithing is taught in the New Testament, they are not trying to justify their desire to give more than 10 percent to God. Usually this person is trying to figure out how little he can give. It makes no sense to try to figure out a way to make God view you as the person who stole from Him. I want you to know without equivocation that tithing is the first step toward receiving God's abundance in your life. It is a foundation on which we stand; if the foundation is faulty, all other efforts of giving will be distorted.

Another question that often comes up is, "Should I tithe on my net income or my gross income?" Exodus 22:29 says, "You must not hold anything back when you give me offerings from your crops and your wine. You must give me your firstborn sons" (NLT). It seems obvious to me that we should tithe on our gross income. The question is, do you want a net blessing or a gross blessing?

Although it is clear that there are consequences for those who withhold the tithe, there are even greater rewards for those who obey the clear command.

> I have held many things in my hand, and have lost them all; but whatever I have placed in God's hands, that I still possess.[6]
> —MARTIN LUTHER

One of the greatest questions regarding tithing is also very controversial: "Where should I give the tithe?" God directs us to bring the tithe into the "storehouse." The Hebrew word for *storehouse* in Malachi 3 literally means "a depository, armory, cellar, garner, store (house), treasure (house)."

I have found that the primary purpose of the storehouse was to supply the provision of the Levitical priests. The storehouse was situated in the vicinity of the temple, where the priests ministered to the Lord. The logical place for us to give our tithe is to the local church, to support those who feed us and are responsible for ministering to us and to our families.

It is my conviction that if you are attending a local church that teaches the whole Bible, you should support that ministry with the tithe. It is very important to plant your life in a local church, submitting yourself to the pastoral authority within that congregation and committing yourself to the vision of the house. It is important to be accountable to someone who has spiritual authority in your life. The bottom line is this: you need to be a part of a local church, submitted to the authority of the spiritual leaders in that house.

2. Firstfruits

> You are to give them the firstfruits of your grain, new wine and
> olive oil, and the first wool from the shearing of your sheep.
> —DEUTERONOMY 18:4

The second type of giving taught in the Bible is firstfruits. Of the four types of giving, only tithes and firstfruits are commanded by God. The firstfruits is actually the first "taste" of any increase you receive, whether it is a raise, a bonus, or any additional source of income. Historically the first yield of your crops and the firstborn of your herds and flocks were all considered firstfruits and therefore holy unto the Lord. By offering them without hesitation and with thanksgiving to God, you acknowledge His sovereignty, and position yourself as a faithful steward.

The Bible teaches that everything we have ultimately belongs to God. We have nothing, including ourselves, that didn't come from Him. Scripture makes it clear that the increase of your possessions is considered firstfruits to be holy and dedicated to God.

> Honor the LORD with your wealth, with the firstfruits of all your
> crops; then your barns will be filled to overflowing, and your vats
> will brim over with new wine.
> —PROVERBS 3:9–10

Basically any time you receive increase, the first "taste" belongs to God. For example, if you are given a raise on your job that results in a twenty-five-dollar-per-week increase, then according to Scripture, the increase should be given to God. You may say, "But I need that extra money!" Or you could say, "I've been living without the increase until now; I can wait one more pay period and show my gratitude to God for His blessing."

I once heard the story about two young boys whose grandfather gave each of them a box of chocolates. After taking his box into his bedroom, the first boy quickly opened it and was soon covered in a chocolate mess, consuming the entire box in one sitting. The other boy, however, remained in the room with his grandfather. After gently opening the box and removing the thin sheet of wax paper that covered the candies, the boy lifted the box to his grandfather and said, "Granddad, thank you for my chocolates. Here, why don't you have the first piece?" I think this illustrates the heart of firstfruits giving, don't you?

When we fail to honor God with the increase, we have to wonder what He must think and feel about it. Either you are ungrateful for what He has done, or you are not impressed with the blessing He gave you. Either way, will there be any motivation for Him to repeat the blessing in the future? God is so generous that even when we simply obey in the area of firstfruits, He promises greater and future blessings. He could threaten us with punishment, but instead He offers abundance.

If the tithe goes to the storehouse, then where should the increase, or firstfruits, go? Ezekiel 44:30 states, "The best of all the firstfruits and of all your special gifts will belong to the priests. You are to give them the first portion of your ground meal so that a blessing may rest on your household."

As you can see, Ezekiel says that we are to give the firstfruits to the priest. I believe the modern-day equivalent of the Old Testament priest would be anyone in fivefold ministry: apostles, prophets, evangelists, pastors, and teachers. As with anything else, you must be led by the Spirit, letting Him direct your increased giving to the ministry that is fulfilling the Great Commission. Do not be motivated by emotion or guilt but by the leadership of the Holy Spirit.

As with the tithe, firstfruits giving is controversial. There are some who say that the giving of firstfruits is not taught in the New Testament; therefore it was only an Old Testament principle and we should not consider it applicable today.

Romans 11:16 says, "If the part of the dough offered as firstfruits is holy, then the whole batch is holy; if the root is holy, so are the branches." That argument is rendered moot by the fact that Romans is clear that the giving of firstfruits was still practiced in the New Testament. Even after the death, burial, and resurrection of Christ, firstfruits was practiced. How do we know? The Apostle Paul, who wrote the Book of Romans, did not come to Christ until after Jesus's death, burial, and resurrection.

Remember, it is never wrong to simply obey God and do the right thing! He has promised that because of our simple obedience He will fill our barns to overflowing, and our vats will brim over with new wine (Prov. 3:10). This is God's way of telling us that when we obey, increase will come.

3. Alms giving

The third type of giving in the Bible is "alms." The Greek word by definition means, "generosity that is motivated by compassion or sympathy towards the poor."

> Now a man who was lame from birth was being carried to the temple gate called Beautiful, where he was put every day to beg from those going into the temple courts. When he saw Peter and John about to enter, he asked them for money.
>
> —ACTS 3:2–3

Of the four types of giving taught in the Bible, alms is the only one in which the giving is directed to man, not God. God is not poor, nor does He want us to pity Him. He does not need our sympathy. Therefore, we do not give alms to God, only to people.

In fact, the Bible cautions us to maintain a level of secrecy regarding alms-giving:

> Be careful not to practice your righteousness in front of others to be seen by them. If you do, you will have no reward from your Father in heaven. So when you give to the needy, do not announce it with trumpets, as the hypocrites do in the synagogues and on the streets, to be honored by others. Truly I tell you, they have received their reward in full. But when you give to the needy, do not let your left hand know what your right hand is doing, so that your giving may be in secret. Then your Father, who sees what is done in secret, will reward you.
>
> —MATTHEW 6:1–4

Many people misinterpret the meaning of Matthew 6 and assume that we are to maintain the same level of secrecy in all of our giving, when in fact the Bible teaches just the opposite.

In Luke 21 we find Jesus and His disciples standing near the offering receptacle observing how and how much each person is giving. Were it not for their curiosity, we would have no record of the story of the "widow's mite." Jesus taught His disciples an important lesson by drawing a comparison between the widow's offering and what others had given. He makes it obvious that God looks more closely at the amount of sacrifice than the dollar amount.

"Truly I tell you," he said, "this poor widow has put in more than all the others. All these people gave their gifts out of their wealth; but she out of her poverty put in all she had to live on."

—LUKE 21:3–4

All this leads back to the fact that when Jesus said we should not tell anyone what we had given, He was speaking only of alms and not in regard to the other three types of giving. Alms giving is a matter of common sense. Think about it: What if you learned that someone did not have enough to eat, and you gave them money to buy food? Don't you think it would be humiliating for them if you told everyone what you had done? I believe Jesus's purpose in telling us to keep it secret was to prevent us from devastating and embarrassing someone. It is tragic enough that he is in a financial crisis; our spreading the news to everyone in town would only make his situation worse.

The Bible is filled with references to the fact that God wants us to be generous toward the poor. The only reason we have so many government programs, handouts, entitlements, and giveaways is because the church has failed in its responsibility to minister to the poor. That is not to say that no one in the church or outside the church is helping those who cannot help themselves. Taking care of the poor has always been part of the assignment of the church, not the government.

Proverbs 14:21 says, "It is a sin to despise one's neighbor, but blessed is the one who is kind to the needy." The meaning is simple: If your neighbor is in need and you are unmoved by his situation, you will eventually suffer the consequence of your indifference. But if you reach out to help him in his time of need, God will bless you.

We read in Proverbs 19:17, "He who has pity on the poor lends to the Lord, and He will pay back what he has given" (NKJV). It is clear that God is saying, "I am going to bless those who give to the poor." Specifically, God takes it personally to reimburse whatever you give.

It is obvious that God is pleased with those who have open and generous hearts toward the poor, and He will reward them accordingly:

+ Proverbs 21:13: "Whoever shuts their ears to the cry of the poor will also cry out and not be answered."
+ Proverbs 22:9: "The generous will themselves be blessed, for they share their food with the poor."

‣ Proverbs 28:27: "Those who give to the poor will lack nothing, but those who close their eyes to them receive many curses."

Our life of poverty is as necessary as the work itself. Only in heaven will we see how much we owe to the poor for helping us to love God better because of them.[7]

—MOTHER TERESA

4. Seedtime and harvest

We have already considered seven dynamic principles of seedtime and harvest (see chapter 13), but I think it is important to go a little deeper into Paul's meaning and motivation when he wrote to the church at Corinth. He encouraged them to keep their commitment. He desired for them to follow through with an offering to the struggling churches of Macedonia.

It was during Paul's plea that he outlined the principles of seedtime and harvest. These principles operate in the natural realm, and they operate on a spiritual level as well:

There is no need for me to write to you about this service to the Lord's people. For I know your eagerness to help, and I have been boasting about it to the Macedonians, telling them that since last year you in Achaia were ready to give; and your enthusiasm has stirred most of them to action. But I am sending the brothers in order that our boasting about you in this matter should not prove hollow, but that you may be ready, as I said you would be. For if any Macedonians come with me and find you unprepared, we—not to say anything about you—would be ashamed of having been so confident. So I thought it necessary to urge the brothers to visit you in advance and finish the arrangements for the generous gift you had promised. Then it will be ready as a generous gift, not as one grudgingly given.

Remember this: Whoever sows sparingly will also reap sparingly, and whoever sows generously will also reap generously. Each of you should give what you have decided in your heart to give, not reluctantly or under compulsion, for God loves a cheerful giver. And God is able to bless you abundantly, so that in all things at all times, having all that you need, you will abound in every good work. As it is written: "They have freely scattered their gifts to the poor; their righteousness endures forever."

Now he who supplies seed to the sower and bread for food will also supply and increase your store of seed and will enlarge the harvest of your righteousness. You will be enriched in every way so that you can be generous on every occasion, and through us your generosity will result in thanksgiving to God.

—2 CORINTHIANS 9:1–11

Like many people, the Corinthian believers had made promises but failed to keep them. In fact, an entire year had gone by and nothing happened. I'm sure they gave many reasons for not following through with their commitment. Paul knew that it would be difficult to get them to participate, so he lifted his teaching to the highest spiritual level possible. He taught them that giving is an act of grace in spite of one's circumstances (2 Cor. 8:1–2). He wanted them to give not out of obligation but as a demonstration of the grace of God working in their hearts.

Paul refers to the Macedonian churches as an example of grace giving in spite of "a great trial of affliction" (v. 2, NKJV). Unlike the church at Corinth, the Macedonian churches needed no prompting or reminding. The Macedonians not only suffered affliction but also were in deep poverty. Although they had hit rock-bottom destitution, their circumstances did not hinder them from giving joyfully and liberally.

There is a great difference between promise and performance. A year earlier these Corinthians had boasted that they would share in the collection, but they did not keep their promise. It is one thing to be willing, but the doing must follow. Sincere desire alone does not translate into action. You may have a sincere desire to walk in abundance, but unless you are willing to obey the Word, it will not happen.

In these verses Paul outlines some important principles:

The principle of multiplication: we reap in the measure that we sow (2 Cor. 9:6).

Every farmer knows that the more seed he plants in the ground, the better his chance for a greater harvest. We also see this principle operating in everyday life. When you take a large investment of money to the bank, it will certainly collect more interest. The more we invest in the gospel of Jesus Christ, the more "fruit" will abound to our account. (See Philippians 4:10–20.)

The principle of motive: we reap when we sow with the right motives (2 Cor. 9:7).

To the farmer who plants his seed, motive makes no difference. If he sows good seed in good ground with good weather, he will reap a harvest. For the Christian, it is different; motive in giving or any other activity is vitally important. Paul is clear: giving must come from the heart to please God, not men. May it never be said of us that we are "sad givers" who give grudgingly or "mad givers" who give because we have to. We should be "glad givers" who cheerfully share what we have because of the many blessings God has given us. "He that hath a bountiful eye shall be blessed" (Prov. 22:9, kjv).

The principle of immediacy: we reap even while we are sowing (2 Cor. 9:8–11).

While the farmer has to wait for his harvest, the believer who practices grace giving begins to reap immediate abundance. Yes, some harvests take longer than others. To be sure, there are long-range benefits, but there are also immediate blessings to enjoy.

Notice the word *abundance*. God is able to make it happen for us. When? Always, in all things. In essence it is God's will that we never lack at any point in time, and that there is no deficiency but "all sufficiency."

The perpetual flow of supernatural abundance means all grace always; all sufficiency for every good work. The word *sufficiency* means "adequate resources within." (See Philippians 4:11.)

We may go through a valley of lack for a season, but we don't stop in the valley. How would we know that our God is the abundant supplier of more than enough if we never experienced a need?

Need is an interesting word. It means "A lack of something requisite, desirable, or useful. A condition requiring supply or relief." We don't like to talk about having needs. It almost sounds as if we don't have faith for the abundant supply. God has some unusual ways of getting my attention. He seems to get my attention not through my success but in my distress.

> Hear me when I call, O God of my righteousness: thou hast enlarged me when I was in distress; have mercy upon me, and hear my prayer.
>
> —Psalm 4:1, kjv

I'm sure you've noticed that every miracle in the Bible started with a need. Without needs you will never know that He is the God of miracles.

You may need a miracle as big as parting the Red Sea, or it may be as small as paying your utility bill. Size is not the issue; it is a matter of recognizing: "And my God shall supply all your need according to His riches in glory by Christ Jesus" (Phil. 4:19, NKJV).

DON'T BE DECEIVED!

It is time for the people of God to stand up and take back everything Satan has stolen! The Bible declares that during the end times we will see the glory of God demonstrated in ways that we never dreamed possible.

Isaiah 40:3–4 declares, "A voice of one calling: 'In the wilderness prepare the way for the LORD; make straight in the desert a highway for our God. Every valley shall be raised up, every mountain and hill made low; the rough ground shall become level, the rugged places a plain.'"

I believe that during the time when this "highway" is being prepared for God, we will see the crooked things made straight:

+ Satan will have to restore all stolen possessions.

+ Family relationships that have been "crooked" will be made straight.

+ Financial and business rip-offs will be made whole.

Dr. John Avanzini writes in *Stolen Property Returned*:

> Red China is often referred to as the slumbering giant. Child of God, I've got news for you—the real slumbering giant is the church of the Lord and Savior Jesus Christ! The church is like Sleeping Beauty. She just needs her prince to come along. That prince will be a people who know who they are in Jesus and could awaken the "sleeping beauty" and solve our identity crisis once and for all. When this happens, you will watch how quickly the church grows into a new, powerful, stirring dimension. The day is upon us when this present generation of Christians does not have to put up with the things that the saints of God put up with in the past generations. It is time to drop the old "pie in the sky, in the sweet by and by" thinking and replace it with the spiritual rights, the heavenly heritage that goes with being a child of the King! Not someday in the future, but right now![8]

THE DAVID FACTOR FOR END-TIMES VICTORY

CHAPTER 15

FACE YOUR FOES

*"Come here," he said, "and I'll give your flesh
to the birds and the wild animals!"*
—GOLIATH, 1 SAMUEL 17:44

DURING WORLD WAR II a submarine sank off the coast of England. It took some time to locate the vessel. When the divers arrived at the sub, they heard a faint tapping. Listening, they recognized a Morse code message: "Is there any hope? Is there any hope?"

This is the question many Christians and non-Christians alike are asking today. It has become apparent that science has failed as a messiah; our world grows bigger and hungrier every day. While speaking of peace, nations are arming themselves to the hilt. Political promises are rampant, while behind closed doors the experts admit that economic, moral, and social problems are insurmountable giants that cannot be defeated.

In affluent America the literature, music, and dramatic arts teach a degraded philosophy of life that sees no hope. Many times I've heard the question asked concerning today's most popular movies, "Do movies reflect the culture or direct the culture?" My answer to that is yes, probably a little of both.

All you have to do is go on the Internet and see the most popular movies of the day. There seem to be two dominant themes: First, movies that depict horror, with a generous blend of the supernatural. For example, *Vampire Academy, Carrie, The Conjuring, Paranormal Activity*, and dozens more. Second, movies that depict the world after some cataclysmic event. One of the most popular series of books/movies of the day is *The Hunger Games*. A brief synopsis of the movie tells us:

> The nation of Panem, formed from a post-apocalyptic North America, is a country that consists of a wealthy Capitol region surrounded by 12 poorer districts. Early in its history, a rebellion led by a 13th district against the Capitol resulted in its destruction and the creation of an annual televised event known as the Hunger Games. In

punishment, and as a reminder of the power and grace of the Capitol, each district must yield one boy and one girl between the ages of 12 and 18 through a lottery system to participate in the games. The "tributes" are chosen during the annual Reaping and are forced to fight to the death, leaving only one survivor to claim victory.[1]

Just as in the fictitious nation of Panem, people today feel they have no control over their lives and must depend on the sympathy of others or the generosity of a nanny state (government) to help them make it through an otherwise gray and dreary life. You really don't have to look very far into the culture to see that when facing giants, most people feel a sense of hopelessness. Even in the framework of the Christian church many people are weak and faithless when facing crisis. The church and the world need to hear the message of the crucified, risen, ascending, and returning Lord as never before!

Sadly enough, instead of turning to the source of help, Jesus Christ, Western culture has decided to mock holy things instead of embracing them. No doubt Simon Peter had it right when he wrote nearly two thousand years ago, "Above all, you must understand that in the last days scoffers will come, scoffing and following their own evil desires" (2 Pet. 3:3).

Peter gives us a sign for the end of the age that fits perfectly with current attitudes. He describes the attitude of "scoffing" and the people as "scoffers." The Greek word literally means "in making fun." It could be an ancient word from which *imposter* is derived. It gives the idea that when discussing the things of God, the first response is to make fun of what is being said. It is a weapon commonly used by liberals to mock people who embrace the truth.

Peter also declares that a part of the scoffing is the sign of "following their own evil desires." It literally means "to journey upward or to the top." These modern-day scoffers treat with sarcasm the things of the Spirit and make fun of biblical truth. They allow their human lust for sex and power to direct their lives!

It would be impossible to mention cultural giants without including what I consider one of the biggest giants of them all—the technology explosion. The prophet Daniel declared that a sign of the last days would be "an increase of knowledge." The technology explosion and the increase of knowledge are not fantasies for the future; they are here now!

But you, Daniel, roll up and seal the words of the scroll until the time of the end. Many will go here and there to increase knowledge.

—DANIEL 12:4

In his book *The Next Story: Life and Faith After the Digital Explosion* Tim Challies says that we don't necessarily need to reject technology altogether. He calls it a gift from God. But he challenges us to use it carefully "for it's a powerful enabler of our idols."[2] Challies suggests that technology has a way of wooing us into a mythical awareness of its power, keeping us from being able to examine it critically.

> Yet each new technology carries hidden ideologies that impact how we live and view the world. From oral transmission, to the written word, to the printed word, to the telegraph, to the television, to the Internet...with each leap forward in the way we communicate and entertain ourselves, power shifts, society morphs, and even our brains change shape.[3]

The author is correct and further challenges us to question how we use technology and be discerning about its impact on our lives. Based on a wonderful review of this book, there are six themes that will help us think about how technology affects our lives.

> *Communication:* Do I value online relationships with people I'll never meet over relationships in my family, church and community?
>
> *Mediation/identity:* Have I begun to feel more comfortable with mediated communication—e-mails, text messages, Twitter—than with face-to-face communication?
>
> *Distraction:* How much do I depend on the constant interruptions of emails, Facebook comments and text messages to make me feel important and valued?
>
> *Information:* Is my mind so flooded with small, constant snippets of information that I am overwhelmed, unable to read and reflect deeply?
>
> *Truth/authority:* Do I seek knowledge from true experts, or are my knowledge and beliefs crowd-sourced?
>
> *Visibility and privacy:* Would I be willing to make my web history public? How careful am I about what I write, view and make public online?"[4]

THERE ARE GIANTS IN THE LAND!

No doubt there are giants in the land. The question is, what are you going to do about it?

When you think of a giant, what is the first name that pops into your head? Is it the Jolly Green Giant? Or Bigfoot? Believe it or not, someone composed a top ten list of the most famous giants in history, mythology, and religion. Topping the list, and the most obvious, is Goliath. Just the mention of the name Goliath instills fear. There have been some infamous names that when spoken cause an immediate emotional response. Some were giants by size, others were giants because of their actions. For example:

+ Jezebel

+ Judas

+ Jack the Ripper

+ Paul Bunyan

+ Lee Harvey Oswald

+ John Wilkes Booth

+ Little John

+ Giants of Jotunheim

+ Gargantua and Pantagruel

Without a doubt, when you hear the name Goliath you are immediately taken back to one of the most famous battles and underdog stories in all of human history!

The Philistines drew up their troops for battle. They deployed them at Socoh in Judah, and set up camp between Socoh and Azekah at Ephes Dammim. Saul and the Israelites came together, camped at Oak Valley, and spread out their troops in battle readiness for the Philistines. The Philistines were on one hill, the Israelites on the opposing hill, with the valley between them.

A giant nearly ten feet tall stepped out from the Philistine line into the open, Goliath from Gath. He had a bronze helmet on his head and was dressed in armor—126 pounds of it! He wore bronze shin guards and carried a bronze sword. His spear was like a fence rail—the spear tip alone weighed over fifteen pounds. His shield bearer walked ahead of him.

Goliath stood there and called out to the Israelite troops, "Why bother using your whole army? Am I not Philistine enough for you? And you're all committed to Saul, aren't you? So pick your best fighter and pit him against me. If he gets the upper hand and kills me, the Philistines will all become your slaves. But if I get the upper hand and kill him, you'll all become our slaves and serve us. I challenge the troops of Israel this day. Give me a man. Let us fight it out together!"

When Saul and his troops heard the Philistine's challenge, they were terrified and lost all hope.

—1 SAMUEL 17:1–11, THE MESSAGE

Ancient Palestine is the region known as the Shephelah, a series of ridges and valleys connecting the Judaean Mountains to the east with the wide, flat expanse of the Mediterranean plain. It is an area of breathtaking beauty, home to vineyards and wheat fields and forests of sycamore and terebinth. It is also of great strategic importance.

Over the centuries, numerous battles have been fought for control of the region because the valleys rising from the Mediterranean plain offer those on the coast a clear path to the cities of Hebron, Bethlehem, and Jerusalem in the Judaean highlands. The most important valley is Aijalon, in the north. But the most storied valley is the Elah. The Elah was where Saladin faced off against the Knights of the Crusades in the twelfth century. It played a central role in the Maccabean wars with Syria more than a thousand years before that, and, most famously, during the days of the Old Testament, it was where the fledgling Kingdom of Israel squared off against the armies of the Philistines.

The Philistines were from Crete. They were seafaring people who had moved to Palestine and settled along the coast. The Israelites were clustered in the mountains, under the leadership of King Saul. In the second half of the eleventh century BCE, the Philistines began moving east, winding their way upstream along the floor of the Elah Valley. Their goal was to capture the mountain ridge near Bethlehem and split Saul's kingdom in two.... The Philistines set up camp along the southern ridge of the Elah. The Israelites pitched their tents along the other side, which left the two armies looking across the ravine at each other. Neither dared to move. To attack meant descending down the hill and then making a suicidal climb up the enemy's ridge on the other side. Finally, the Philistines had enough. They sent their greatest warrior down into the valley to resolve the deadlock one on one.[5]

Here was no ordinary warrior. Goliath would have been about nine feet nine inches tall. His armor consisted of a bronze helmet, a coat of scale armor weighing about one hundred twenty-five pounds, and a pair of bronze leggings. His weapons were a bronze spear with a fifteen-pound tip, a sword, a javelin, and a shield that was carried by an armor-bearer who walked before him.

Standing there in the valley, Goliath presented an awesome appearance. He was a mighty warrior who could overpower any enemy. Then he spoke, crying out in defiance, mocking and ridiculing the Israelites. I often wondered why they bothered to line up when the entire army was frozen in fear. Not a single soldier dared to face Goliath in hand-to-hand combat. Day after day he shouted a challenge to fight. He challenged the army of Israel to representative combat, a common practice in the ancient world. It meant the mightiest warrior of Israel would fight a one-on-one dual with Goliath. Each warrior represented his nation, and the loser became the subject of the winner. The idea was to avoid as much carnage that open battle represented by choosing one combatant to represent each side. As with so many of the things in life we are faced with, it sounded good on paper, but in reality there were no takers!

DAVID: THE ULTIMATE UNDERDOG!

This is a true underdog story. "There's no need to fear! Underdog is here!" Remember that cartoon show? We enjoyed seeing the puny dog take on the villains and accomplish impossible feats of strength and derring-do. We like to root for the underdog. We like to see the little guy beat the big guy. We like to see teams beat the odds and walk away with the amazing upset. We cheer when the one who received no respect triumphs. But why do we care so much about the underdog? Probably because we all see a little bit of ourselves in the underdog. When we see someone else rise above the insurmountable odds and come away victorious, we are inspired to believe that we can be winners too.

A casual observer would look on the scene and declare, "This fight has to be stopped, or somebody is going to get killed!" I don't think anyone would disagree that this was not going to be a fair fight. Historians tell us that the height of an average man in that day was around five feet two inches. There were exceptions (such as Saul, who was "head and shoulders" above his brethren), but for the most part, this was going to be a slaughter.

History is filled with many examples of underdogs who came out on top. My all-time favorite has been called "The Miracle on Ice." That's what they called the United States hockey team's victory over the Soviet Union in the semifinals of the 1980 Winter Olympics:

> The odds were against the Americans in so many ways. They were a group of untested college and amateur players in a culture that was hardly hockey-centric, and they entered the 1980 Games as the seventh seed amongst twelve teams. The Soviets, meanwhile, were essentially full-time hockey players who had played together for years, and they were representing a country which had produced eight of the last nine gold medalists in the sport. The two countries were rivals in every sense of the word, with the political differences between them serving to further the meeting between the two teams on the ice. And to top it all off, the USSR and USA had already played each other in 1980, with the Americans suffering a 10–3 thrashing in a February exhibition match. If they played 100 times, the Soviet Union probably would have won 99 times. But they only played once, and on that day, the United States was the better team, winning 4–3 in what *Sports Illustrated* has called the greatest sporting moment of the 20th century.[6]

As awesome and improbable as the United States's victory over the Soviet Union was, it was nothing compared to what David did when he faced Goliath. No one would believe that David was capable of taking down such a brute. I heard someone describe the confrontation this way: Here is a skinny, scrawny David against a bulky, brutish giant. The toothpick versus the tornado. The minibike attacking the eighteen wheeler. The toy poodle taking on the Rottweiler. What odds do you give David against this giant? Perhaps better odds than you give yourself when faced with your own Goliath. At some point we are all called on to face our giants. The question is not if, but when:

> Your Goliath doesn't carry a sword or shield; he brandishes blades
> of unemployment, abandonment, sexual abuse, or depression. Your

giant doesn't parade up and down the hills of Elah; he prances through your office, your bedroom, your classroom. He brings bills you can't pay, grades you can't make, people you can't please, whiskey you can't resist, pornography you can't refuse, a career you can't escape, a past you can't shake, and a future you can't face....

David shows up discussing God. The soldiers mentioned nothing about him, the brothers never spoke his name, but David takes one step onto the stage and raises the subject of the living God [1 Sam. 17:26]....

A subplot appears in the story. More than "David versus Goliath," this is "God-focus" versus "giant-focus."

David sees what others don't and refuses to see what others do. All eyes, except David's, fall on the brutal, hate breathing hulk....

David majors in God. He sees the giant, mind you; he just sees God more so [1 Sam. 17:45]....

David sees the armies of God. And because he does, David hurries and runs toward the army to meet the Philistine [1 Sam. 17:48].[7]

So how did David win the biggest fight of his life? Are there any strategies that we can apply when faced with our own giants? I mean, really? How did this skinny kid do it?

PUT YOUR HAND DOWN!

The "sound" of this generation is to face your giants and stay in the game. I believe without a doubt Jesus is coming back—that is a given for me! After all these years of studying the Bible, I have learned that I don't have all the answers, especially when it comes to God's timing. My responsibility is not to hide in a cave or sit on top of a mountain somewhere longingly waiting for His return. I refuse to cower in the trenches with Saul's army in fear. The Holy Spirit's challenge to me is to actively engage the culture in which He has placed me.

If you have ever watched a football game, you may have noticed that when a player gets tired and wants to come out of the game he raises his hand and looks at the bench. It is a nonverbal communication to the coach that says, "I need a breather; take me out of the game."

I have developed the attitude of *build a legacy and lasting value for generations to come* as if Jesus is not coming back for a thousand years. But I live my life as if He could come back at any minute. To the church, the old expression "It ain't over until the fat lady sings" should say, "It ain't over until the trumpet sounds!" It's time for the church to stop whining and start winning.

When Jesus comes back is not up to us, but what we do until He gets here is entirely up to us. The Spirit of the Lord is saying to this generation, "Put your hand down; you're not coming out of the game until it's over!"

Stop running from Goliath and start running toward him! In the next chapter I will show you four keys to David's victory.

CHAPTER 16

APPLY THE KEYS TO VICTORY

The very thing that gave the giant his size was also the source of his greatest weakness.... The powerful and the strong are not always what they seem.[1]
—MALCOLM GLADWELL

DAVID HAD A strategy. It was simple, direct, and to the point. Looking on, you might think there wasn't any way this strategy would work. After all, Goliath was the undefeated all-time champion of the world!

What was David's strategy?

+ Apply what he already knew.

+ Choose the terms of the fight.

+ Not allow his emotions to overload based on Goliath's words.

+ Keep it simple—take a few rocks and a sling, and kill Goliath from a distance.

DAVID'S FOUR KEYS TO VICTORY

Key #1: He was obedient to his assignment.

> Now Jesse said to his son David, "Take this ephah roasted grain and these ten loaves of bread for your brothers and hurry to their camp. Take along these ten cheeses to the commander of their unit. See how your brothers are and bring back some assurance from them. They are with Saul and all the men of Israel in the Valley of Elah, fighting against the Philistines."
> —1 SAMUEL 17:17–19

David was given an assignment from his father: "Go take food and check on your brothers." He could have said yes and wandered off somewhere else, distracted by other things. He could have thought, "This assignment is too dangerous," or, "This is a waste of time," or whatever excuse he could have come up with for not completing his assignment. After all, he was still a teenager, and we all know that teenagers can be easily distracted.

Half the battle is already won when you just show up where you're supposed to be. You may not win all the battles all the time, but I promise you will lose all the battles all the time if you don't show up.

> Whenever, wherever, however You want me, I'll go. And I'll begin this very minute. Lord, as I stand up from this place, and as I take my first step forward, will You consider this is a step toward complete obedience to You? I'll call it the step of yes.[2]
> —BROTHER ANDREW, "GOD'S SMUGGLER"

Why was it important that David knew that he was in the right place at the right time? God's primary purpose is to get us in the place of proper assignment. Proper assignment will release supernatural abundance. In the case of David, there is no doubt that God supernaturally intervened and gave him a great victory.

David was willing to prepare for his assignment. Even though he had been anointed king, David tended his father's sheep and obeyed his father's voice without even realizing he was "training for reigning." Each assignment has a preparation period. The greater the assignment, the longer the preparation time. When the door of opportunity opens, it's too late to begin making preparations.

Consider Moses.

Moses spent forty years learning about the wisdom of Egypt (the enemy). He spent the next forty years learning about sheep (the people he was going to lead). He spent eighty years in preparation—many people today cannot wait eighty days. Jesus spent thirty years preparing for three and a half years of ministry. We want three and a half years of preparation for a thirty-year ministry. Things of the kingdom don't work that way.

Consider Elijah.

Elijah had prophesied that there would be no rain (1 Kings 17:1–9). God told Elijah to stand before the king and declare that he was shutting off the waterworks. As a result of the lack of rain, there was a famine in the land. For several years there was no rain—so what was Elijah to do? I'm sure he asked the Lord more than one time, where do I go from here? It was God's idea for Elijah to go to the brook. The brook was a place of supply, and I'm sure that Elijah thought that he had everything he needed. He had water to drink; room service was delivered every day by the ravens, so he had plenty of food. He must have thought, "I'm in the right place. What could go wrong?"

Elijah learned that even in the place of proper assignment there is training and there are lessons to learn. He also discovered there is a difference between truth and facts. The facts said, "The brook is drying up and there is nothing to drink." But the truth said, "God is your source and supply; continue to obey His voice." It's important to remember that we can't always go by what we see; instead, we must go by what God has told us! God is constantly placing us in situations so that we can determine our place of proper assignment:

+ Noah building an ark.

+ Abraham offering his son as a sacrifice.

+ Moses leading his people.

+ Elijah at a dried-up brook.

+ Peter at the house of Cornelius.

+ Paul in prison.

+ John on the Isle of Patmos.

We must know our place of assignment! David ran toward his assignment and defeated the giant. Are you in your place of proper assignment? How can you know?

+ What you love reveals the gifts you contain.

+ What troubles you reveals what you are called to correct. (You will never change what you're willing to tolerate.)

+ What breaks your heart reveals what you're called to heal.

Jonah flunked the assignment test!

If David is the poster boy for being in the place of proper assignment, then Jonah is the poster boy for running from one's assignment. Remember this: you don't have to go through the things Jonah went through to learn the lessons Jonah learned.

Jonah had an assignment. God told him to go to Nineveh. He partly obeyed; he got up and bought a ticket on a boat, but he went the wrong way. Partial obedience is still disobedience. God never ignores my acts of disobedience. Sometimes God will use pain to bring me back toward my assignment.

> No discipline seems pleasant at the time, but painful. Later on, however, it produces a harvest of righteousness and peace for those who have been trained by it.
> —Hebrews 12:11

Jonah had to endure three miserable days and nights in the belly of a big fish before he accepted his assignment. The pain he endured must have been horrible. But God used even his pain to bring him to his senses and focus his attention back on his original mission. If you are in pain, don't waste it; maybe God is trying to tell you something.

Pain can be a good thing when viewed with the proper perspective. Pain in the physical body is a warning that something is terribly wrong. Jonah was in physical and spiritual pain, and it forced him to

- look to the word of the Lord again;

- lean on the arm of the Lord; and

- listen to his assignment instructions again.

Key #2: He refused to listen to the negative.

It is interesting to me that Eliab is the one giving David sharp and unnecessary criticism. He was David's oldest brother. I thought the oldest brother was supposed to take care of the younger brother. It is obvious that Eliab had his own issues:

> When Eliab, David's oldest brother, heard him speaking with the men, he burned with anger at him and asked, "Why have you come down here? And with whom did you leave those few sheep in the wilderness? I know how conceited you are and how wicked your heart is; you came down only to watch the battle."
> "Now what have I done?" said David. "Can't I even speak?" He then turned away to someone else and brought up the same matter, and the men answered him as before. What David said was overheard and reported to Saul, and Saul sent for him.
> —1 Samuel 17:28–31

If you go back to 1 Samuel 16, you will read that it was this brother, not David, who everyone expected would be anointed the next king of Israel.

> When they arrived, Samuel saw Eliab and thought, "Surely the Lord's anointed stands here before the Lord." But the Lord said to Samuel, "Do not consider his appearance or his height, for I have rejected him. The Lord does not look at the things people look at. People look at the outward appearance, but the Lord looks at the heart."
> —1 Samuel 16:6–7

It must have been a blow to Eliab's ego to hear Samuel say, "You are not the man." Reading his words of criticism to David, there is no doubt in my mind that Eliab had a jealous heart toward David. There was a national crisis brewing. The future of the nation hung in the balance, and all he wanted to do was criticize his young brother for coming to check on his family.

It may be a shock to your system to realize that we all have our own Eliabs. There will always be those who are more willing to tell you what not to do. Then, when you try to do the right thing, they stand over your shoulder and criticize even that. The truth is, they never seem to get in the game themselves, and they don't want you to be successful.

David was focused on his assignment. He knew that something had to be done. He asked, "Is there not a cause?" (1 Sam. 17:29, nkjv). Even in his youth he focused on the problem like a laser beam and determined to do something about it.

In general we have become a nation of critics. We have art critics, food critics, movie critics, and political critics. It's easy to criticize but very difficult to deal with criticism when it comes your way.

What was it about David that brought him such sharp criticism? There could be many reasons; I don't know all of them, but let me suggest two:

You haven't paid your dues.

David was young and inexperienced in the way of war. But one thing people already knew about David was that he had been anointed king—and they didn't like it. Some people are like water boys on a football team. They wait until you look like you're "getting hot" and then they want to throw water in your face. There will always be those who are waiting for your success just so they can be there to cool you off when you start getting too far ahead.

Anybody but him

It is obvious from reading 1 Samuel 16 that David was not the first choice to be king. As a matter of fact, he was the last choice in the minds of his brothers. They must have thought, "Anybody but *him*."

It's called the "lead dog" principle. You know the old saying—it may be humorous but it's true: "If you're not the lead dog, the view never changes." "They" can always do a better job, so they are always heaping criticism on you. It's always something. You're too young or too old, or you don't have enough education because you haven't been on the job long enough. The list is endless! You name it, and the critics will come up with something to say.

The best way to avoid criticism is to isolate yourself and do nothing, say nothing, and be nothing! Then someone will come along and criticize you for wasting your talent! The greatest men and women of the Bible and in human history were criticized, so you are in good company if you too have your critics.

It is obvious to me that Eliab was so jealous of David's courage that he fell into the trap of criticizing what he didn't understand. At the heart of his criticism were three accusations.

First, he accused David of *pride*. "I know how conceited you are and how wicked your heart is" (1 Sam. 17:28). Eliab developed X-ray vision and looked into David's heart. It is not unusual for a critic to impugn your motives.

Second, he accused David of *neglect*. "And with whom did you leave those few sheep in the wilderness?" (v. 28). Eliab was basically saying, "You should be a good little boy and go back and take care of the sheep; you have no business here."

Third, he accused David of a *wicked curiosity*. "You came down only to watch the battle" (v. 28). No matter what David said, it would be wrong. So David spoke what was in his heart: "Is there not a cause?" (v. 29, NKJV). David's heart was stirred, and bold courage began to bubble up out of his spirit. He knew that shrinking back and hiding from the enemy would only lead to humiliation, destruction, defeat, and enslavement.

Success is the best antidote for unwarranted and hateful criticism. The last time I checked, parades and celebrations are given only for heroes, not critics!

Key #3: He celebrated past victories.

When David told the king that he would be the one to face Goliath, I am not surprised at Saul's reaction. There was nothing about this shepherd boy to suggest he had the ability to bring down mighty Goliath. No doubt the army was filled with men who had been victorious in battle, and if the bravest of the brave were filled with fear, what made this mere kid think he could tackle this situation by himself? David, however, knew what God could do:

> But David said to Saul, "Your servant has been keeping his father's sheep. When a lion or a bear came and carried off a sheep from the flock, I went after it, struck it and rescued the sheep from its mouth. When it turned on me, I seized it by its hair, struck it and killed it. Your servant has killed both the lion and the bear; this uncircumcised Philistine will be like one of them, because he has defied the armies of the living God. The LORD who rescued me from the paw of the lion and the paw of the bear will rescue me from the hand of this Philistine. Saul said to David, "Go, and the Lord be with you."
>
> —1 SAMUEL 17:34–37

Don't ignore personal experiences with God. In verse 34 David answers the challenge by citing experiences with God against a lion and a bear. Verse 37 sums it up as far as David is concerned: "I've seen the faithfulness of God. The same God who delivered me from them is upon me to deliver me now." Too often we remember what we should forget and forget what we should remember.

The next time Goliath shows up and knocks on your door, remember that you are not alone. It's encouraging to remember those times in the past when God came through for us. I am convinced we don't celebrate enough past victories. The reason is simple: when a new challenge shows up, instead of being filled with faith we are filled with fear. The example of Saul's army is not one we should emulate. Instead, look to the shepherd boy who was not intimidated but celebrated the power and strength God would give him!

Giants come in many forms. It may be a Goliath, a mountain, or a storm. It really doesn't matter the shape or size—if it instills fear and we are paralyzed, then it qualifies as an obstacle to our destiny.

Jesus said that we should have peace, not fear, when faced with difficulty. When you walk away from the doctor's office after receiving a bad report, or when you stand beside the bed of a loved one who doesn't have long to live, remember these words of Jesus: "Be of good cheer, I have overcome the world" (John 16:33, NKJV).

Many people spend much of their lives dreading things that will never happen. Take Scottish philosopher and historian Thomas Carlyle, for example:

> In his house in Chelsea in London, they'll show you the sound-proof chamber which [Scottish-born historian Thomas] Carlyle had built in his house so that all the noise of the street would be shut out and he could do his work in unbroken silence. One of his neighbours, however, had a rooster that would crow loudly in the early morning. Carlyle protested to the owner of the rooster; but the man pointed out to him that the rooster crowed only once per day, and that could not be such a terrible annoyance. "But," Carlyle said to him, "if you only knew what I suffer waiting for that cock to crow!" In the same way, there are a lot of people like that who live their lives waiting for something disastrous and unpleasant to happen. And what's worse, these are people who in many cases never accomplish the tasks God has in store for them, because they're fearful of what might happen to them if they attempt such tasks.[3]

Key #4: He chose his weapons carefully.

Everything was in place. The two armies stared at each other from high atop the ridges. When word spread that young David would face Goliath, the army of Saul held its collective breath waiting for David to meet Goliath in a no-holds-barred, hand-to-hand fight to the death. If this had been a boxing match, I'm sure the betting line would have been that David would not last through the first minute of the first round. It was obvious to all that it was a mismatch—a fight that should never take place.

Use your imagination with me for a moment and picture this improbable scene as if it were a drama being played out on a stage.

Act I: David refuses Saul's armor.

Saul listens as David talks about the lion and the bear, and he makes a decision. He might say something like this: "Hey, kid, I've killed thousands of Philistines, I am a well-trained killing machine—hostile, mobile, and agile—so here, put on my armor." David could say, "Hey, King, if you're so tough, how come your armor is hanging in the tent?" That would be a legitimate question, but probably not something David would say. Saul should have been out front leading the army and, if necessary, taking on the giant himself. Instead he hid in fear like everyone else.

Of course David tries on the armor, and as you might suspect, it doesn't fit. Saul is a size forty-eight, and David is a size thirty. But Saul is the expert here. David suits up, only to discover he can hardly walk. So David does what he has to do—even though it's not easy. David loves Saul. He admires Saul. He serves Saul. Saul is splendid and powerful. Saul loves him and is doing his best to help him. Despite that, David takes off the helmet, unbelts the sword, and removes the armor.

It could not have been easy for David to walk away from all that loving expertise Saul offered him. But David knows that to go meet Goliath wearing Saul's armor would be a disaster; Goliath would kill him. David needs to fight the battle using what he knows—the weapon of the shepherd. If he gets close enough to Goliath to need armor, he's already lost. It's game over.

The lesson for us is obvious—you can't walk in someone else's anointing. David was walking in something greater than physical armor, and so are we:

> Put on the full armor of God, so that you can take your stand against the devil's schemes. For our struggle is not against flesh and blood, but against the rulers, against the authorities, against the powers of this dark world and against the spiritual forces of evil in the heavenly realms. Therefore put on the full armor of God, so that when the day of evil comes, you may be able to stand your ground, and after you have done everything, to stand.
>
> —EPHESIANS 6:11–13

God will never allow a situation to occur without giving you the proper equipment to meet the challenge head-on. You may not take on the challenge as I would, and you may not feel that you are as qualified as someone else, but God will "suit you up" to take on your giant. The size of your anointing will always equal the size of your giant!

The response of David to King Saul, his brothers, and even Goliath demonstrated his supreme confidence. His confidence was not in his knowledge of the slingshot but in God's anointing on his life.

You may be in the fight of your life today; but remember, when it comes to the anointing, one size does not fit all. Many times we exhaust all of our resources to find answers to deal with our giants. We go to family, friends, books, and anything else we can get our hands on to find solutions. There is nothing wrong with getting wise counsel, but when it comes to facing Goliath we need more than counsel. We need a powerful anointing.

When the pressure of circumstances is great on the outside, the Holy Spirit will give equal pressure on the inside so that there will be no cracks or crack-ups. We can trust that regardless of what happens, the Holy Spirit is there to provide everything we need.

Act II: David slings his way to victory!

Much has been made of the five smooth stones in David's pouch. While I agree that the stones represent a prophetic picture of great significance, I believe it's of equal importance to focus on the sling. Not much has been said about the sling.

David faced Goliath in his own way, on his own terms. He refused to listen to his critics, wear Saul's armor, or employ traditional combat techniques. Also, as a "slinger," though he wasn't military trained, David possessed a deadly skill:

> Ancient armies had three kinds of warriors. The first was cavalry—armed men on horseback or in chariots. The second was infantry—foot soldiers wearing armor and carrying swords and shields. The third were projectile warriors, or what today would be called artillery: archers and, most important, slingers...Slinging took an extraordinary amount of skill and practice. But in experienced hands, the sling was a devastating weapon. Paintings from medieval times show slingers hitting birds in midflight...In the Old Testament Book of Judges, slingers are described as being accurate within a "hair's breadth." An experienced slinger could kill or seriously injure a target at a distance of up to two hundred yards. The Romans even had a special set of tongs made just to remove stones that had been embedded in some poor soldier's body by a sling. Imagine standing in front of a Major League Baseball pitcher as he aims a baseball at your head. That's what facing a slinger was like.[4]

Act III: David reaps the rewards of courage.

The biggest giants produce the greatest results and rewards. As we move toward our assignment, there will be giants blocking the road ahead. Each new level will produce an even bigger enemy. It's obvious that David was "training for reigning," and the next step was to take on Goliath. The sooner we learn that we have an enemy blocking our way the better off we will be. Whatever is sent to destroy you will actually become a footstool to promote you, as was the case with David:

> David asked the men standing near him, "What will be done for the man who kills this Philistine and removes this disgrace from Israel? Who is this uncircumcised Philistine that he should defy the armies of the living God?" They repeated to him what they had been saying and told him, "This is what will be done for the man who kills him."
>
> —1 Samuel 17:26–27

First Samuel 17:25 tells us that after killing Goliath, David

- received great riches;
- married the king's daughter;
- moved into the king's house; and
- was given greater responsibility.

Even his father's house was declared to be tax-exempt! Yes, David received a reward. But for many believers that does not add up at all. The church has been pulled in opposite directions for centuries—on one side is the mind-set that to be totally spiritual is to be totally broke and to live in poverty; on the other side are the "name it and claim it" prosperity teachers who say that if you ever have a need then you're not right with God. As with all things, truth is found in the middle.

There is no advantage to being broke. Being penniless doesn't mean you're spiritual any more than having $10 million in the bank makes you closer to God. But many in the church would have you believe that if you have money you're automatically evil. Remember this—it is not what you have that makes you evil; it is what you love that makes you evil.

The Bible does not say that having money is evil. Instead, it says that loving money is evil: "For the love of money is the root of all evil" (1 Tim. 6:10, KJV). You see, anything we love more than God becomes sin, regardless of what or whom it may be.

In Mark 10 we find the story of the rich young ruler. He came to Jesus telling him of all the things he had done to please God. He then asked, "What else should I do?" Jesus plainly told him to sell everything he had and give it away to the poor. After hearing what Jesus said, the young man became sorrowful and realized that he loved money more than he loved God. The Bible says that he walked away sad, leaving the master behind.

The disciples who were observing this conversation must have been puzzled by the outcome. Jesus looked at them and said that it was easier for a camel to go through the eye of the needle than for a rich person to enter the kingdom of God. Jesus identified the one thing in this young man's life that he loved more than God. In order to help this young person see that God was not really first in his life, Jesus put his finger on the very thing that was stopping him: his possessions.

Many Christians have misinterpreted the meaning of Jesus's statement, thinking that it is impossible to be a Christian and have wealth at the same time. Jesus did not say it was impossible for a rich person to be saved; only that it is more difficult. When a person has great riches and does not know Christ, he has a tendency to become dependent on his financial standing and the lifestyle that his wealth provides. In order for him to accept Christ, he has to make Him first in his life—even before his financial portfolio.

If Christ is first in your life and you have a generous heart, I believe that God wants you to become a conduit of His blessing. He wants you to be rich, according to 2 Corinthians 9:11. God is looking for generous people!

There is more to this story than David asking about the reward for killing Goliath. Obviously David wanted to know what he would gain from taking on such a huge assignment. David had developed the heart of a servant, tending his father's sheep and doing the necessary things in obedience to his father. Guarding sheep and living at home seemed like an unlikely place for a king. Yet all God's great people, including David, were faithful in small things.

The fear of the impossible has stopped many of God's people from moving to the next level of anointing. Many times the impossible is simply the untried. Don't let fear keep you from growing wherever you're planted.

American moral and social philosopher Eric Hoffer said: "The fear of becoming a 'has-been' keeps some people from becoming anything."[5]

Yes, there are giants in the land. At some point we, like the army of Israel, will face one. They may not all be over nine feet tall, but trust me, when you're facing one it may appear to be.

Enemy after enemy confronts us as we walk through life. Sometimes these enemies are defiant and frightening, and we feel overpowered and overwhelmed. These enemies may be people who ridicule, mock, oppose, bypass, ignore, abuse, assault, curse, lie, or steal. The enemies might include circumstances that create all kinds of trials, temptations, accidents, disease, financial difficulty, depression, discouragement, purposelessness, or death of a loved one. None look alike, yet all produce the same result: fear!

The bottom line is that any circumstance, person, or thing that stands in your way to prevent you from completing your assignment becomes your giant.

SPEAK AND DECLARE YOUR INTENTIONS!

David spoke to the giant and declared his intentions. He didn't run around camp asking everybody what they thought about Goliath and getting their opinions on how he should handle the situation. We spend more time talking about our problems than doing anything about them. We call our friends, talk about our problems at church, and complain to our neighbors and anybody else who will listen. We do everything except what we're supposed to do as Spirit-filled believers: *Speak to your giant (mountain), not just about it.*

> "Have faith in God," Jesus answered. "Truly I tell you, if anyone
> says to this mountain, 'Go, throw yourself into the sea,' and does
> not doubt in their heart but believes that what they say will happen,
> it will be done for them. Therefore I tell you, whatever you ask for
> in prayer, believe that you have received it, and it will be yours."
> —MARK 11:22–24

David spoke his future and saw victory before it ever happened. David knew the battle belonged to the Lord and that it was He who would give him the victory. *There is power in the spoken word!* Faith will help you face the last days without fear.

CHAPTER 17

UNTIL THEN

A certain nobleman went into a far country to receive for himself a kingdom, and to return. And he called his ten servants, and delivered them ten pounds, and said unto them, Occupy till I come.

—LUKE 19:13, KJV

T HE WORD OCCUPY used in Luke 19:13 means, "to engage the attention or energies of…to take or fill…to take or hold possession or control of…to reside in as an owner or a tenant."[1]

Taking all the definitions together, what Jesus was really saying was, "Do business till I come!" For too long the church has used the word *occupy* to mean "sit down and do nothing." It's called a "hold the fort" mentality—hiding behind the four walls of the church on Sunday morning and hoping against hope that Satan will not pay any attention. As long as we can sing our praise songs, hear a little sermon, and go home, everything is fine with the world. That is totally opposite from what God told the children of Israel about their Promised Land and what we are to do to live in the land of our promises.

THERE IS A PARALLEL BETWEEN THE TWO

See, I have given you this land. Go in and take possession of the land the LORD swore he would give to your fathers—to Abraham, Isaac and Jacob—and to their descendants after them.

—DEUTERONOMY 1:8

Destroy completely all the places on the high mountains, on the hills and under every spreading tree, where the nations you are dispossessing worship their gods.

—DEUTERONOMY 12:2

In order to possess something you have to dispossess what is already there. The Hebrew word for dispossess is *yaresh*, which means, "by implication, to seize, to rob, to inherit; also to expel, to impoverish, to ruin." You see, to enjoy the abundance and prosperity that God wants you to have, you must understand that you have an enemy who wants to keep you from your promised land. He is telling us, "Take what I have given you to enjoy!" just as He told Joshua, "Now you are the leader; *go* and take the land":

> After the death of Moses the servant of the LORD, the LORD said to Joshua son of Nun, Moses' aide: "Moses my servant is dead. Now then, you and all these people, get ready to cross the Jordan River into the land I am about to give to them—to the Israelites. I will give you every place where you set your foot, as I promised Moses. Your territory will extend from the desert to Lebanon, and from the great river, the Euphrates—all the Hittite country—to the Mediterranean Sea in the west. No one will be able to stand against you all the days of your life. As I was with Moses, so I will be with you; I will never leave you nor forsake you. Be strong and courageous, because you will lead these people to inherit the land I swore to their ancestors.
>
> —JOSHUA 1:1–6

There came a time when Israel needed to possess their land of promise. Today we need to possess the land of our promises. We can't afford to keep getting together to talk about how great it is to be out of Egypt. We need to start looking for some walls to tear down!

You will never possess your promised land or receive the promises of God by just knowing about them. The children of Israel spied out the land and knew all about it. They looked it over and said, "It's great!" But they didn't possess it just by knowing about it. Some people know so much but are not doing anything with the knowledge they have. People think that if they keep studying or going to committee meetings, somehow the promised land will fall into their laps.

It is one thing to recognize that something belongs to you legally; it is another thing to enjoy it. For example, let's say you were rummaging through your attic one day and discovered a box that had been hidden away for many years. In that box was a letter addressed to you from a relative that used to own the house. You open the letter and read the note: "I am so happy you have finally found my note. You are my sole surviving relative, and I have a wonderful surprise for you. In the back-yard, in the very corner of the lot, by the old oak tree, I have buried a box. Start at the base of the tree, walk six paces north and start digging.

In that box is my inheritance to you. You will find $2 million in stocks and bonds. It's all yours! Your favorite uncle, Tim."

I think you would agree with me that in order to enjoy your inheritance you would have to take action. Having the letter in your possession does not mean you have the money in your bank account. Although it is legally yours, you still have to grab a shovel and start digging!

In order for the children of Israel to claim their inheritance, they not only had to realize the land was legally theirs, but they also had to do something about it. The Lord said to Joshua, "Every place on which the sole of your foot treads I have given to you" (Josh. 1:3). As soon as their feet touched the ground it became theirs.

As believers we have to do the same thing as they did. We have to believe that God has given us legal right to all the promises, and we have to act on those promises.

Did you know that more than forty times in the Book of Deuteronomy alone God commands Israel to "possess the land"? He is telling them over and over again that the land is already theirs for the taking, but they have to drive out the tenants and possess the land in their place. They will never enjoy the fruits of their Promised Land until they cross the Jordan River and take action. The word that God used to describe what they were to do was a military word. It was an action word.

DON'T DIG IN!

The church of Jesus Christ is supposed to be an advancing army, not a peacekeeping force. In today's world peacekeepers don't take territory; they are there to keep sides from killing each other. The objective of a peacekeeping force is to maintain the status quo. They define *peace* as the absence of conflict. An advancing army will fight to take territory, and fight to keep it!

Alan Axelrod writes in *Patton on Leadership* about US Army General George S. Patton:

> The Battle of the Bulge was the last major German offensive of World War II, and it caught the Allied forces off guard, completely surrounding the 101st Airborne and elements of other units. The allies had generally assumed that the Germans had been defeated, that the war was drawing to a close. Patton and others understood, however, that if the German all-or-nothing offensive succeeded, the war would be prolonged at a very great cost. Pushing back the

offensive and rescuing the surrounded 101st required immediate action, Patton believed, and he could not wait for ideal conditions. Leadership is often a matter of balancing timing against available resources. Opportunities are easily lost while waiting for "perfect" conditions.[2]

In military strategy one of the earmarks of victory is who claims the land after the battle is over. The American Civil War is a great example. Every Civil War historian will tell you that the military determined the winner of a particular battle based on which side had the land at the end of the day. More likely than not, the winner was whoever held the ground, not whoever had the fewest casualties. The North was determined to be the winner of the battle of Gettysburg in 1863 because after three days of fighting, the Southern army withdrew. Casualties were just about even for both sides, yet the North was declared victorious. Why? The North held the ground!

The reason the United States and her allies were victorious in World War II was because decisions were made and strategies given for the invasion of Europe that began on June 6, 1944. The invasion of Normandy is one of the greatest examples of what an invasion force looks like. Before the allies could ever totally occupy, they had to land on the beach and move inland, and not stop until they achieved victory. The church today is still on the beach, afraid to move!

What we need today is a strategy to help the church live in the land of our promises and walk in abundance. God is raising up spiritual strategists (apostles and prophets) who will take biblical insight and outline the road to victory.

Let's look back in the Book of Joshua and discern certain principles that apply today. There is a very simple parallel between what happened to the children of Israel under the leadership of Joshua and the New Testament principle of walking in the new covenant established by Jesus. In the old covenant it was the Promised Land; in the new covenant it is a magnificent "land of promises."

SEVEN STEPS TO VICTORY

1. Action: They crossed over.

So when the people broke camp to cross the Jordan, the priests carrying the ark of the covenant went ahead of them. Now the

Jordan is at flood stage all during harvest. Yet as soon as the priests who carried the ark reached the Jordan and their feet touched the water's edge, the water from upstream stopped flowing. It piled up in a heap a great distance away, at a town called Adam in the vicinity of Zarethan, while the water flowing down to the Sea of the Arabah (that is, the Dead Sea) was completely cut off. So the people crossed over opposite Jericho. The priests who carried the ark of the covenant of the LORD stopped in the middle of the Jordan and stood on dry ground, while all Israel passed by until the whole nation had completed the crossing on dry ground.

—JOSHUA 3:14–17

The children of Israel did not look at the circumstances but focused on the promise. Even though they had stopped short forty years before, this time they determined to possess their promises.

At the Red Sea they had "crossed over"—which is a picture of salvation. Now they were about to cross the Jordan River on dry ground, a picture of the baptism of the Spirit. Crossing the Jordan River at flood stage was nothing short of a miracle and a release of the power of God.

Now the Jordan is at flood stage all during harvest. Yet as soon as the priests who carried the ark reached the Jordan and their feet touched the water's edge, the water from upstream stopped flowing.

—JOSHUA 3:15–16

It took many miracles just to get them to this place. God took care of the Israelites in the wilderness in spite of their unbelief. They went in circles for forty years. When they finally arrived at the point when it was time to cross over and claim their inheritance, the Jordan River was at flood stage! They must have thought, "You have to be kidding. The river is flooded. Anybody notice that?" It was as if God was playing some kind of cruel joke on them.

Have you ever thought that you were so close to the fulfillment of your dreams and vision, and then all of a sudden a roadblock (a flooded Jordan River) stood in your way? One thing I have learned about the Lord is this: He loves us too much to let us go straight through to our promised land.

If there were no obstacles to overcome, there would be no development of our character. The process is very important to God. There are many believers who think that if you face pressure, trials, or obstacles, you are not right with God. Disappointment is the major roadblock to the promised land. You will soon find out what people are made of when they get to the edge of the promised land, the land of fulfillment, and things don't go according to their plan.

> Answer me when I call to you, my righteous God. Give me relief from my distress; have mercy on me and hear my prayer.
>
> —PSALM 4:1

> Remember how the LORD your God led you all the way in the wilderness these forty years, to humble and test you in order to know what was in your heart, whether or not you would keep his commands. He humbled you, causing you to hunger and then feeding you with manna, which neither you nor your ancestors had known, to teach you that man does not live on bread alone but on every word that comes from the mouth of the LORD. Your clothes did not wear out and your feet did not swell during these forty years. Know then in your heart that as a man disciplines his son, so the LORD your God disciplines you.
>
> —DEUTERONOMY 8:2–5

Instead of focusing on the flood, focus on the harvest! Lift up your eyes beyond the flood (obstacles) and see a bountiful harvest of abundance that God has prepared. If you wait for the water to go down, your harvest will rot on the vine. Whatever you focus on will become the driving force of your life. Focus is the key to success or failure. Whatever you spend your time thinking about you will spend your time doing.

In order to possess our possessions, we must walk in the baptism of the power of God. It's not enough to know that our sins are forgiven (leaving Egypt); we must also be endued with power to accomplish what only God can accomplish through us. Acts 1:8 is very clear: "But you will receive power when the Holy Spirit comes on you; and you will be my witnesses in Jerusalem, and in all Judea and Samaria, and to the ends of the earth."

2. Legacy: They left a sign.

> Go over before the ark of the LORD your God into the middle of the Jordan. Each of you is to take up a stone on his shoulder, according to the number of the tribes of the Israelites, to serve as a sign among you. In the future, when your children ask you, "What

do these stones mean?" tell them that the flow of the Jordan was cut off before the ark of the covenant of the LORD. When it crossed the Jordan, the waters of the Jordan were cut off. These stones are to be a memorial to the people of Israel forever.
—JOSHUA 4:5–7

Twelve stones were placed in the dry riverbed as a testimony to God's awesome power and a sign for future generations. It is significant to note the number twelve:

+ Twelve is the signature of the nation of Israel.

+ There were twelve tribes of Israel.

+ Twelve spies were sent in to spy out Canaan.

+ Jesus visited the temple at twelve years of age.

+ Jesus chose twelve disciples.

+ There are twelve gates in New Jerusalem, twelve angels at the gates, and twelve foundations with the names of the twelve apostles.

What is this saying? When the Israelites crossed over the flooded Jordan, God's rulership and government was established in the Promised Land. Twelve is the number of government. Even though the vision was released to the children of Israel, government and order had to be established. So the twelve stones were not only a memorial but also a "sign" that God was in charge.

Vision brings order out of chaos. Proverbs 29:18 says, "Where there is no revelation, people cast off restraint; but blessed is the one who heeds wisdom's instruction."

God's government does not bring restriction but freedom. To "cast off restraint" is a picture of a horse spitting the bit out of its mouth. That is the literal meaning of the Hebrew phrase. This tells me that when there is no God-given revelation the people will "spit the bit" of God's order.

3. Courage: They faced their enemies.

Now when all the Amorite kings west of the Jordan and all the Canaanite kings along the coast heard how the LORD had dried up the Jordan before the Israelites until they had crossed over, their

hearts melted in fear and they no longer had the courage to face
the Israelites.

—JOSHUA 5:1

Once the decision was made to cross over and proper order was established, the enemy heard and was afraid. When a blessed people come
into a territory, a region, or a culture walking in proper order and the
power of God, the enemy knows he is defeated!

The melting of the hearts of the enemies had already begun. In
Joshua 2 the enemy was already confessing defeat:

> I know that the LORD has given you this land and that a great
> fear of you has fallen on us, so that all who live in this country are
> melting in fear because of you. We have heard how the LORD dried
> up the water of the Red Sea for you when you came out of Egypt,
> and what you did to Sihon and Og, the two kings of the Amorites
> east of the Jordan, whom you completely destroyed.
>
> —JOSHUA 2:9–10

In the natural world it is said that when an animal such as a bear or
lion smells fear, it attacks. The same is true in the spiritual world. God
is raising up an army of "no names" who do not have the smell of fear but
walk in the power of God. The greatest untapped power source in the
universe is God's covenant people walking in abundance and power—
understanding that it is not the powerful or persuasive but common
people such as you and me taking back everything the enemy has stolen.
The enemy is a thief and a robber, and until we realize we don't have to
take it anymore, he will continue to destroy lives.

4. Commitment: The covenant of circumcision restored.

> All the people that came out had been circumcised, but all the
> people born in the wilderness during the journey from Egypt
> had not. The Israelites had moved about in the wilderness forty
> years until all the men who were of military age when they left
> Egypt had died, since they had not obeyed the LORD. For the
> LORD had sworn to them that they would not see the land he
> had solemnly promised their ancestors to give us, a land flowing
> with milk and honey.
>
> —JOSHUA 5:5–6

Circumcision was a seal of the covenant God established with Abraham.

> Then he gave Abraham the covenant of circumcision. And Abraham became the father of Isaac and circumcised him eight days after his birth. Later Isaac became the father of Jacob, and Jacob became the father of the twelve patriarchs.
>
> —Acts 7:8

The administration of this covenant involved three things:

1. The cutting of the flesh, involving shedding of blood (Gen. 17:9–11).

2. The invocation of the name of the child (Gen. 21:4; Luke 1:59).

3. The circumcision took place on the eighth day (Gen. 17:12).

The covenant of circumcision is significant in that only by obedience to the commandment could any of Abraham's seed begin covenantal relationship with God. This entitled them to the promises, privileges, and blessings of the covenant. To reject or neglect this sign of the covenant would break the covenant and mean being cut off from its benefits. (See Genesis 17:14.) Circumcision was the outward evidence of their inward commitment to the terms of the covenant.

How does this apply to us today? The spiritual implications are many.

> Then the LORD said to Joshua, "Today I have rolled away the reproach of Egypt from you." So the place has been called Gilgal to this day.
>
> —Joshua 5:9

Moses and the prophets used the term circumcise as a symbol of purity of heart and a readiness to hear and obey.

> Which made me hostile toward them so that I sent them into the land of their enemies—then when their uncircumcised hearts are humbled and they pay for their sin, I will remember my covenant with Jacob and my covenant with Isaac and my covenant with Abraham, and I will remember the land.
>
> —Leviticus 26:41–42

*Jeremiah characterized rebellious Israel as having "uncircumcised"
ears and an "uncircumcised" heart.*

> To whom shall I speak and give warning, that they may hear?
> Indeed their ear is uncircumcised, and they cannot give heed.
> Behold, the word of the LORD is a reproach to them; they have no
> delight in it.
>   —JEREMIAH 6:10, NKJV

> Egypt, Judah, Edom, the people of Ammon, Moab, and all who are
> in the farthest corners, who dwell in the wilderness. For all these
> nations are uncircumcised, and all the house of Israel are uncir-
> cumcised in the heart.
>   —JEREMIAH 9:26, NKJV

Fast-forward...because the people did not understand the spiritual
meaning of circumcision, a huge controversy erupted in the early church
between the Jewish believers and the Gentile believers (Acts 15:1–2).
Abraham was saved by faith, not by circumcision. Circumcision is of no
value if not accompanied by obedience.

> Circumcision has value if you observe the law, but if you break the
> law, you have become as though you had not been circumcised. So
> then, if those who are not circumcised keep the law's requirements,
> will they not be regarded as though they were circumcised?
>   —ROMANS 2:25–26, NKJV

We must have circumcision of our hearts to deal with our flesh
(Col. 2:11–15). And in order to hear and receive revelation from God we
need circumcision of our hearing (Heb. 5:11–14).

5. Intimacy: Passover was reestablished.

> On the evening of the fourteenth day of the month, while camped
> at Gilgal on the plains of Jericho, the Israelites celebrated the
> Passover.
>   —JOSHUA 5:10

As Passover was renewed there was a renewal of intimacy with God.
It served as a reminder of what God did when He brought them out of
Egypt. They would get a picture of what David would eventually write in
Psalm 23:5: "You prepare a table before me in the presence of my enemies.
You anoint my head with oil; my cup overflows."

What was natural to them becomes spiritual to us. The Apostle Paul wrote to the church at Corinth: "Get rid of the old yeast, so that you may be a new unleavened batch—as you really are. For Christ, our Passover lamb has been sacrificed. Therefore let us keep the Festival, not with the old bread leavened with malice and wickedness, but with the unleavened bread of sincerity and truth" (1 Cor. 5:7–8).

One of the most amazing illustrations of this truth is found in the conversation Jesus had with the Emmaus disciples in Luke 24. The two disciples in this story are much like the modern church. We find "itching ears," but what we need are "burning hearts." Instead of having a church of "Amens" we have the church of the "So what?"

> He asked them, "What are you discussing together as you walk along?" They stood still, their faces downcast. One of them, named Cleopas, asked him, "Are you the only one visiting Jerusalem who does not know the things that have happened there in these days?" "What things?" he asked. "About Jesus of Nazareth," they replied. "He was a prophet, powerful in word and deed before God and all the people. The chief priests and our rulers handed him over to be sentenced to death, and they crucified him; but we had hoped that he was the one who was going to redeem Israel. And what is more, it is the third day since all this took place."
>
> —Luke 24:17–21

These disciples had lost their hope because they did not realize the reality of the Resurrection. Look at what they had:

+ Facts but no fire
+ Head knowledge but no heart knowledge
+ More questions than answers
+ Theology but no doxology

They knew some things about Jesus. They acknowledged that He was a prophet—which is a good start, but there is obviously so much more. A church with no intimacy with Him will end up like these two disciples—hopeless and sad.

The Apostle Paul said it best in Philippians 3:10: "I want to know Christ—yes, to know the power of his resurrection and participation in his sufferings, becoming like him in his death."

When we get that close to Jesus, we will know His heart. Knowing His heart will drive away sadness, depression, and hopelessness. Many believers are like a car with no gas in the tank. It looks good on the outside, but it can't go anywhere.

The good news of this account is that they didn't stop; they pursued Christ. They "constrained Him," which literally means they pulled on Him so He would stay with them. He stopped at their house, and the guest became the host. In the breaking of bread, which is a picture of intimacy, these two disciples are infected with holy heartburn.

> As they approached the village to which they were going, Jesus continued on as if he were going farther. But they urged him strongly, "Stay with us, for it is nearly evening; the day is almost over." So he went in to stay with them. When he was at the table with them, he took bread, gave thanks, broke it and began to give it to them. Then their eyes were opened and they recognized him, and he disappeared from their sight. They asked each other, "Were not our hearts burning within us while he talked with us on the road and opened the Scriptures to us?" They got up and returned at once to Jerusalem. There they found the Eleven and those with them, assembled together and saying, "It is true! The Lord has risen and has appeared to Simon." Then the two told what had happened on the way, and how Jesus was recognized by them when he broke the bread.
>
> —LUKE 24:28–35

The word *opened* in verse 32 is the key. The same word is used again in verse 45: "Then He opened [*dianoigo*] their minds so they could understand the Scriptures."

> The term "opened" in Luke 24:32 means to open the sense or significance of a thing, hence, to explain, expound, or interpret.[3] It is derived from the Greek term *dianoigo* (dee-an-oy'-go), figuratively, to make understanding possible.[4]

The verb *open* appears 106 times in various forms in the New Testament. The specific word translated here is *dianoigo* and is used only seven times. It means to "open thoroughly," as the opening of the womb in giving birth. (See Luke 2:23.)

Something happened to these two disciples that changed them forever. According to Luke 24:16, their eyes were prevented from recognizing

Jesus. He revealed His identity only after taking great pains to explain to them "the things concerning Himself in all the Scriptures" (Luke 24:27, MEV).

> Luke concludes this story with another bit of irony. The disciples had been staring into the face of the risen Jesus, yet they were prevented from seeing Him until they buried their faulty expectations. Then, a careful review of the Scriptures gave them a divine perspective on what they once saw as dismal circumstances. Once their eyes were opened to the reality and implications of the resurrection, Jesus became visible to their physical eyes. The Greek phrase *ophthalmos dianoigo epiginosko*, translated "eyes were opened and they recognized Him," literally means "their eyes were completely opened" and "they came to fully comprehend Him." This action was more than a mere recognition of His features. They came to recognize Jesus in all His significance as the Messiah, the Son of God, and their risen Lord! Then Jesus literally became "invisible"— *aphantos*—meaning that He suddenly vanished from their midst once their eyes were open. Now, their new, resurrected hope carried them back to Jerusalem to bear the good news to others (24:33–35).[5]

There are many believers who are "filled with the Spirit" and still do not move in revelation knowledge. In order to have a burning heart and revelation knowledge, we must be willing to totally surrender to Him, much like the disciples did in Luke 24. The Old Testament picture of total surrender is seen when a slave voluntarily became a permanent "bond slave" to his master. (See Exodus 21:1–6.)

When God opens your spiritual hearing as He did with the disciples on the Emmaus road, your heart will begin to burn within you as the Spirit opens the Scripture. You will not just have a case of holy heartburn—it will translate to your feet as well, much like it did for those disciples who ran approximately eleven miles back to the other disciples to tell them that Jesus was alive!

6. Interdependence: They ate the firstfruits of the land.

> The manna stopped the day after they ate this food from the land; there was no longer any manna for the Israelites, but that year they ate the produce of Canaan.
>
> —JOSHUA 5:12

After the Israelites entered the land, they ate the produce of the land and the manna stopped. Manna was only temporary. It was never intended to be permanent.

The Hebrew word for *manna* literally means, "What is this?" It was wilderness food. The manna started in Exodus 16, and it didn't take long for the children of Israel to forget the bitterness and hardship of Egypt and complain about this miracle of creation that God used to sustain them:

> The rabble with them began to crave other food, and again the Israelites started wailing and said, "If only we had meat to eat! We remember the fish we ate in Egypt at no cost—also the cucumbers, melons, leeks, onions and garlic. But now we have lost our appetite; we never see anything but this manna!"
> —NUMBERS 11:4–6

God gave them bread from heaven, a type of both the written Word and the living Word. Manna is a type of the ABCs of the Word—a picture of milk, not meat. A baby can handle milk for only so long before it has to progress to something more substantial. The same is true with us. We start out as babies requiring the milk of the Word, but we must progress to the meat of the Word in order to move in the revelation that God wants to impart to us so we can occupy the land of promises. It is imperative to move from "faith to faith" and "glory to glory."

> Jesus said to them, "Very truly I tell you, it is not Moses who has given you the bread from heaven, but it is my Father who gives you the true bread from heaven. For the bread of God is the bread that comes down from heaven and gives life to the world." "Sir," they said, "always give us this bread." Then Jesus declared, "I am the bread of life. Whoever comes to me will never go hungry, and whoever believes in me will never be thirsty."
> —JOHN 6:32–35

7. Strategy: Occupation revelation is now given.

> Now when Joshua was near Jericho, he looked up and saw a man standing in front of him with a drawn sword in his hand. Joshua went up to him and asked, "Are you for us or for our enemies?" "Neither," he replied, "but as commander of the army of the LORD I have now come." Then Joshua fell facedown to the ground in reverence, and

asked him, "What message does my Lord have for his servant?" The commander of the Lord's army replied, "Take off your sandals, for the place where you are standing is holy." And Joshua did so.

—JOSHUA 5:13–15

Now that proper order had been restored, it was time for the Israelites to face their first test. Standing before them was the city of Jericho, immovable and impenetrable. As the commander-in-chief of the army, Joshua needed more than a plan; he needed revelation to take the city.

Old strategies and well-worn vision will not suffice to take the next level of occupation! Joshua needed imparted vision:

> Now the gates of Jericho were securely barred because of the Israelites. No one went out and no one came in. Then the LORD said to Joshua, "See, I have delivered Jericho into your hands, along with its king and its fighting men. March around the city once with all the armed men. Do this for six days. Have seven priests carry trumpets of rams' horns in front of the ark. On the seventh day, march around the city seven times, with the priests blowing the trumpets. When you hear them sound a long blast on the trumpets, have the whole army give a loud shout; then the wall of the city will collapse and the army will go up, everyone straight in."
>
> —JOSHUA 6:1–5

More than anything else, Joshua needed a God-given vision to take on such a difficult task. As he stood before Jericho, the walls were just as impregnable as they had always been! God was imparting something to Joshua. It was a vision of the future—his future.

George Barna, in his excellent book *The Power of Vision*, gives one of the best definitions of vision I have found. He says, "Vision...is a clear mental image of a preferable future imparted by God to His chosen servants and is based upon an accurate understanding of God, self and circumstances."[6]

What mental image do you have of your destiny? If it is an image conjured by wishes and hopes, tremendous frustration will follow. If, however, it is an image of the will of God, it cannot fail. Since time isn't an issue with God, He is able to say to us, "See [present tense!] I have given [completed action] Jericho *into your hand*." (See Joshua 6:2.)

Of course the desired result was, "The wall of the city will fall down flat!" Joshua couldn't do it by his own schemes, designs, or plans. It had to come from God. Real vision always produces desired results. The hard part is giving up our good ideas for God's ideas. Someone said it well: "The worst enemy of that which is best is that which is good." If we are to see a preferable future, we must be willing to set aside all the things that interfere with God's best plan, even though some of those things may be very good. God has not called any of us to omnipotence—that is His area.

Traditionally leaders, especially church leaders, have been expected to be all things to all people. Thousands of men and women leave ministry positions each year, toasted to a crisp by the expectations of those around them. We need to be focused (not narrow-minded) on our vision, enabled by our gifting, in order to conquer our foes and see the walls of our opposition fall down flat!

Joshua had been walking around those walls, no doubt trying to find some way for this thing to happen. It was not until God showed up that Joshua could accomplish what God had told him to do earlier. (See Joshua 1.) As you read this, you quite possibly may be thinking, "I've seen the thing that God has shown me. I've sold out to the plan. I'm ready to accomplish what God has revealed, but I don't have a clue how to do it!" Be assured, fellow leader, that God has a plan, and you shall soon know it. The vision of God to the people of God of the plan of God is always accompanied by the power of God.

Joshua will also learn that God didn't come to take sides but to take over. There is only one way God operates in our destiny: God in charge. His way. Without limitation. Sorry, but God is not anyone's copilot. He is not a partner, and He is not a consultant. When God came to Joshua, He came as the unquestioned supreme commander. True understanding of God is based upon the realization that He hardly ever moves as we want or expect Him to move! Are we willing to accept Him on His terms?

What a relief it was when Joshua realized that taking Jericho was not his responsibility but God's! We can almost feel the emotion in Joshua's response. Falling down before the presence of the Lord can be as much a sign of relief as worship! Have you ever been in that place where, if God didn't show up, all would be lost? Everything that we can do has been done, and victory is still far away. Certainly Joshua was worshipping. At the Word of God he removed his shoes. His first words to the Lord, however, revealed his uppermost thoughts: "What saith my Lord?" (Josh. 5:14, KJV). God, in order to be God, will allow us to come to the end of ourselves and realize that we must have Him. Don't be guilty of the response of one church leader who, when told it was time to pray about a difficult situation, exclaimed, "Has it come to that?"

During this whole experience Joshua was having a major reality check. Can you imagine what it was like when he got back to camp and told them he had God's plan (vision) for taking the city?

They all knew this was an impossible situation: green troops, never really tested in battle, and a leader who was just as inexperienced as they were. Joshua came back, called everyone together, and declared: "I have a vision from God! Here is what we are going to do. We will march around the city once a day for six days, and seven times on the seventh day, shout real loud, blow some trumpets, and the walls will fall down. And, by the way, we're going to let the praise team lead the way." By this time they were beginning to form a pulpit search committee; the pastor had lost his mind! Joshua discovered that when God reveals occupation strategy, it may not look like anything anyone has seen before. No matter what the plan sounded like or looked like, when Joshua and the people obeyed the revealed strategy, the walls of the city collapsed and total victory was given!

To occupy our land of promises is going to take a different spirit and mentality from what we see in the church today. We must start by knowing what we want.

The blind man in Mark 10 knew what he wanted.

Think of the blind man in Mark 10:47–52 who cried out, "Jesus, Son of David, have mercy on me!" He knew what he wanted. The religious crowd said to him, "Be quiet! Don't be so loud. You're embarrassing us. Can you be a little more respectable?" What do you think the blind man did? He got louder and cried out even more, "Jesus, Son of David, have mercy on me!"

When Jesus heard a man who knew what he wanted, He stopped and told people to bring the man to Him. When they brought the blind man to Jesus, He simply asked him, "What do you want?" The blind man said, "I want to see." How did Jesus respond to such a statement? Did He rebuke the man? No! He healed him.

Caleb knew what he wanted.

I pray the spirit of Caleb will invade the church. Here was a man who knew what he wanted. Numbers 13 tells us that after the men spied out the land, only Joshua and Caleb said, "Let us go up at once and take possession, for we are well able to overcome it" (Num. 13:30, NKJV). Caleb didn't want to talk about Egypt or the pillar of cloud and the pillar of fire. He didn't want to talk about manna or how difficult it might be to move forward. He wanted to possess the land! It was said of Caleb, according to Numbers 14:24, "But because my servant Caleb has a different spirit and follows me wholeheartedly, I will bring him into the land he went to, and his descendants will inherit it."

Caleb did not follow the crowd or do what was acceptable. He followed God fully. Because Joshua and Caleb were faithful, Caleb came to Joshua after the land was taken and said, "Now therefore give me this mountain" (Josh. 14:12, KJV). Caleb knew what he wanted, and Joshua blessed him and told him to go and get it.

God is asking us today, "What do you want?" Once you know what you want, go after it! Do not be paralyzed in these last days; occupy till He comes!

CHAPTER 18

FULLY PREPARED FOR THE LAST DAYS

*Knowing this first: that scoffers will come in the last
days, walking according to their own lusts.*

—2 PETER 3:3, NKJV

HERE AGAIN WE find the phrase "last days." Peter gives us a new sign for the end of the age. This sign fits our Western culture.

Notice that they are described as "scoffers." The Greek word here is *empaiktoi*. It comes from two words that mean "in making fun." It could be an ancient word from which we get *imposter*. The idea is of a teacher making fun of the Second Coming.

Mocking people who embrace the truth is the weapon being used by liberals. Left-wing entertainers and comedians mock all truth and those who hold to the truth. Also, these "scoffers" who make fun of God's truth about the last days model immoral lifestyles. This sign includes "walking after their own lusts." The word *walking* is *poreomai*, which means "to journey upward or to the top." These scoffers have a burning desire—a lust to get to the top in the world system.

Here are leaders who will laugh at and treat with sarcasm the things of the Spirit and of doctrine. They allow their human lusts for sex, for power, and for things to drive their lives!

Can you see that our Western culture mocks holy things? God-hating, mocking, immoral voices are heard across the vast spectrum of politics, business, and entertainment!

How do we meet this society saturated with blasphemy, sexual immorality, and unholy desires to be on top? With power!

THREE THINGS WE MUST NEVER FORGET

1. The prophetic word

> Beloved, I now write to you this second epistle (in both of which I stir up your pure minds by way of reminder), that you may be mindful of the words which were spoken before by the holy

prophets, and of the commandment of us, the apostles of the Lord and Savior, knowing this first: that scoffers will come in the last days, walking according to their own lusts, and saying, "Where is the promise of His coming? For since the fathers fell asleep, all things continue as they were from the beginning of creation."

—2 Peter 3:1–4, NKJV

Notice the words "stir up your pure minds." The word *to stir up* is to "stand up alert or wide awake." It means a mental awakening. The word *pure* comes from *eilikrinés*, which means "to be judged in the sunlight." This is where we get our English word *eye*. The idea is to see with clear judgment what God is saying out of the prophetic word to our day.

The word *reminding* is the Greek word *dianous*, which means "deep, clear thoughts and understanding." Our English word *diagnose* comes from a similar root. It is translated as "understanding."

Here we are told to take both the Old Testament and New Testament seriously so that we can "understand" what is happening. The same word translated "understanding" is found in Ephesians.

That the God of our Lord Jesus Christ, the Father of glory, may give to you the spirit of wisdom and revelation in the knowledge of Him, the eyes of your understanding being enlightened; that you may know what is the hope of His calling, what are the riches of the glory of His inheritance in the saints.

—Ephesians 1:17–18, NKJV

Here we are promised the gift of revelation knowledge and wisdom as we read Scripture. This wisdom will open our eyes to last-days truth.

2. The past judgments

Saying, "Where is the promise of His coming? For since the fathers fell asleep, all things continue as they were from the beginning of creation." For this they willfully forget: that by the word of God the heavens were of old, and the earth standing out of water and in the water, by which the world that then existed perished, being flooded with water. But the heavens and the earth which are now preserved by the same word, are reserved for fire until the day of judgment and perdition of ungodly men.

—2 Peter 3:4–7, NKJV

Here the scoffers make fun of last-days truth, even citing the Creation. Peter turns this upside down by pointing to the fact that we are on the second Earth!

He describes Genesis 1:1–2:

> In the beginning God created the heavens and the earth. The earth was without form, and void; and darkness was on the face of the deep. And the Spirit of God was hovering over the face of the waters.
>
> —NKJV

Here is that timeless netherworld that existed after a solar system catastrophe took place. According to Genesis and our text, the earth was bobbing like a cork in water! This conflagration caused a "world that then was" to perish. *Perish* is *appollumi*, from *apo* and *ole thros*. It means to utterly rain and destroy. *Apo* means "to cease" and *olethros* means "to die, destroy, ruin."

Our world has been judged completely once before, and as we shall observe later in this chapter, this second Earth will be destroyed as well. (The Flood of Noah did not destroy the solar system—we live on the same planet Noah lived on.) We catch glimpses of that world in Isaiah 14 and Ezekiel 28 and hints of it in unexplained archaeological findings. Take warning: this world will end!

3. The promises of God

> But, beloved, do not forget this one thing, that with the Lord one day is as a thousand years, and a thousand years as one day. The Lord is not slack concerning His promise, as some count slackness, but is longsuffering toward us, not willing that any should perish but that all should come to repentance.
>
> —2 PETER 3:8–9, NKJV

Notice that these promises are timeless. God is not restricted to our three dimensions, our twenty-four-hour clock, and our weekly or monthly calendar! His promises may seem slow sometimes, but they will certainly be fulfilled. His promises are also not delayed but will be fulfilled on time. These promises are saving to all who will repent.

TWO THINGS AHEAD IN THE FUTURE

> But the day of the Lord will come as a thief in the night, in which
> the heavens will pass away with a great noise, and the elements
> will melt with fervent heat; both the earth and the works that are
> in it will be burned up. Therefore, since all these things will be dis-
> solved, what manner of persons ought you to be in holy conduct
> and godliness, looking for and hastening the coming of the day
> of God, because of which the heavens will be dissolved, being on
> fire, and the elements will melt with fervent heat? Nevertheless we,
> according to His promise, look for new heavens and a new earth in
> which righteousness dwells.
>
> —2 PETER 3:10–13, NKJV

1. The coming of the Lord

The day of the Lord represents His return to judge a world that has
rejected His Son, His people, and His Word! All through Scripture the
day of the Lord for the unsaved is called the Great Tribulation, the Time
of Jacob's Trouble, and Great Day of His Wrath, among other names.
Seven years of sheer terror are coming on the earth.

Many of us believe that the Rapture of the church will occur before
that happens.

> For this we say to you by the word of the Lord, that we who are
> alive and remain until the coming of the Lord will by no means
> precede those who are asleep. For the Lord Himself will descend
> from heaven with a shout, with the voice of an archangel, and with
> the trumpet of God. And the dead in Christ will rise first. Then
> we who are alive and remain shall be caught up together with them
> in the clouds to meet the Lord in the air. And thus we shall always
> be with the Lord.
>
> —1 THESSALONIANS 4:15–17, NKJV

Seven years later the Lord will return with His mighty angels to exercise vengeance:

> Now, brethren, concerning the coming of our Lord Jesus Christ and
> our gathering together to Him, we ask you, not to be soon shaken in
> mind or troubled, either by spirit or by word or by letter, as if from
> us, as though the day of Christ had come. Let no one deceive you
> by any means; for that Day will not come unless the falling away

comes first, and the man of sin is revealed, the son of perdition, who opposes and exalts himself above all that is called God or that is worshiped, so that he sits as God in the temple of God, showing himself that he is God.

Do you not remember that when I was still with you I told you these things? And now you know what is restraining, that he may be revealed in his own time. For the mystery of lawlessness is already at work; only He who now restrains will do so until He is taken out of the way. And then the lawless one will be revealed, whom the Lord will consume with the breath of His mouth and destroy with the brightness of His coming. The coming of the lawless one is according to the working of Satan, with all power, signs, and lying wonders, and with all unrighteous deception among those who perish, because they did not receive the love of the truth, that they might be saved. And for this reason God will send them strong delusion, that they should believe the lie, that they all may be condemned who did not believe the truth but had pleasure in unrighteousness.

—2 THESSALONIANS 2:1–12

After we are gathered to Him in the Rapture, the Lord will come to judge the Antichrist and all lost sinners!

2. The new heaven and earth

Looking for and hastening the coming of the day of God, because of which the heavens will be dissolved, being on fire, and the elements will melt with fervent heat? Nevertheless we, according to His promise, look for new heavens and a new earth in which righteousness dwells.

—2 PETER 3:12–13, NKJV

After the judgments and the millennial reign of one thousand years, the great white throne judgment will occur.

Now when the thousand years have expired, Satan will be released from his prison.

—REVELATION 20:7, NKJV

Then I saw a great white throne and Him who sat on it, from whose face the earth and the heaven fled away. And there was found no place for them. And I saw the dead, small and great, standing before

God, and books were opened. And another book was opened, which
is the Book of Life. And the dead were judged according to their
works, by the things which were written in the books. The sea gave
up the dead who were in it, and Death and Hades delivered up the
dead who were in them. And they were judged, each one according
to his works. Then Death and Hades were cast into the lake of fire.
This is the second death. And anyone not found written in the Book
of Life was cast into the lake of fire.

—Revelation 20:11–15, nkjv

According to verse 11, our solar system will vanish! In its place will
come a new heaven and Earth.

Looking for and hastening the coming of the day of God, because
of which the heavens will be dissolved, being on fire, and the elements will melt with fervent heat? Nevertheless we, according to
His promise, look for new heavens and a new earth in which righteousness dwells.

—2 Peter 3:12–13, nkjv

Now I saw a new heaven and a new earth, for the first heaven and
the first earth had passed away. Also there was no more sea.

—Revelation 21:1, nkjv

The Response of Faith

Therefore, beloved, looking forward to these things, be diligent
to be found by Him in peace, without spot and blameless; and
consider that the longsuffering of our Lord is salvation—as also
our beloved brother Paul, according to the wisdom given to him,
has written to you, as also in all his epistles, speaking in them of
these things, in which are some things hard to understand, which
untaught and unstable people twist to their own destruction, as
they do also the rest of the Scriptures. You therefore, beloved,
since you know this beforehand, beware lest you also fall from your
own steadfastness, being led away with the error of the wicked;
but grow in the grace and knowledge of our Lord and Savior Jesus
Christ. To Him be the glory both now and forever. Amen.

—2 Peter 3:14–18, nkjv

Our response of faith to these certain events should be as follows:

Live in the reality of God's unchanging love

Notice the following:

+ "Beloved":

Beloved, I now write to you this second epistle (in both of which I stir up your pure minds by way of reminder).

—2 PETER 3:2, NKJV

+ "But, beloved":

But, beloved, do not forget this one thing, that with the Lord one day is as a thousand years, and a thousand years as one day.

—2 PETER 3:8, NKJV

+ "Therefore, beloved":

Therefore, beloved, looking forward to these things, be diligent to be found by Him in peace, without spot and blameless.

—2 PETER 3:14, NKJV

+ "You therefore, beloved":

You therefore, beloved, since you know this beforehand, beware lest you also fall from your own steadfastness, being led away with the error of the wicked.

—2 PETER 3:17

Agapetoi means "loved by God." In the middle of the fire and judgment is God's love, His long-suffering, and His desire for all to be saved!

Live with godly character a faithful life

Therefore, beloved, looking forward to these things, be diligent to be found by Him in peace, without spot and blameless.

—2 PETER 3:14, NKJV

Being diligent, blameless, and spotless produces peace!

Live close to the cross

And consider that the longsuffering of our Lord is salvation—as also our beloved brother Paul, according to the wisdom given to him, has written to you.

—2 PETER 3:15, NKJV

Embrace sound teaching

As also in all his epistles, speaking in them of these things, in which are some things hard to understand, which untaught and unstable people twist to their own destruction, as they do also the rest of the Scriptures. You therefore, beloved, since you know this beforehand, beware lest you also fall from your own steadfastness, being led away with the error of the wicked.

—2 PETER 3:16–17, NKJV

Pursue spiritual growth

But grow in the grace and knowledge of our Lord and Savior Jesus Christ.

—2 PETER 3:18, NKJV

Glorify God in worship

To Him be the glory both now and forever. Amen.

—2 PETER 3:18, NKJV

NOTES

INTRODUCTION
YES, THERE IS HOPE FOR THE LAST DAYS!

1. René Schlaepfer, "The Effect of Hope," http://www.hopeexperience.com /day26 (accessed May 18, 2015).

CHAPTER 2
MOVING AT THE SOUND

1. Charles Stanley, *How to Listen to God* (Nashville, TN: Thomas Nelson, 1985), 94.

2. Alan Axelrod, *Patton on Leadership* (Paramus, NJ: Prentice Hall Press, 1999), 228–229.

3. Larry Lea, *The Hearing Ear* (Altamonte Springs, FL: Creation House Publishing, 1988), 12.

4. "Inspirational Quotes on Prayer" Thoughts About God, http://www .thoughts-about-god.com/quotes/quotes-prayer.htm (accessed May 4, 2015).

5. Eugene Peterson, as quoted in Bob Lerod, "Happiness Is an Oily Beard," SermonCentral, http://www.sermoncentral.com/sermons/happiness-is-an-oily -beard-robert-leroe-sermon-on-unity-48129.asp (accessed May 4, 2015).

6. A. W. Tozer, *The Pursuit of God* (Ventura, CA: Regal Books from Gospel Light, 2013), 31.

7. As quoted in Lee McGlon, ed., *The Minister's Manual* (San Francisco, CA: Jossey-Bass, 2011), 397; Charles Schulz, *Celebrating Peanuts: 60 Years* (Kansas City, MO: Andrews McMeel Publishing, 2009), 144.

8. Sermonillustrations.com, "Obedience," http://www.sermonillustrations .com/a-z/o/obedience.htm (accessed May 4, 2015).

9. Taken from the United States Marines website, http://www.marines.com /global-impact/toward-chaos (accessed May 4, 2015).

CHAPTER 3
THE KEY OF SUPPORTING ISRAEL

1. Pat Robertson, "Why Evangelical Christians Support Israel," speech before the Herzliya Conference, Herzliya, Israel, December 17, 2003.

2. Religious News Service, "'Two-Covenant Theology' Wins Wide Acceptance," *The Bakersfield Californian*, October 12, 1990, http://www.eaec.org/dove /dove1990aw/two_covenant_theology.htm (accessed May 8, 2015).

3. Ibid.

4. Nahum N. Glatzer, *Franz Rosenzweig: His Life and Thought* (New York: Schocken Books, 1961), 162.

5. Joseph P. Gudel, "To the Jew First: A Biblical Analysis of the 'Two Covenant' Theory of Atonement," Christian Research Institute, March 30, 2009,

http://www.equip.org/article/to-the-jew-first-a-biblical-analysis-of-the-two
-covenant-theory-of-the-atonement/#christian-books-1 (accessed May 18, 2015);
Jakob J. Petuchowski, "The Christian-Jewish Dialog: A Jewish View," *Lutheran
World*, October 1963, 383.

6. Gudel, "To the Jew First: A Biblical Analysis of the 'Two Covenant'
Theory of Atonement"; Arthur Gilbert, "The Mission of the Jewish People in
History and in the Modern World," *Lutheran World*, July 1964, 308.

7. Kenneth A. Myers, "Do Jews Really Need Jesus?", *Christianity Today*,
August 1, 2002, http://www.christianitytoday.com/ct/2002/augustweb-only/8
-12-52.0.html?start=2 (accessed May 8, 2015).

8. Ibid.

9. Ibid.

10. Ibid.

11. Religious News Service, "'Two-Covenant Theology' Wins Wide Acceptance"; for more information about Moishe Rosen and Jews for Jesus, see http://
www.jewsforjesus.org/washington-dc.

12. Carl E. Braaten, as quoted in Pinchas Lapide, *The Resurrection of Jesus*
(Minneapolis, MN: Augsburg Publishing House, 1983), 19.

13. Gudel, "To the Jew First: A Biblical Analysis of the 'Two Covenant'
Theory of Atonement"; George Sheridan, as quoted in Mitch Glasser, "Critique of
the Two Covenant Theory," *Mishkan: A Theological Forum on Jewish Evangelism* 11
(1989): 2, 45.

14. Clarence H. Wagner Jr., "The Error of Replacement Theology," http://
www.therefinersfire.org/replacement_theology.htm (accessed May 7, 2015).

15. Ibid.

16. Ibid.

17. Ibid.; Clarence H. Wagner Jr., *Lessons from the Land of the Bible* (Jerusalem, Israel: Bridges for Peace, 1998).

18. "Ephesians 2:11–18: Community Through the Cross," October 24, 1999,
http://my.execpc.com/~crnrstn/sermons/Ephesians2_11.htm (accessed May 8,
2015).

19. Paul David Tripp, *Instruments in the Redeemer's Hands* (Phillipsburg, NJ:
P&R Publishing, 2002), 116.

CHAPTER 4
JERUSALEM, ISRAEL'S CAPITAL

1. Benjamin Disraeli, as quoted in Tracy Frydberg, "Jerusalem: Eat, Pray,
Love in the Capital of the Jewish World," *Times of Jerusalem*, http://www
.timesofisrael.com/the-jewish-planet/jerusalem/about/jerusalem-eat-pray-and
-love-in-the-capital-of-the-jewish-world/ (accessed May 4, 2015).

2. "Famous Quotes About Israel From World Leaders," Jerusalem Prayer
Team, http://jerusalemprayerteam.org/famous-quotes.asp (accessed May 4, 2015).

3. Charles H. Dyer, *The Rise of Babylon* (Wheaton IL: Tyndale House Publisher, 1991).

4. Mike Evans, *Jerusalem Betrayed* (Dallas, TX: Word Publishing, 1997), 5.

5. "Famous Quotes About Israel From World Leaders," Jerusalem Prayer Team, http://jerusalemprayerteam.org/famous-quotes.asp (accessed May 4, 2015).

6. Richard F. Ames, "The Future of Jerusalem," *Tomorrow's World*, May–June 2007, http://www.tomorrowsworld.org/magazines/2007/may-june/the -future-of-jerusalem (accessed May 7, 2015). Printed with permission.

7. Ibid.

CHAPTER 6
KNOW THE END-TIMES ENEMY

1. See "Islam's War Against the Jews: Quotes from the Palestinian Authority," Aish.com, July 21, 2001, http://www.aish.com/jw/me/48883732.html (accessed May 7, 2015).

2. Mitchell G. Bard, "Myths and Facts: A Guide to the Arab-Israeli Conflict," American-Israeli Cooperative Enterprise, 2006, http://www.jewishvirtuallibrary .org/jsource/myths3/MFattitudes.html (accessed May 4, 2015).

3. Ibid.

4. Dennis Davidson, "A Survey of Islam," SermonCentral, May 2013, http:// www.sermoncentral.com/sermons/a-survey-of-islam-dennis-davidson-sermon-on -apologetics-general-156936.asp?Page=9 (accessed May 7, 2015); "Top 10 Reasons Eric Holder Should Not Be Attorney General," Human Events, April 9, 2011, http://humanevents.com/2011/04/09/top-10-reasons-eric-holder-should-not-be -attorney-general/ (accessed May 7, 2015).

5. Cathy Lynn Grossman, "Number of US Mosques Up 74% Since 2000," *USA Today*, February 29, 2012, http://usatoday30.usatoday.com/news/religion /story/2012-02-29/islamic-worship-growth-us/53298792/1 (accessed May 7, 2015).

6. Yahoo! Answers, "Why Ppl Worship....," https://answers.yahoo.com /question/index?qid=1006050129605 (accessed May 18, 2015).

7. Yahoo! Answers, "What's the Difference Between Allah & God?", https:// answers.yahoo.com/question/index?qid=20121103014956AAnaVeg (accessed May 18, 2015).

8. "The Five Pillars of Islam," Royal Embassy of Saudi Arabia, http://www .saudiembassy.net/about/country-information/Islam/five_pillars_of_Islam.aspx (accessed May 4, 2015).

9. William M. Miller, *A Christian's Response to Islam* (Phillipsburg, NJ: Presbyterian & Reformed Publishing Co., 1976); Dennis Davidson, "A Survey of Islam," SermonCentral, May 2013, http://www.sermoncentral.com/sermons/a -survey-of-islam-dennis-davidson-sermon-on-apologetics-general-156936 .asp?Page=9 (accessed May 7, 2015).

10. "Radical Islam," Discover the Networks.org: A Guide to the Political Left, http://www.discoverthenetworks.org/guide (accessed May 4, 2015).

11. As quoted by Andrew Webb, "A More Realistic Assessment of Islam," PCANews.com, http://www.starwire.com/partner/Article_Display_Page /0,,PTID34418_CHID578460_CIID1194802,00.html (accessed May 7, 2015).

12. Ibid.

13. Charles Krauthammer, *Things That Matter: Three Decades of Passions, Pastimes and Politics* (New York: Crown Forum, 2013).

14. Organisation of Islamic Cooperation, http://www.oic-oci.org/oicv2/states/ (accessed May 7, 2015).

15. Ramesh R. Desai, "Islamization of the World by the Year 2501: Is It Possible?", FaithFreedom.org, https://www.faithfreedom.org/Articles/Desai/islamization_of_the_world.htm (accessed May 4, 2015).

16. Chris Surber, "What About Islam," SermonCentral, November 2008, http://www.sermoncentral.com/sermons/world-religions--1-islam-chris-surber-sermon-on-grace-128533.asp?Page=4 (accessed May 4, 2015).

17. From the biography of missionary Samuel Zwemer, https://urbana.org/go-and-do/missionary-biographies/faithful-hero (accessed May 4, 2015).

18. "There Is a Fountain Filled With Blood" by William Cowper. Public domain.

CHAPTER 7
IS THERE A FUTURE IN ISRAEL'S HOPE?

1. As quoted in Martin Gilbert, *Churchill and the Jews: A Lifelong Friendship* (New York: Henry Holt and Company, 2007), 308.

2. Walter B. Knight, *Knight's Treasury of Illustrations for Christian Service* (Grand Rapids, MI: Wm. B. Eerdmans, 1963).

3. As quoted in Ray Pritchard, "Does Israel Have a Future?," Keep Believing Ministries, August 11, 2006, http://www.keepbelieving.com/sermon/does-israel-have-a-future/ (accessed May 8, 2015).

4. Jack Van Impe, *Israel's Final Holocaust* (Nashville, TN: Thomas Nelson Publishers, 1979).

5. Warren W. Wiersbe, *Be Right* (Wheaton, IL: Victor Books, 1977), 125.

6. John Phillips, *Exploring Romans: An Expository Commentary* (Chicago, IL: Moody Press, 1969).

CHAPTER 8
THE MYSTERY OF PHOENICIA

1. Notable-Quotes.com, "Cicero Quotes," http://www.notable-quotes.com/c/cicero_quotes.html (accessed May 4, 2015).

2. Salim George Khalaf, "A Bequest Unearthed, Summary and Introduction." http://phoenicia.org/noframe.html#ixzz3ZYPy1t2H (accessed May 8, 2015).

3. Sanford Holst, "Origin of the Phoenicians," paper presented at Queen Mary College in London, England, June 29, 2008, http://www.phoenician.org/origin_of_phoenicians.htm (accessed May 8, 2015).

4. Kerry W. Cranmer, *Tyre the Invincible* (Tulsa, OK: Word and Spirit Publishing, 2012), 10.

5. Ibid., 91.

6. Pliny the Elder, *The Natural History*, ed. John Bostock and Henry T. Riley (London: Taylor and Francis, 1855).

7. Diodorus of Sicily, *Diodorus of Sicily*, trans. C. H. Old Father (Cambridge, MA: Harvard University Press, 1968).

8. Cranmer, *Tyre the Invincible*, 93.

9. Kevin McCaffrey, "Who Discovered the Americas? Ancient Coins May Map New Understandings of Antiquity," https://www.mtholyoke.edu/offices /comm/vista/9606/4.html (accessed May 4, 2015).

10. Ibid.

11. Alan Campbell is the pastor of the Cregagh Covenant People's Fellowship in Belfast, Northern Ireland, and director of Open Bible Ministries. Read the entire article at http://www.cai.org/bible-studies/israelites-were-america-columbus (accessed May 8, 2015).

12. Cyrus H. Thomas, "Report on the Mound Explorations of the Bureau of Ethnology," *Twelfth Annual Report of the Bureau of American Ethnology to the Secretary of the Smithsonian Institution 1890–1891* (Washington, DC: Government Printing Office, 1894), 393.

13. J. Huston McCulloch, "The Bat Creek Stone," September 2010, http:// economics.sbs.ohio-state.edu/jhm/arch/batcrk.html (accessed May 7, 2015).

ADDENDUM TO CHAPTER 8
HIRAM, THE PHOENICIANS, AND THE CHEROKEE NATION

1. Donald N. Yates, *Old World Roots of the Cherokee* (Jefferson, NC: McFarland Publication, 2012).

2. Ibid.

3. Ibid.

4. Ibid.

5. Sakiyah Sanders, *Cherokee History of the World*. Public domain.

6. Lia Mandelbaum, "Hitler's Inspiration and Guide: The Native American Holocaust," *Jewish Journal*, June 18, 2013, http://www.jewishjournal.com/sacred intentions/item/hitlers_inspiration_and_guide_the_native_american_holocaust (accessed May 18, 2015).

CHAPTER 9
UNLOCKING THE HIRAM CODE

1. Flavius Josephus, *The Antiquities of the Jews* VIII, trans. William Whiston (Grand Rapids, MI: Kergel Publications, 1980), 174.

2. Jesse L. Cotton, "Hiram," International Standard Bible Encyclopedia Online, http://www.internationalstandardbible.com/H/hiram.html (accessed May 4, 2015).

CHAPTER 10
THE HIRAM CODE ACTIVATED TODAY

1. Spurgeon's address to the British Society for the Propagation of the Gospel Amongst the Jews. Delivered at the Metropolitan Tabernacle on June 16, 1864, "The Restoration and Conversion of the Jews"; Dennis M. Swanson, "Charles H.

Spurgeon and the Nation of Israel," 2000, http://www.spurgeon.org/misc
/eschat2.htm#note48 (accessed May 4, 2015).

2. Mike Evans, *Jerusalem Betrayed* (Dallas, TX: Word Publishing, 1997), 199.

3. Wikipedia.org, s.v. "List of Wars Involving Israel," http://en.wikipedia.org
/wiki/List_of_wars_involving_Israel (accessed May 4, 2015).

4. Maurice Sklar, "The New Tabernacle of David," 2010; read the entire
article at http://www.mauricesklar.com/Teachings/The_New_Tabernacle_of
_David/the_new_tabernacle_of_david.html (accessed May 8, 2015).

CHAPTER 11
LIVING WITH CONTRADICTION

1. Brainyquote.com, "Saint Francis de Sales Quotes," http://www.brainyquote
.com/quotes/quotes/s/saintfranc143989.html (accessed May 4, 2015).

2. The Free Dictionary, s.v. "contradiction," http://www.thefreedictionary
.com/contradiction (accessed May 4, 2015).

3. Warren W. Wiersbe, *Be Real* (Wheaton, IL: Victor Books, 1972), 70.

4. Michael P. Walther, "Blessed Is He Who Comes in the Name of the Lord,"
SermonCentral, May 25, 2011, http://www.sermoncentral.com/sermons/blessed
-is-he-who-comes-in-the-name-of-the-lord-michael-walther-sermon-on-judgment
-157342.asp (accessed May 8, 2015).

5. Charles Spurgeon, *Spurgeon's Sermons on the Death and Resurrection of
Jesus* (Peabody, MA: Hendrickson Publishers Inc., 2005).

6. Erwin Lutzer, *Pastor to Pastor* (Grand Rapids, MI: Kregel Publications,
1998), 76.

7. As quoted at Bible.org, "Double Minded Man," https://bible.org/illustra-
tion/double-minded-man (accessed May 18, 2015).

8. Warren W. Wiersbe, *The Wycliffe Handbook of Preaching and Preachers*
(Chicago: Moody Press, 1984), 209; Bible.org, "Moody's Epitaph," https://bible
.org/illustration/moody%E2%80%99s-epitaph (accessed May 8, 2015).

CHAPTER 12
THE ISAAC EFFECT

1. George Pearsons, "Become Kingdom-Inside-Minded," Eagle Mountain
International Church, September 23, 2011, http://www.emic.org/blog/?p=181
(accessed May 8, 2015).

2. Parker J. Palmer, as quoted in Luis Rodriguez, *Hearts and Hands: Creating
Community in Violent Times* (New York: Seven Stories Press, 2001), 185.

3. Charles Rush, "From Abundance to Abundance," November 18, 2007,
http://archive.christchurchsummit.org/Sermons-2007/071118-FromAbundance
ToAbundance.html (accessed May 8, 2015).

4. Source material in this section taken from Matthew Henry's *Commentary
on the Whole Bible* (Grand Rapids, MI: Zondervan Publishing, 1961).

5. Bob Deffinbaugh, "27. Isaac Walks in His Father's Steps (Genesis 26:1–
35)," Bible.org, May 12, 2004, https://bible.org/seriespage/27-isaac-walks-his
-father-s-steps-genesis-261-35 (accessed May 8, 2015).

CHAPTER 13
LAST DAYS GENEROSITY

1. Oral Roberts, *Abundant Life* 24, Oral Roberts Evangelistic Association Inc., 1970.

2. C. S. Lewis, *The World's Last Night and Other Essays* (New York: Harcourt Brace Jovanovich, 1960), 9.

3. SermonIndex.net, "Christian Quotes on Obedience," http://www.sermon index.net/modules/articles/index.php?view=article&aid=30586 (accessed May 4, 2015).

4. Mark Gorman, *God's Plan for Prosperity* (New Orleans, LA: Mark Gorman Ministries, 2004).

5. As quoted at Evelyn Lim, "20 Inspirational Abundance Quotes," Abundance Tapestry, October 4, 2010, http://www.abundancetapestry.com/20 -inspirational-abundance-quotes/ (accessed May 7, 2015).

CHAPTER 14
PROSPERING IN THE LAST DAYS

1. As quoted in *The Westminster Collection of Christian Quotations*, ed. Martin H. Manser (Louisville, KY: Westminster John Knox Press, 2001), 361.

2. Al Mohler, "A Christian View of the Economic Crisis," http://www.albert mohler.com/2008/09/24/a-christian-view-of-the-economic-crisis/ (accessed May 7, 2015).

3. C. H. MacIntosh, *Notes on Numbers* (New Jersey: Loizeaux Brothers, 1972). Quoted in Tom Rose, *Economics: Principles and Policy From a Christian Perspective* (Mercer, PA: American Enterprise Publications, 1996), 16.

4. Goodreads.com, "Francis A. Schaeffer Quotes," http://www.goodreads .com/quotes/485241-people-have-presuppositions-by-presuppositions-we-mean -the-basic-way (accessed May 4, 2015).

5. Sermonillustrations.com, "Giving," http://www.sermonillustrations.com /a-z/g/giving.htm (accessed May 4, 2015).

6. As quoted in Ray Comfort, *Luther Gold* (Alachua, FL: Bridge Logos Foundation, 2010), 50.

7. Brainyquote.com, "Mother Teresa Quotes," http://www.brainyquote.com /quotes/quotes/m/mothertere158110.html (accessed May 8, 2015).

8. John Avanzini, *Stolen Property Returned!* (Joplin, MO: His Image Ministry, 1984).

CHAPTER 15
FACE YOUR FOES

1. "Synopsis for *The Hunger Games* (2012)," http://www.imdb.com/title /tt1392170/synopsis (accessed May 4, 2015).

2. Jean Williams, "The Next Story: Life and Faith after the Digital Explosion," review of *The Next Story: Life and Faith after the Digital Explosion*, by Tim Challies, The Briefing, May 10, 2012, http://matthiasmedia.com/briefing

/2012/05/the-next-story-life-and-faith-after-the-digital-explosion/ (accessed May 7, 2015).

3. Ibid.

4. Ibid.

5. Malcolm Gladwell, *David and Goliath: Underdogs, Misfits, and the Art of Battling Giants* (New York: Little, Brown and Company, 2013), 4.

6. Shell Harris, "Top 10 Greatest Upsets in Sports History," TopTenz, September 21, 2008, http://www.toptenz.net/top-10-upsets-in-sports-history.php (accessed May 7, 2015).

7. Max Lucado, *Facing Your Giants* (Nashville, TN: Thomas Nelson, 2013), 2–6.

CHAPTER 16
APPLY THE KEYS TO VICTORY

1. Gladwell, *David and Goliath*.

2. Goodreads.com, "Quotes About Obedience Christianity," http://www .goodreads.com/quotes/tag/obedience-christianity (accessed May 4, 2015).

3. Harold L. White, "God's Gonna Do Great Things!", http://www.angelfire .com/fl5/hleewhite/ser323godsgonnado.html (accessed May 8, 2015).

4. Gladwell, *David and Goliath*, 9–12.

5. Brainyquote.com, "Eric Hoffer Quotes," http://www.brainyquote.com/quotes /quotes/e/erichoffer100979.html (accessed May 4, 2015).

CHAPTER 17
UNTIL THEN

1. Merriam-Webster.com, s.v. "occupy," http://www2.merriam-webster.com /cgi-bin/mwdictsn?book=Dictionary&va=occupied (accessed May 8, 2015).

2. Axelrod, *Patton on Leadership*, 69.

3. William D. Mounce, *The Analytical Lexicon of the Greek New Testament* (Grand Rapids, MI: Zondervan, 1993), s.v. "*dianoigo*," 140.

4. Walter Bauer, *A Greek-English Lexicon of the New Testament and Other Early Christian Literature*, 3rd Edition, ed. Frederick William Danker (Chicago: University of Chicago, 2000), s.v. "*dianoigo*," 234; Johnson A. Beaven III, "Preaching Theory and Tips," Impact Training Center, 2006, http://www .impacttrainingcenter.com/articles.html (accessed May 8, 2015).

5. "Encountering Jesus Along Life's Road," Insight for Living, http://www .insight.org/resources/articles/pastors/lifes-road.html?print=t (accessed May 4, 2015); adapted from Charles R. Swindoll, *Jesus: The Greatest Life of All* (Nashville: Thomas Nelson, 2008), 245–258.

6. George Barna, *The Power of Vision* (Ventura, CA: Regal Publishing, 1992), 13.